SHORTLIST

London
2012

WHAT'S NEW | WHAT'S ON | WHAT'S BEST

www.timeout.com/london

Time Out
London

Contents

London by Area

Essentials

Published by Time Out Guides Ltd
Universal House
251 Tottenham Court Road
London W1T 7AB
Tel: + 44 (0)20 7813 3000
Fax: + 44 (0)20 7813 6001
Email: guides@timeout.com
www.timeout.com

Managing Director Peter Fiennes
Editorial Director Ruth Jarvis
Business Manager Daniel Allen
Editorial Manager Holly Pick
Management Accountants Margaret Wright, Clare Turner

Time Out Guides is a wholly owned subsidiary of Time Out Group Ltd.

© Time Out Group Ltd
Chairman & Founder Tony Elliott
Chief Executive Officer David King
Chief Operating Officer Aksel Van der Wal
Group Financial Director Paul Rakkar
Group General Manager/Director Nichola Coulthard
Time Out Communications Ltd MD David Pepper
Time Out International Ltd MD Cathy Runciman
Time Out Magazine Ltd Publisher/Managing Director Mark Elliott
Group Commercial Director Graeme Tottle
Group IT Director Simon Chappell
Group Marketing Director Andrew Booth

Time Out and the Time Out logo are trademarks of Time Out Group Ltd.

London 2012 emblems © The London Organising Committee of the Olympic Games and
Paralympic Games Ltd (LOCOG) 2007. London 2012 mascots © LOCOG 2009-2010.
London 2012 Pictograms © LOCOG 2009. All rights reserved.

This edition first published in Great Britain in 2011 by Ebury Publishing
A Random House Group Company
Company information can be found on www.randomhouse.co.uk
Random House UK Limited Reg. No. 954009
10 9 8 7 6 5 4 3 2 1

Distributed in the US and Latin America by Publishers Group West (1-510-809-3700)

For further distribution details, see www.timeout.com

ISBN: 978-1-84670-291-4

A CIP catalogue record for this book is available from the British Library.

Printed and bound in Germany by Appl.

The Random House Group Limited supports the Forest Stewardship Council® (FSC®),
the leading international forest certification organisation. All our titles that are printed on
Greenpeace approved FSC® certified paper carry the FSC® logo. Our paper procurement
policy can be found at www.randomhouse.co.uk/environment.

Time Out carbon-offsets all its flights with Trees for Cities (www.treesforcities.org).

London Shortlist

The **Time Out London Shortlist 2012** is one of a series of annual guides that draws on Time Out's background as a magazine publisher to keep you current with everything that's going on in town. As well as London's key sights and the best of its eating, drinking and leisure, it picks out the most exciting new venues and gives a full calendar of events from September 2011 to December 2012. Whether you're visiting for the first time in your life or the first time this year, you'll find the *Time Out London Shortlist* contains all you need to know, in a portable, easy-to-use format.

Time Out Guides is proud to be the official book publisher of travel and tourism guides for the **London 2012 Olympic & Paralympic Games**. In this edition of the Shortlist, we have included all the information you need to enjoy the 2012 Games, whether you're a ticket-holder or in town just for the atmosphere.

The guide divides central London into five areas, each containing Sights & Museums, Eating & Drinking, Shopping, Nightlife and Arts & Leisure, and maps pinpointing their locations. At the front of the book are chapters rounding up these scenes city-wide, and giving a shortlist of our overall picks. We also include itineraries for days out, plus essentials such as transport information and hotels.

Our listings give phone numbers as dialled if you're in London. To dial them from elsewhere in the UK, preface them with 020. From abroad, use your country's exit code then 44 (the country code for the UK), 20 and the number given.

We have noted price categories by using one to four pound signs (**£-££££**), representing budget, moderate, expensive and luxury. Major credit cards are accepted unless otherwise stated. We also indicate when a venue is NEW, and give **Event highlights**.

All our listings are double-checked, but places sometimes close or change their hours or prices, so it's a good idea to call a venue before visiting. While every effort has been made to ensure accuracy, the publishers cannot accept responsibility for any errors that this guide may contain.

Venues are marked on the maps using symbols numbered according to their order in the chapter and colour-coded thus:

❶ Sights & Museums
❶ Eating & Drinking
❶ Shopping
❶ Nightlife
❶ Arts & Leisure

Map Key	
Major sight or landmark	
Railway or coach station	
Underground station	⊖
Park	
Hospital	
Casualty unit	✛
Church	✚
Synagogue	✡
District	MAYFAIR
Theatre	●

Time Out **London** Shortlist 2012

CONTRIBUTORS
This guide was researched and written by Carol Baker, Simon Coppock, Guy Dimond, Dominic Earle, Janice Fuscoe, Rob Greig, Kate Hutchinson, Zoe Kamen, Hui Shan Khoo, Caroline McGinn, Kathryn Miller, Leo Miranda, Emma Perry and the writers of *Time Out London*.

Photography by page 7 Belinda Lawley; pages 8, 18, 59 ODA; pages 13, 60, 66, 86, 123, 124, 182 (left) Ben Rowe; pages 15, 16, 29 LOCOG; pages 20, 113 (bottom), 155 (top right and bottom left), 191 Michelle Grant; pages 22, 182 (right) Christina Theisen; pages 24, 61, 155 (top left and bottom right), 168 Jonathan Perugia; pages 26, 33 Ed Marshall; pages 27, 72 (top), 105 (top), 106, 137, 148, 163 (top left and bottom) Rob Greig; pages 28, 82, 92, 97, 113 (top), 173 Michael Franke; pages 32, 62, 72 (bottom), 105 (bottom), 109, 140, 166, 192, 195 Britta Jaschinski; page 34 Vickie Parker; page 37 Tom Chambers; page 39 Nick Ballon; page 44 Pride London/One Sunny Day; page 46 Heloise Bergman; page 46 (bottom left) Catherine Clark; page 48 James O Jenkins; page 49 Matt Golowczynski; pages 52, 54 Getty Images; page 56 www.simonleigh.com; page 58 Getty Images/ODA; page 75 Ming Tang-Evans; page 88 Karen McGaul; page 120 Abi Lelliott; page 127 Scott Wishart; page 153 Courtesy of the Trustees of Sir John Soane's Museum; page 163 Andrew Brackenbury; page 180 Arcelor Mittal Orbit, designed by Anish Kapoor and Cecil Balmond; page 188 Oliver Knight; page 190 Elisabeth Blanchet; page 203 Chris Tubbs.

The following images were provided by the featured establishments/artists: pages 23, 40, 81, 145, 160, 198.

Cover photograph: Millennium Bridge and Tate Modern Gallery. Credit: Getty Images.

MAPS
JS Graphics (john@jsgraphics.co.uk).

About **Time Out**

Founded in 1968, Time Out has expanded from humble London beginnings into the leading resource for those wanting to know what's happening in the world's greatest cities. As well as our influential what's-on weeklies in London, New York and Chicago, we publish nearly 30 other listings magazines in cities as varied as Beijing and Mumbai. The magazines established Time Out's trademark style: sharp writing, informed reviewing and bang up-to-date inside knowledge of every scene.

Time Out made the natural leap into travel guides in the 1980s with the City Guide series, which now extends to over 50 destinations around the world. Written and researched by expert local writers and generously illustrated with original photography, the full-size guides cover a larger area than our Shortlist guides and include many more venue reviews, along with additional background features and a full set of maps.

Throughout this rapid growth, the company has remained proudly independent, still owned by Tony Elliott four decades after he started *Time Out London* as a single fold-out sheet of A5 paper. This independence extends to the editorial content of all our publications, this Shortlist included. No establishment has been featured because it has advertised, and no payment has influenced any of our reviews. And, for our critics, there's definitely no such thing as a free lunch: all restaurants and bars are visited and reviewed anonymously, and Time Out always picks up the bill.

For more about the company, see www.timeout.com.

Don't Miss 2012

Olympic Park

The 2012 Games

The **London 2012 Olympic & Paralympic Games** are fast approaching. When this guide hits the shelves, there will be less than a year until the Opening Ceremony on 27 July 2012.

The Olympic Park

Centre of the London 2012 Games is the combination of permanent and temporary venues that make up east London's **Olympic Park** (map p208). This is already a major sightseeing destination, with the raised Greenway foot- and cycle-path, and towpaths north and south along the River Lea, making casual viewing from outside the Park's perimeter fence a joy. In the run-up to the Games, the **View Tube** (see box p182) is a cracking viewpoint, which is why we've incorporated it into our **Itinerary** on pp58-60.

The Park is an extraordinary feat of ingenious planning and massive construction, from its huge bridges and wheelchair-accessible paths to plantings developed to bloom right on time for the sporting events.

Of the Park venues (a complete list is on p206), the key ones are the Olympic Stadium, Aquatics Centre and Velodrome. On its own island in the south section of the Park, the **Olympic Stadium** sits between three rivers, crossed by five bridges. It hosts the Opening and Closing Ceremonies, as well as both Olympic and Paralympic Athletics. It looks like a giant mechanical lotus flower, especially when you see its 14 stanchions of floodlights, open like 60m-long petals, reflected in the junction of the Lee Navigation and Hertford Union Canal. Most of the Stadium's non-sporting functions have, unusually, been moved outside: refreshments, merchandising and information desks are located around the perimeter, giving the venue a festival feel.

Between the Olympic Stadium and Westfield Stratford City (p181), the **Aquatics Centre** is the first building many spectators will see as they take the main approach from Stratford station. Designed by Iraqi-born architect Zaha Hadid, its talking point is the huge, wave-shaped, steel-and-glass roof, now flanked by 42m-high temporary stands on either side.

At the north end of the North-East Concourse, the **Velodrome** is the hardest to see from outside the park, but it's a stunner; indeed, it won an architecture award from RIBA in 2011. Inside, the slope of the Siberian pine track and best racing temperature have been exactly worked out to produce optimal conditions for fast rides. There should be great views of east London via a glass wall between upper and lower seating.

Perhaps the most dramatic structure of all, however, is the **Orbit**, designed by sculptor Anish Kapoor and due to be completed by spring 2012. Towering above the Olympic Stadium, this 374ft-tall roller-coaster of bright red, steel girders will have a lift up to a lofty viewing platform.

All of the Park venues have points of interest: the stretched white material on the **Basketball Arena** will be used as a screen for light projections during London 2012, in a style reminiscent of the Beijing 2008 Water Cube, and the copper-clad exterior of the **Handball Arena** is designed to weather and age. Even the blue colour of the pitches at the **Hockey**

SHORTLIST

Breathtaking happenings
- London 2012 Festival (see box p54)
- Olympic Games Opening Ceremony (p13)

Best of the tests
- Aquatics – Water Polo (p49)
- Athletics (p49)
- Paralympic Athletics (p49)
- Track Cycling (p47)

Best of Olympic Park
- Orbit (left)
- Velodrome (left)

Best outside the Park
- Lee Valley White Water Centre (see box p190)
- View Tube (see box p182)

Key Olympic contests
- 30 July, 1 Aug: Ian Thorpe v Michael Phelps
- 5 Aug: Usain Bolt

Potential big days for Brits
- 4 Aug: Jessica Ennis & Mo Farah
- 5 Aug: Paula Radcliffe & Christine Ohuruogu
- 9 Aug: Phillips Idowu

Best non-ticketed events
- Marathon (p16)
- Road Cycling (p16)

Key clash in the Paralympic Athletics
- Oscar Pistorius v Jerome Singleton

Paralympic home heroes
- Ellie Simmonds
- David Weir

Great Paralympic sports
- 5-a-side Football (p16)
- Wheelchair Rugby (p16)

DON'T MISS: 2012

Centre was carefully chosen to improve visibility both for fans and for players.

Around London

Although the Olympic Park is the focus, there will be Games activity right across town. In fact, you'll be able to visit historic and sporting venues with important Games roles until close to the start of the Olympics. **Horse Guards Parade** (p85), **Hampton Court Palace** (p188), **Hyde Park** (p95) and **Greenwich Park** (p181) are key London sights; **Lord's Cricket Ground** (p169), **Wimbledon** (p189) and **Wembley Stadium** (p188) are already world-famous for sport.

London's most successful concert venue, the O2 Arena (p184; formerly the Dome), is also getting involved as the **North Greenwich Arena**, while the **ExCeL** conference centre – across the Thames from North Greenwich Arena, on the edge of a vast decommissioned dock – will host the largest number of events of any venue outside the Olympic Park.

Further afield, rural **Hadleigh Farm** and the vast lake at **Eton Dorney**, owned by the private school that educated both Mayor Boris Johnson and Prime Minister David Cameron, will be grand settings, but there's only one place where you can try out an actual 2012 venue: **Lee Valley White Water Centre** (see box p190). For a complete list of the London 2012 venues, see pp206-207.

In the run-up to the Games, the city will be 'dressed' with Games symbols and London 2012 colours. **St Pancras International Station** (p125), home to a dedicated London 2012 Shop (p126) and a key transport hub for the Games (the Javelin® will run to the Olympic Park from here), was decked out with Olympic rings in spring 2011; plans are afoot to do the same to London icons new and old as we near the Games.

Helping to build anticipation, the electronic counter on the top of the **BT Tower** (p114) has been joined by an official clock in **Trafalgar Square** (p83), one side ticking away the seconds to the Olympic Games, the other to the Paralympic Games. Meanwhile, **Live Sites** are being chosen – big screens, where spectators without tickets can enjoy the action in a festival atmosphere. **Potters Field** (near City Hall, p62), Hyde Park and **Victoria Park** in the Host Borough of Hackney are likely locations for these screens.

Many organisations not directly responsible for the delivery of the London 2012 Games are coming up with exciting ideas for Games-time. Funding has been secured for the **London River Park**, for example. This will be a 39ft-wide, half-mile-long temporary river pontoon providing a section of unbroken walkway along the north bank of the Thames under Blackfriars Bridge, on which eight pavilions will explore different aspects of life in London. There is also a **cable car** (see box p177) planned to connect the North Greenwich Arena and ExCeL across the Thames, although this may not be completed in time for the Games.

We're expecting a good deal of international frivolity as well during the Games, with national delegations setting up 'home' camps in London. **Somerset House** (p152) is to become Casa Brazil (Rio hosts the 2016 Games), **Alexandra Palace** will turn Dutch orange and resonate to brass bands, while the Russians hope to promote the Sochi 2012 Winter Games with an unseasonal 1,000-capacity ice-rink beside Hyde Park.

A celebration of great sporting moments

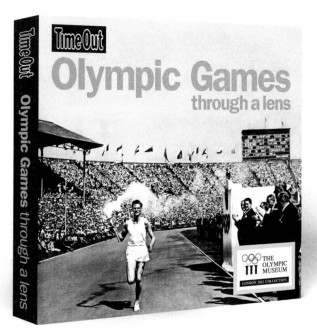

DON'T MISS: 2012

St Pancras International Station p11

Before the Games

Plenty of events – sporting and cultural – are planned for the run-up to the Games. In sport, keep an eye out for the **London Prepares** test events, some of which are ticketed and thus give the public a chance to see the Olympic Park and other venues in action well in advance of the Games themselves. Confirmed Olympic test events are given in the Calendar (pp47, 49); for more on Paralympic test events, see p16 and the London Prepares website (www.londonpreparesseries.com).

In addition, the Cultural Olympiad will be hotting up, with exhibitions and artistic events, before reaching a climax with the **London 2012 Festival** (see box p54). But the key symbolic precursor to the Games is the arrival of the Olympic Torch at Land's End, in the far west of the country, on 19 May. The **Torch Relay** will arrive in London on 21 July to complete a 70-day, 8,000-mile journey that encompasses the whole country, with the last of the long chain of Torchbearers – half of whom will be young people –

entering the Olympic Stadium for the Opening Ceremony.

The Olympic Games

The Olympic Games will open on 27 July 2012 with an elaborate **Opening Ceremony**, overseen by Oscar-winning film directors Danny Boyle and Stephen Daldry. For a **day-by-day schedule** of the Olympic events that follow, see pp14-15.

Two contests are likely to stand out at the 2012 Olympic Games. The **100m Final** (5 Aug) is one of the centrepieces of any Games, but the prospect of seeing the extraordinary Usain Bolt pitted against a crop of young pretenders is irresistible. The other mouth-watering showdown is between American Michael Phelps, the eight-times gold medallist of Beijing 2008, and Australian Ian Thorpe, a five-times career Olympic gold medallist who is returning from retirement. They could be competing with each other in the **100m Freestyle** (30 July) and **200m Freestyle** (1 Aug).

London 2012 Olympic Games Schedule

SPORT	VENUE	JULY							AUGUST											
		W 25	Th 26	F 27	Sa 28	Su 29	M 30	Tu 31	W 1	Th 2	F 3	Sa 4	Su 5	M 6	Tu 7	W 8	Th 9	F 10	Sa 11	Su 12
Opening Ceremony	Olympic Stadium			•																
Closing Ceremony	Olympic Stadium																			•
Archery	Lord's Cricket Ground			•	•	•	•	•	•	•	•									
Athletics	Olympic Stadium										•	•	•	•	•	•	•	•	•	•
Athletics – Marathon	The Mall												•							•
Athletics – Race Walk	The Mall											•							•	
Badminton	Wembley Arena				•	•	•	•	•	•	•	•	•							
Basketball	Basketball Arena				•	•	•	•	•	•	•	•	•	•	•	•	•			
	North Greenwich Arena															•	•	•	•	•
Beach Volleyball	Horse Guards Parade				•	•	•	•	•	•	•	•	•	•	•	•	•			
Boxing	ExCeL				•	•	•	•	•	•	•	•	•	•	•	•	•	•	•	•
Canoe Slalom	Lee Valley White Water Centre					•	•	•	•	•										
Canoe Sprint	Eton Dorney														•	•	•	•	•	•
Cycling – BMX	BMX Circuit																•	•	•	
Cycling – Mountain Bike	Hadleigh Farm																		•	•
Cycling – Road	The Mall				•	•			•											
	Hampton Court Palace								•											
Cycling – Track	Velodrome									•	•	•	•	•	•					
Diving	Aquatics Centre					•	•	•	•	•	•	•	•	•	•	•	•	•		
Equestrian – Dressage	Greenwich Park									•	•	•			•		•			
Equestrian – Eventing	Greenwich Park				•	•	•	•												
Equestrian – Jumping	Greenwich Park											•	•	•		•				
Fencing	ExCeL				•	•	•	•	•	•	•	•								
Football	Wembley Stadium												•		•		•			
	Outside London	•	•	•	•	•	•	•	•	•	•	•								

Sport	Venue
Gymnastics – Artistic	North Greenwich Arena
Gymnastics – Rhythmic	Wembley Arena
Gymnastics – Trampoline	North Greenwich Arena
Handball	Handball Arena Basketball Arena
Hockey	Hockey Centre
Judo	ExCeL
Modern Pentathlon	Handball Arena, Aquatics Centre & Greenwich Park
Rowing	Eton Dorney
Sailing	Weymouth & Portland
Shooting	Royal Artillery Barracks
Swimming	Aquatics Centre
Swimming – Marathon	Hyde Park
Synchronised Swimming	Aquatics Centre
Table Tennis	ExCeL
Taekwondo	ExCeL
Tennis	Wimbledon
Triathlon	Hyde Park
Volleyball	Earls Court
Water Polo	Water Polo Arena
Weightlifting	ExCeL
Wrestling – Freestyle	ExCeL
Wrestling – Greco-Roman	ExCeL

NOTES
For more information, see www.london2012.com.

For British female athletes, highlights should include World Champion Jessica Ennis in the **Heptathlon** (3-4 Aug), Paula Radcliffe's return from injury to attempt to win her first Olympic **Marathon** gold (5 Aug), Rebecca Adlington in the 800m Freestyle **Swimming** (2-3 Aug), Christine Ohuruogu in the **400m** (5 Aug) and Vicky Pendleton in the **Track Cycling** (7 Aug).

The **Cycling** team hopes to do as well as at Beijing 2008; Chris Hoy and Bradley Wiggins are likely to be in the Velodrome (2-7 Aug), Manx sprinter Mark Cavendish on the road (28 July). There should be a mighty battle between Phillips Idowu (from Hackney, one of the boroughs that contains the Park) and Frenchman Teddy Tamgho in the **Triple Jump** (9 Aug), while Mo Farah will seek to turn European into Olympic golds in the **10,000m** (4 Aug) and **5000m** (11 Aug). There are high hopes in **Diving** (Tom Daley; 7, 11 Aug) and **Sailing** (Ben Ainslie, Iain Percy, Andrew Simpson; 29 July-11 Aug), and brothers Alistair and Jonathan Brownlee share medal aspirations in the **Triathlon** (7 Aug).

Several events are **free** to watch: just bag a roadside spot to see the **Cycling Road Race** (28, 29 July), the cycle element of the **Triathlon** (4, 7 Aug), the **Race Walks** (4, 11 Aug), or the **Marathon** (5, 12 Aug). The **Closing Ceremony** (12 Aug), on the other hand, is TV viewers and ticket-holders only. Choreography will be by Kim Gavin, responsible for Take That's impressive Circus Tour, and the stage design by Es Devlin, the woman behind Lady Gaga's Monster Ball tour.

The Paralympic Games

On 8 September 2011, the biennial **International Paralympic Day** (p44) will be held outside Germany for the first time. It marks the next day's opening of the Paralympic Games **ticket ballot** (9-30 September). All 20 Paralympic sports will be represented in Trafalgar Square (p83) – with the public encouraged to try some out.

Following this, there are several **London Prepares** test events: both Wheelchair Tennis and Paralympic Athletics (p49) take place in the Olympic Park, another chance to admire the venues.

The Paralympic Games has its own **Torch Relay**, with the flame arriving in the Olympic Stadium for the **Opening Ceremony** on the 29 August. The **day-by-day schedule** (right) then begins. The Paralympic Games mixes sports with Olympic counterparts (Cycling, Athletics, Judo and so on) and unique sports such as **Boccia** ('botcha'; 2-8 Sept), a game similar to petanque or bowls. For visually impaired athletes, both **Goalball** (30 Aug-7 Sept) and **5-a-side Football** (31 Aug-8 Sept) are played with a ball with a sound-making device inside, so spectators remain silent until the game is over. Right at the opposite end of the noise spectrum is the intensely physical **Wheelchair Rugby** (5-9 Sept), originally called 'murderball' due to the ferocity of the clashes between competitors.

The headline event for the Paralympic Games is also likely to be the 100m, with South African **Oscar Pistorius** – 'the Blade Runner' – facing **Jerome Singleton**, the US athlete who took silver to Pistorius's 100m (T44) gold at Beijing 2008. Also watch out for Irishman **Jason Smyth**, who matched Pistorius in taking both 100m and 200m golds at Beijing 2008, but in the T13 (visually impaired) rather than T44 category. Among the local stars, support will be strong for wheelchair athlete **David Weir** and swimmer **Ellie Simmonds**, both double gold winners at Beijing 2008.

On 9 September, the Paralympic **Closing Ceremony** will mark the end of London 2012 Games.

Essentials

Our chapter **Essentials: The 2012 Games** (pp206-213) provides succinct practical details and advice on tickets, basic orientation and the 2012 venues across London, transport, health & safety advice and accommodation. Also included in that chapter are **indicative venue maps**: the Olympic Park on pp208-9; the Greater London venues on p213.

London 2012 Paralympic Games Schedule

		AUGUST							SEPTEMBER			
SPORT	**VENUE**	W 29	Th 30	F 31	Sa 1	Su 2	M 3	Tu 4	W 5	Th 6	F 7	Sa 8	Su 9
Opening Ceremony	Olympic Stadium	•											
Closing Ceremony	Olympic Stadium												•
Archery	The Royal Artillery Barracks		•	•	•	•	•	•	•				
Athletics	Olympic Stadium			•	•	•	•	•	•	•	•	•	
Athletics – Marathon	The Mall												•
Boccia	ExCeL				•	•	•	•	•	•	•	•	
Cycling – Road	Brands Hatch								•	•	•	•	
Cycling – Track	Velodrome		•	•	•	•							
Equestrian	Greenwich Park		•	•	•	•	•	•					
Football 5-a-side	Hockey Centre			•			•		•		•		
Football 7-a-side	Hockey Centre					•		•	•		•		•
Goalball	Handball Arena		•	•	•	•	•		•	•	•		
Judo	ExCeL		•	•	•								
Powerlifting	ExCeL		•	•	•	•	•	•	•				
Rowing	Eton Dorney			•	•	•							
Sailing	Weymouth & Portland				•	•	•	•	•	•			
Shooting	The Royal Artillery Barracks		•	•	•	•	•	•	•	•			
Swimming	Aquatics Centre		•	•	•	•	•	•	•	•	•	•	
Table Tennis	ExCeL		•	•	•	•	•	•	•	•	•	•	
Volleyball (Sitting)	ExCeL		•	•	•	•	•	•	•	•	•	•	
Wheelchair Basketball	North Greenwich Arena		•	•	•	•	•	•	•	•	•		
	Basketball Arena		•	•	•	•	•	•	•	•	•		
Wheelchair Fencing	ExCeL							•	•	•	•	•	
Wheelchair Rugby	Basketball Arena								•	•	•	•	•
Wheelchair Tennis	Eton Manor				•	•	•	•	•	•	•	•	
ExCeL day pass				•	•	•	•	•	•	•	•	•	
Olympic Park day pass				•	•	•	•	•	•	•	•	•	

NOTES
Correct as at 10 May 2011; for more information, see www.london2012.com.

Olympic Park

Sights & Museums

London winning the bid for the 2012 Olympic and Paralympic Games back in 2005 ensured, at a stroke, that 2012 became the de facto deadline for all major projects. Reality – in the shape of a savage recession and cost-cutting government – has since intervened. Even as the venues in the **Olympic Park** (pp179-181) are serenely completed, a number of ambitious plans – the expansions of the **British Museum** (p118) and **Tate Modern** (p70), interior redevelopment of **Tate Britain** (p83), the Triforium Galleries at **Westminster Abbey** (p83) – are quietly and sensibly aiming fundraising expectations towards post-Games completion.

It's not as though London lacks amazing sights. We're blessed with no fewer than four UNESCO World Heritage Sites: the **Tower of London** (p161), the cluster of fine buildings round Parliament Square in **Westminster** (pp78-83), soothing **Kew Gardens** (p189) and, above all, the numerous attractions in **Greenwich** (pp181-184). **Discover Greenwich** has been doing a superb job of pulling the disparate Greenwich sites together since it opened in 2010, and the opening of the repaired **Cutty Sark** tea clipper and new Sammy Ofer Wing of the **National Maritime Museum** are perfectly timed to entertain spectators after the London 2012 Equestrian events in Greenwich Park. An ambitious, Games-led plan to link the Greenwich Peninsula to the Royal Docks business hub with a cross-river **cable car** (see box p177) is likely to help shift the sightseeing map of London eastwards, even beyond **Docklands** (pp178-179), while the reopening as London Overground of train lines that will form an orbital route round the city are already immensely useful.

The **South Bank** (p62-71) remains London's key tourist destination. The principal attractions are well established: Tate Modern, **Shakespeare's Globe** and **Borough Market** (p74), the lively **Southbank Centre** (p77), the **Sea Life London Aquarium** and – each pod lovingly refurbished – the **London Eye**. Do take the time also to explore minor highlights such as the **Garden Museum** and **Topolski Century** mural.

Across the river, the **City** authorities have been making a concerted effort to alter the reputation of the most ancient part of London as a place for bank workers rather than pleasure-seekers. It's been a pretty easy sell, given the number of historic attractions – the Tower of London and **St Paul's** (p159) are only the best known – and easy access from the South Bank over the Millennium Bridge. St Paul's and the **Monument** (p159) have been vividly refurbished, and the **Museum of London** (p159) is approaching its rightful place in locals' affections with four amazing new galleries, inviting street-level windows (through which you can see the Lord Mayor's golden coach) and a revitalised events programme.

The other London essentials are South Kensington and Bloomsbury. In **South Kensington**, the Medieval & Renaissance Galleries at the lovely **V&A** (p93) have been a huge hit, propelling this superb Victorian mansion up the visitors' lists. The **Natural History Museum** (p89) has an ultra-modern white Cocoon,

SHORTLIST

Most exciting developments
- Expansion at the Sir John Soane Museum (p152)
- Sammy Ofer Wing at the National Maritime Museum (p183)
- TM2 extension at Tate Modern (p70)

Most welcome returns
- Cutty Sark (p183)
- Grant Museum of Zoology (p119)

Best views
- London Eye (p67)
- Monument (p159)
- Top deck of a Heritage Routemaster bus (p80)
- View Tube at the Olympic Park (see box p182)

Finest free attractions
- British Museum (p118)
- Museum of London (p159)
- National Gallery (p80)
- Victoria & Albert Museum (p93)

Unsung museums
- Old Operating Theatre (p69)
- Petrie Museum (p121)
- Wellcome Collection (p125)

Best late events
- Science Museum (p93)
- Sir John Soane's Museum by candlelight (p152)
- Tate Britain (p83)
- Victoria & Albert Museum (p93)

Best outdoor
- Swimming in the ponds on Hampstead Heath (p188)
- Royal Botanic Gardens, Kew (p189)
- Watching the pelicans in St James's Park (p85)

Kew Gardens p18

and the neighbouring **Science Museum** (p93) been following a steady programme of new openings: the up-to-the-minute, all-bells-and-whistles Atmosphere gallery for climate change and an old-fashioned reconstruction of James Watt's attic workshop appeared within a few months of each other last year. In **Bloomsbury**, half a dozen new rooms had been completed at the world-class **British Museum** (p118) before work on the north-west extension even began. To the north, the ancient Egyptiana at the **Petrie** (p121) and the ghoulish animal remains at the **Grant Museum of Zoology** (p119) are tiny but atmospheric treats, while the **Wellcome Collection** (p125) by Euston station has carved itself a special niche for arresting themed exhibitions, often drawing together cutting-edge science and unusual or underground art.

Fans of art are especially well catered for in London these days. It isn't just the superstars – Tate Modern, Tate Britain, the **National Gallery** (p80) – that keep our visual culture vibrant: visitors can check out unabashedly modern work at east London's **Whitechapel** (p174), and the constellation of private galleries that cluster in Shoreditch and north into Hackney, as well as at the **Saatchi** (p99) in Chelsea. Not at all contemporary is the creaky old **Courtauld** (p148), which enjoyed a gentle rehang in summer 2011.

For students of changing London, a great deal of fun can be had by paying a visit to the city's biggest building sites: the Olympic Park is so nearly complete it barely qualifies any more (we show you how to peek from the perimeter on pp58-60), but large areas of King's Cross are still under transformation as this once drug-addled part of London slowly clears its head.

The key problem with a visit to London remains what it's always been: how do you do it all? The answer is simple: you can't… not in a single trip, not in a single lifetime. So relax, do whatever you fancy and – if you've only a couple of days of holiday – consider following our two-day **itinerary** (pp56-57).

Doing the geography

This book is divided by area. The **South Bank** primarily covers riverside Bankside, home of Tate Modern, and the revamped Southbank Centre. Over the river, **Westminster & St James's** cover the centre of UK politics, while the impressive Victorian museums of **South Kensington**, the Knightsbridge department stores, and the boutiques and eateries of **Chelsea** lie to the west.

The **West End** includes most of what is now central London. We start north of unlovely Oxford Street, in the elegant, slightly raffish shopping district of **Marylebone**. South, between Marylebone and St James's, is **Mayfair**, as expensive as its reputation but less daunting, with fine mews and pubs. Eastward are **Fitzrovia**, its elegant streets speckled with inviting shops and restaurants; the squares and Georgian terraces of literary **Bloomsbury**, home of academia and the British Museum; and up-and-coming **King's Cross**. Head south for **Covent Garden**, so popular with tourists that locals often forget about the charms of its boutique shopping, and **Soho**, formerly notorious centre of fun.

The **City** comprises the once-walled Square Mile of the original city, now adjoined by the focal area for bars and clubs, **Shoreditch**; **Holborn & Clerkenwell** have wonderful food.

Around these central districts **neighbourhood London** has clusters of fine restaurants, bars and clubs, servicing mainly residential zones (as well as **Greenwich** and the **Olympic Park**), while further London must-sees are **worth a day-trip**: among them, gorgeous **Kew** and grand **Hampton Court Palace**.

Making the most of it

Don't be scared of London's public transport: it's by far the best way around town. Invest in an **Oyster travel smartcard** (p216) and roam cashless through the city by bus, tube (underground trains) and train. The excellent London Overground – considered part of the underground network when it comes to ticketing – is developing into a handy rail orbital and already a neat north–south link across the river on the east of town, running right through Shoreditch.

The tube is the easiest mode of transport for newbies, but buses are best to get a handle on the city's topography. Some good sightseeing routes are RV1 (riverside), 7, 8 and 12, but hop on a **Routemaster Heritage bus** (p80) to enjoy a ride on a classic red double-decker.

Crime in central London is low, so walk whenever you can to really get a feel for the character of different areas of the city. No one thinks any the less of someone consulting a map – so long as they dive out of the stream of pedestrian traffic while doing so. And, despite Londoners' not entirely undeserved reputation for being sullen and unhelpful, most of us are quietly delighted to show off the breadth of our local knowledge by assisting with directions.

To avoid the worst of the crowds, avoid big attractions at **weekends** and on late-opening nights, and aim to hit blockbuster exhibitions in the middle of a run; January to March are the quietest months for visiting attractions, July to September the busiest. **Last entry** can be up to an hour before closing time (we specify when it is more than an hour before), so don't turn up at the last minute and expect to get in. Some sights close at Christmas and Easter – ring ahead to confirm opening hours.

Cutty Sark p18

Koya

WHAT'S BEST
Eating & Drinking

The last few years have been especially hard for London's restaurateurs, with the country's fragile economy ensuring there's been no shortage of restaurant closures. Even so, new openings continue apace, many of them surprisingly high profile, but with a growing trend for quality dining at the lower end of the scale.

Of the spate of new restaurants at top-end hotels, Gordon Ramsay's renewed **Savoy Grill** (p143), Jean-Georges Vongerichten's **Spice Market** (p134) at the W Leicester Square and **Dinner by Heston Blumenthal** at the Mandarin Oriental Hyde Park got plenty of press, but the one that really captured our tastebuds was the far more casual **Bar Boulud** (for both, see box p97), which is also at the Mandarin Oriental.

Eats & attractions

Over the last decade, even London's museums and galleries have begun to look beyond the shrink-wrapped sandwich to provide visitors with quality food. The **National Dining Rooms** (p84) has long led the field (and the pricing if you stray from the set lunch), but **Gallery Mess** (p99) at Chelsea's Saatchi Gallery and **Restaurant at St Paul's** (p162) are both also fine eateries in their own right.

Hot zones & Brit cuisine

These days you can eat well all over London, but our favourite restaurants still seem to cluster around Soho and Clerkenwell.

In the heart of Soho, **Hix** (p133), **Polpo** (p134) and **Arbutus** (p132) are reliably excellent (and, in the case of Arbutus, competitively priced), but among numerous appealing new arrivals are the Japanese noodle bar **Koya** (p133), New York diner **Spuntino** (p135) and ice-cream shop **Gelupo** (p141).

In Clerkenwell, Anna Hansen – one of the original co-owners of Marylebone's Providores & Tapa Room – has quietly jolted the tired concept of 'fusion food' out of its torpor at **Modern Pantry** (p154), and Exmouth Market has been rediscovering that foodie is fun with long-term Moorish favourite **Moro** opening a nicely relaxed new version next door: 'little Moro' or **Morito** (p156). **St John** (p156) is just down the road: this restaurant was the game-changer in modern British cooking in the 1990s and continues to serve brilliantly simple, classic combinations of gutsy, carefully sourced ingredients. A third outpost, this with bedrooms too, opened in early 2011 in the West End (p200).

Towards Covent Garden, we're still loving Paul Merrony's **Giaconda Dining Room** (p142), amid the guitar shops of London's 'Tin Pan Alley', and **Great Queen Street** (p142), but the area has had a real restaurant revival over the last year: steakhouse **Hawksmoor Seven Dials** (p142), classy Indian cafe **Dishoom** (p141) and tapas venue **Opera Tavern** (p143) have become instant favourites.

Following the lead set by St John, Brit bites continue to be very much in vogue. **Hereford Road** (p186) is a great exponent at the upper end of the scale, while **Clerkenwell Kitchen** (p154) is a leader in terms of support for traditional farming. The British nostalgia trend is exemplified at Sir Terence Conran's Boundary Project by **Albion** (p174), a casual ground-floor cafe that serves unpretentious, nostalgic dishes from kedgeree to welsh rarebit. Not far away, by Spitalfields Market,

S H O R T L I S T

Best new restaurants
- Bar Boulud (see box p97)
- Morito (p156)
- Viajante (p175)

Best new cheap eats
- Dishoom (p141)
- Koya (p133)
- Zucca (p74)

Best of British
- Great Queen Street (p142)
- Hereford Road (p186)
- St John (p156)

Best global scoff
- Barshu (p132)
- Modern Pantry (p154)
- Song Que (p175)

Best drop-in nosh
- Hummus Bros (p121)
- Lantana (p115)
- Princi (p134)

Best coffee
- Espresso Room (p121)
- Prufrock Coffee (p156)

Best ice-cream
- Gelupo (p141)
- Scoop (p143)

Best gastropubs
- Cadogan Arms (p99)
- Eagle (p154)

Best pubs
- Euston Tap (p126)
- Ye Olde Mitre (p157)

Best for wine
- Terroirs (p144)
- Vinoteca (p156)

Best new cocktails
- Experimental Cocktail Club (p132)
- Zetter Townhouse (p157)

DON'T MISS: 2012

Comptoir Libanais

Poppies (p174) is a fun new retro setting for fish and chips, produced by a fryer who learnt his trade in the 1950s on the Roman Road – proper East End, in other words.

Ethnic eats

Against the backdrop of all this Britishness, it's pleasing that ethnic eateries flourish. Everyone says it – and we really believe it's true: the whole world's food can be found here. Recent years have seen more sophisticated takes on Chinese cuisine, such as at **Barshu** (p132). Indian food is still strong – ranging from the haute cuisine of **Cinnamon Club** (p84) through Dishoom's take on the Irani cafe to cheap-and-cheerful chains such as **Masala Zone** (p169) – but you'll also find Koya's Japanese noodles in Soho, Middle Eastern just off Oxford Street at **Comptoir Libanais** (p102), brilliant Vietnamese at Shoreditch's **Song Que** (p175), authentic burritos at **Benito's Hat** (p114) and great tapas all over the place.

Drinking it all in

London's top-end cocktail venues are drawing the capital's drinking scene ever closer to the quality of New York or Sydney – **Mark's Bar** (p133) has been joined by the **Experimental Cocktail Club** (p132) in Soho, for example – but variety is the key. Shoreditch is home to both the events-driven **Book Club** (p164) and the crazy back room of **Callooh Callay** (p165). Covent Garden has the 'natural' wines of **Terroirs** (p144). **69 Colebrooke Row** (p171) and **Zetter Townhouse** (p157) serve inventive cocktails. There's also a notable revival in venues for great beer: **Euston Tap** (p126) is just one.

Gastropubs have contributed hugely to the revolution in modern British dining, their ambition to turn

Viajante p25

out top nosh in relaxed surroundings becoming an enduring part of the city's culinary repertoire, despite pale imitations. Newer stars include the **Cadogan Arms** (p99) and the **Orange Public House** (p98), but don't neglect old favourites such as the **Anchor & Hope** (p71) and, widely accepted as the pioneer of the genre, the **Eagle** (p154).

Dishoom p25

Neighbourhood watch

The **South Bank**, close to foodie-magnet Borough Market (p74), offers plenty of quality chain options on the riverside – you should also check out Skylon (p73) for a drink with fantastic views – but **Soho**, in the West End just across the river, is probably the best place in London for eats, both cheap and chic: canteen-style Busaba Eathai (p132), Hummus Bros and Princi do a brisk trade near upmarket neighbours such as Bocca di Lupo (p132), Arbutus and Dehesa (p132). Also in the West End, **Covent Garden** remains a busy tourist trap, but some very decent options have emerged, from Mexican at Wahaca (p144) to tapas at the Opera Tavern. Expense-account eats are concentrated in **Mayfair**: top-name chefs here include Claude Bosi at Hibiscus (p108), while celebrity executive chefs populate the posh hotel dining rooms. Further west, **Marylebone** is another foodie enclave, replete with top-notch delis, cafés and – on Sundays – a farmers' market. Superb options here include the formidable L'Autre Pied (p102) and cafe-style La Fromagerie (p102). Both **South Kensington** and **Chelsea** do expensive, special-occasion destinations, such as Zuma (p96), but the arrival of the likes of the Cadogan Arms has brought in more affordable fare. **The City** remains relatively poor for evening and weekend eats, but Clerkenwell next door is famously a culinary hotspot: from the Modern Pantry to the Eagle, St John and Moro, most London restaurant trends have been kicked off here. Shoreditch, just north-east of the City, is still the place for a top night out – the edgy bars have been joined by interesting restaurants, and are themselves beginning to head upmarket.

London 2012 Shop p31

Shopping

Londoners are unstoppable shoppers. They were battered by the recession, but the economic downturn underlined their tenacity: unable to resist a bargain, they're still out there trawling the city's markets and superluxe department stores, sniffing out the snips in London's flagship fashion outlets, tradition-soaked arcades and world-class boutiques.

In the past couple of years, London's shopkeepers have fallen back on their creative instincts, thinking up increasingly wily ways to tempt in the customers. High-concept pop-up shops, packed with limited edition products, appear and disappear across the capital each month; high-street outlets stock young design talent at budget prices; and department stores are refreshed and renewed.

We're even learning to love the shopping centre: at least when they combine good eating, quirky events and a mix of chains and higher-end fashion. Key players are **St Martin's Courtyard** (p146), **One New Change** (p164) and, due to open as Europe's biggest urban mall just as this guide comes out, **Westfield Stratford City** (p181), gateway to Olympic Park.

Fashionable young things

London's design strength has long been its young upstarts: recent graduates firmly entrenched in the youth scene they create for. Most young Londoners mix vintage with high street, shopping in chain stores full of high-profile design collaborations at rock-bottom prices (Japanese chain **Uniqlo**,

LINKS
LONDON

Official Jewellery Collection of Team GB

linksoflondon.com

p112; the indefatigable **Topshop**, p107. For the vintage side of the equation, Shoreditch still does the maths: **123 Boutique** (p176) and **Vintage Emporium** (p177) are exemplary but certainly not without local challengers. Heading elsewhere might take you upmarket (**Lucy in Disguise**, see box p140, in Covent Garden) or cheerfully downmarket (**Camden Market**, p170, still rewards rummaging).

To find something a little more unusual, get the low-down on sample sales, pop-up shops and one-off shopping events in *Time Out* magazine's weekly Shopping & Style section, or indulge Londoners' obsession with the concept store – try newcomers **Wolf & Badger** (p187) on Ledbury Road, Clerkenwell's **Out of Town** (p157) and edgy Dalston's **LN-CC** (p175). When money is no object, Mayfair's hallowed **Dover Street Market** (p111) is the city's most revered example.

It's worth checking out the well-established department stores: **Selfridges** (p104) and **Liberty** (p136), the latter having been revamped at the hands of fashion consultant Yasmin Sewell, are our long-term favourites, but even **Harrods** (p96) is no longer the byword among locals for 'more money than sense'.

Luxury labels continue to open on **Mount Street** (p111), the historic pink-brick Mayfair road that is fast replacing Sloane Street as the 'in' place to shop: we would have loved to have been a fly on the wall at the gunsmith, antique galleries and traditional butcher when they first clapped eyes on goth-rock designer Rick Owens or the five-floor Lanvin flagship. At the other side of the blade, **Redchurch Street** (p176) is a primer in why Shoreditch remains the fashionista's first port of call.

SHORTLIST

Best new
- Acne Studio (p110)
- Apple Store Covent Garden (p144)
- Lucy in Disguise (see box p140)
- Louis Vuitton Maison (p111)
- Mary's Living & Giving Shop (p187)
- Shop 24 (p112)

Best department stores
- Harrods (p96)
- Liberty (p136)
- Selfridges (p104)

Best shopping streets
- Broadway Market (p175)
- Mount Street (p111)
- Redchurch Street (p176)

Best books & music
- Foyles (p135)
- London Review Bookshop (p122)
- Rough Trade East (p176)

Best retro clothing
- 123 Boutique (p176)
- Vintage Emporium (p177)

Cutting-edge concepts
- Dover Street Market (p111)
- LN-CC (p175)
- Wolf & Badger (p187)

Best markets
- Borough Market (p74)
- Camden Market (p170)
- Portobello Road Market (p187)

Best London souvenirs
- London Transport Museum shop (p139)
- London 2012 Shop (p126)

Best old-style British
- Burlington Arcade (p110)
- James Smith & Sons (p144)

Liberty p31

Get cultural

In a city bursting with history,
the steady closure of London's
independent bookshops is sad, even
incongruous. Still, you can browse
travel literature in the Edwardian
conservatory of Daunt Books on
Marylebone High Street (p104)
or the never-ending selection of new
titles at **Foyles** (p135), where you
can try before you buy in the fine
café. Persephone Books on **Lamb's
Conduit Street** (p122) and the
London Review Bookshop
(p122) are new London classics,
while **Cecil Court** (p144) is an
irrepressible old stager – long may
the landlord stay benevolent.

Don't neglect the museum stores,
either: the **London Transport
Museum** (p139) and **Southbank
Centre** (p77) led the way with
strikingly designed gifts, but the
renewed **Museum of London**
(p159) and the **V&A** (p93) are
also terrific for original gifts.

Record and CD shops have also
taken a beating, but second-hand
vinyl and CDs linger on **Berwick
Street** (p135). Indie temple **Rough
Trade East** (p176) now feels like
it's been on Brick Lane forever, but
HMV (p118) – last of the big beasts
roaring on Oxford Street – seems
rather isolated.

Markets valued

Neighbourhood markets remain
the lifeblood of London shopping,
but few are the domain of Cockney
costermongers. Instead, you'll
find fashion kids flashing new
vintage sunglasses over a soy latte.
Borough Market (p74) is superb
for foodies (the more adventurous
might prefer Maltby Street, see
box p75), but canalside **Broadway
Market** (p175) is well worth the
trek into Hackney. Lush flower
market **Columbia Road** (p175)
is a classic Sunday morning outing;
try to get there before 11am, then
follow Brick Lane down to **Old
Spitalfields Market** (p176) and
the nearby Sunday (Up)Market,
which is great for fashion, crafts
and vintage clobber. You'll be an
expert in East End street-style by
early afternoon.

London's most famous markets
are also both going strong: despite
ongoing major redevelopment,
Camden's markets remain a major
tourist attraction, and – if you can

stomach the crowds – **Portobello Road Market** (p187) is terrific for antiques, bric-a-brac and star-spotting. Also in the vicinity, **Alfie's** (p170) is more laid-back and full of odd characters.

Neighbourhood watch

With more than 40,000 shops and 80 markets, shopping in London can be exhausting, so limit the territory you cover in each outing, sticking to one or two earmarked areas at a time. **Regent Street** is home to the flagships of many mid-range high-street clothing ranges. For a taste of retail past, the area around **St James's Street** is full of anachronistic specialists, including London's oldest hatter and the royal shoemaker; **Savile Row** has been given a shake-up in recent years by a handful of tailoring upstarts. **Mayfair** – especially Conduit Street, Bond Streets Old and New, and now Mount Street – remains the domain of major catwalk names.

To the north, it's best to hurry across heaving **Oxford Street** with its department stores, budget fashion and language schools. Duck instead into pedestrianised Gees Court and St Christopher's Place – pretty, interconnecting alleyways lined with cafés and shops that lead to the bottom of Marylebone. Curving **Marylebone High Street** has excellent fashion, perfumeries, gourmet shops and chic design stores.

A couple of London's most celebrated streets have recently been lifted out of chain-dominated doldrums. **Carnaby Street** has been salvaged by an influx of quality youth-clothing brands and Kingly Court; the decline of the **King's Road** has been arrested with some hip new stores, taking cues from the Shop at Bluebird.

Similarly, **Covent Garden** can no longer be written off as a tourist trap. New flagships have opened up in the piazza, while, to the north-west, cobbled Floral Street and the offshoots from Seven Dials remain fertile boutique-browsing ground. Don't miss sweet little Neal's Yard, with its wholefood cafés and herbalist. A little further north, **Lamb's Conduit Street** crams in appealing indie shops.

Unless you're working the plastic in the designer salons of Sloane Street or plan to marvel at the art nouveau food halls of Harrods, there's little reason to linger in **Knightsbridge**. Instead, for deluxe designer labels without the crush of people, try **Notting Hill**, especially where Westbourne Grove meets Ledbury Road.

On the other side of town, **Brick Lane** (mostly around the Old Truman Brewery and, at its northern end, Redchurch Street) has a dynamic collection of offbeat clothing and homeware shops.

The boutiques of **Islington** are also worth having a nose around, along Upper Street and on former antiques haven Camden Passage.

123 Boutique
p31

Proud2

WHAT'S BEST
Nightlife

While the last few years have been filled with the grim litany of club closures and doomy prognostications about the death of live music, this year has been looking rather more cheerful.

Yes, we lost the only recently relocated T Bar and hugely loved, generously staffed, brilliantly run Luminaire gig space, but it has been feeling like there are at least as many openings as closures at the moment.

In the railway arches behind the major tourist draws along the South Bank, **Cable** (p74) has been joined by the new superclub **Pulse** (p76). Further to the east, the unlucky Matter in the O2 Arena has reopened as **Proud2** (see box p185), which is run by the people behind a favoured indie-disco joint in Camden and a burlesque bar in

the City. Longer established venues are thriving too: **Fabric** (p157), despite all the worries about its financial strength when it was forced to close down Matter, is still doing a roaring trade in leftfield electronic wiggery, while the **Ministry of Sound** (p76) has kept right on hauling in big-name DJs for marquee-sign nights… now beyond its 20th birthday.

Shoreditch & Dalston

It's many years since Shoreditch was the watchword for clubbing cool, but it has seen a revival of sorts. Venues such as the **Book Club** (p164) continue to make a virtue of diverse programming, but the appearance of **XOYO** (p167) has seemed a bit more like the good old days: great music in an old-fashioned loft setting. One of the remaining fixtures from way back when, **Plastic People** (p167), has had a brush-up too.

If recession has forced some promoters out of business, it made the survivors get creative. Any space is up for grabs now: hence the unlikely birth of Dalston (easily accessible on the new Overground) as London's centre of edgy nights out, a land where surreal bars used to open every week under Turkish cafés and in not massively altered former video shops. Even here licensing and opening hours have begun to become more formalised, with the much-loved but barely organised Bardens Boudoir, for example, reopening as **Nest** (p178). A hit ever since it opened, the **Dalston Superstore** (p178) is already a clubbing reference point in the area, but there are still plenty of smaller dive bars – on Stoke Newington Road, you can try Moustache Bar (no.58) or Vogue Fabrics (no.66) – that keep the scene from ossifying.

Naughty, naughty

Burlesque continues to cover the mainstream in kitsch and feathers, with many a regular club night adding a stripper, some twisted magic or a bit of surreal cabaret. The best nights are at the sweet supper club **Volupté** (p158), **RVT** (p185) and the **Bethnal Green Working Men's Club** (p177), with **Bathhouse** (p164) a lively addition to the scene. In the West End, the hype is about celeb-magnet the **Box** (see box p137). The basement at the **Leicester Square Theatre** (p136) divides opinion (our cabaret critic likes it, one of our theatre critics doesn't), but we're all interested to see how the new cabaret space at the **Soho Theatre** (p139), ahem, takes off.

S H O R T L I S T

Best new clubs
- Nest (p178)
- Proud2 (see box p185)
- XOYO (p167)

Best superclub
- Fabric (p157)

Best stadium gigs
- O2 Arena (p184)

Rockin' pub-clubs
- Nest (p178)
- Old Blue Last (p167)
- Paradise (p187)
- Proud Camden (p170)

Best for bands
- Koko (p170)
- Scala (p128)

Best leftfield dance action
- Plastic People (p167)
- XOYO (p167)

Best for jazz
- Ronnie Scott's (p138)
- Vortex Jazz Club (p178)

For the outer limits
- Café Oto (p177)

Best comedy
- Comedy Store (p136)
- Soho Theatre (p139)

Best gay clubbing
- Dalston Superstore (p178)
- Fire (p184)

Best new cabaret
- The Box (see box p137)
- Soho Theare (p139)

Burlesque on the edge
- Bethnal Green Working Men's Club (p177)
- RVT (p185)

DON'T MISS: 2012

Small stage, big music

London's music scene is defined by rampant diversity. On any night, you'll find death metal, folk whimsy and plangent griots on one or other of the city's many stages.

At the top of the tree, and the most popular concert venue for four successive years (in 2010 it sold 1.7m tickets), is the **O2 Arena** (p184). This enormodome has pretty much cornered the market for classic rock and retro gigs (from Led Zeppelin to Duran Duran), as well as booking pop stars (Britney to Barry Manilow).

Although club/gig mash-ups have taken up some of the slack, London's mid-size venues have suffered carnage over the last several years: **Koko** (p170) and the **Scala** (p128) are the pick of the survivors, and the roster at upmarket jazz classic **Ronnie Scott's** (p138) is much improved over the last couple of years, after a brief period of bland rebranding.

There's also plenty of microscene life. Camden and Shoreditch are thriving with guitar-heavy music bars like **Proud** (p170) and the **Old Blue Last** (p167), and Dalston shines bright on the cutting edge: the **Vortex Jazz Club** (p178) and **Café Oto** (p177) both have ridiculously diverse programmes. Even Oxford Street's redoubtable **100 Club** (p118) has contrived to stay afloat – through sponsorship from Converse sneakers, starting in spring 2011 – but the loss of the Luminaire is still mourned.

Gay disco

Despite the influx of straight ravers to some club nights, 'Vauxhall Village' remains the hub for all folks gay and out who want to party hard. **RVT** (p185) is the key venue, a friendly, historic gay

Nest p35

tavern that hosts comedy nights, arty performance parties and discos. **Fire** (p184) and its rave-tastic Lightbox room remains the key party place, opening through to very, very late. The closure of numerous West End venues has also encouraged plenty of club nights to up sticks to Shoreditch and Dalston, creating a third gay scene to add to Vauxhall and, of course, Soho. **Dalston Superstore** (p178) is the stand-out venue for the new breed of young, gay Shoreditch hipster.

Just for laughs

Stand-up comedy has gone stadium-sized: Michael McIntyre is likely to follow the likes of Peter Kay in selling out the **O2** enormodome (p184) in 2012. It's not all supernova shows, though: on an extremely boisterous scene, check out the **Comedy Store** (p136), still the one that all the comedians want to play, and **Soho Theatre** (p139), great for interesting solo shows from breaking comics, for starters.

While London's nightlife is lively all year, anyone who's come here to see some comedy in late July or August is likely to be disappointed. Most of the city's performers head to Scotland for the Edinburgh Festival and consequently many venues are dark. Come in June or October instead: comedians are either trying out fresh shows or touring their Edinburgh triumph.

Making the most of it

Whatever you're doing, check the transport before you go: festivals, repairs and engineering tinkerage throw spanners in the works all year, notably on public holidays, but also many weekends. Regularly updated information can be found at **www.tfl.gov.uk**. Public

transport isn't as daunting as you might think. The tube is self-evident, even to newcomers, but it doesn't run much after midnight (New Year's Eve is the exception). Black cabs are pricey and hard to find at night, but safe. There are also licensed minicabs; on no account take an illegal minicab, even though they're touted outside every club. Far better to research the slow but comprehensive **night bus** system (p217) before leaving your hotel (see www.tfl.gov.uk's Journey Planner). A few minutes working out which bus gets you safe to bed can save hours of blurry-visioned confusion later.

You'll also kick yourself if you came all this way to see an event, only to arrive the one weekend it isn't on – or to find dates have changed. We've done our best to ensure the information in this guide is correct, but things change with little warning: www.timeout.com has the latest details or, if you're already here, buy *Time Out* magazine for weekly listings. Record shops are invaluable for flyers and advice – try the friendly folk at **Rough Trade East** (p176) for starters.

If the dates won't quite work out, don't despair. There's something going on here, no matter the day, no matter the hour. So if a useless mate forgets to get tickets, it isn't the end of the world. Even long-in-the-tooth Londoners fall across brand new happenings just by taking the wrong street, and the best way to get a taste of 'real London' – instead of the city every postcard-collecting tourist sees – is to go with the flow. Someone tells you about a party? Check it out. Read about a new band? Get a ticket. Sure, you've some 'essentials' in mind, but if you miss them this time... hell, come back next year.

Sadler's Wells p41

WHAT'S BEST

Arts & Leisure

London isn't just the political hub of Britain. It's the country's cultural and sporting capital too. Classical music of all types is studied and performed here, ambitious and inventive actors, directors and dancers learn their chops, and films are premièred and shot. The city also has two of the nation's top three football teams, national stadiums for football and rugby, and international centres of tennis and cricket. In the run-up to the **2012 Games** (pp8-17), sports and culture are going to be having a lot to do with each other, as cannier arts operators seize the opportunities of the **Cultural Olympiad** and **London 2012 Festival** (see box p54), even as vicious cuts in arts funding mean that this will be as challenging a year as it will be exciting.

Theatre & musicals

London's theatreland is looking oddly healthy and wealthy. It seems economic hard times have sent people to the theatre in search of distraction, rather than chasing them away – *The Lion King* beat its own record for highest annual West End takings. Nonetheless, producers remain cautious: for 2011/12 you can expect the usual crop of celebrity-led revivals and musicals piggy-backed on nostalgia for hit movies. The excellent *Billy Elliot* (Victoria Palace Theatre, p84), *Priscilla, Queen of the Desert* and a take on *Legally Blonde* (the Savoy, p147) that's sassy enough to have won four What's On Stage awards last year are joined in 2011 by *Shrek the Musical* (Theatre Royal Drury Lane, p147), the home-grown

DON'T MISS: 2012

Betty Blue Eyes (Novello Theatre, p147) with its animatronic pig voiced by Kylie, and a stunningly staged *Wizard of Oz* (London Palladium, p138).

The blockbuster musical's dominance in London is certainly under no immediate threat – the 25th anniversary of *Les Misérables* (Queen's Theatre, p138) saw two versions playing simultaneously in central London – but straight plays have been making a comeback. The success of new plays (*Clybourne Park* followed *Jerusalem* as a successful transfer from the **Royal Court Theatre**, p100) and starry classics (Ralph Fiennes is in *The Tempest* at the Theatre Royal Haymarket until 29 Oct 2011) have shown there is appetite for drama without a score, and there are also interesting new takes on dramatic entertainment – try the frankly terrifying *Ghost Stories* (Duke of York's, p147). Despite decreasing theatrical subsidies, the **National Theatre** (p76) has had a terrific couple of years. Its programme for this year includes a musical by Tori Amos (Apr 2012) and Zoe Wanamaker in Chekhov's *The Cherry Orchard* (May 2012). Even as Michael Grandage's successful reign as artistic director comes to an end, the **Donmar Warehouse** (see box p145) continues to show great resourcefulness: in addition to bringing real star power to its tiny space (Nicole Kidman, Ewan McGregor), it has made blockbuster successes of serious plays in the West End and, as 'Donmar Trafalgar', runs a showcase for coming directors.

A seemingly endless procession of London *Hamlet* productions still pulls in the punters. (Rory Kinnear at the National remains our pick, but we're excited about Michael Sheen's take at the **Young Vic**, p77). **Shakespeare's Globe** (p70)

SHORTLIST

Best of the West End
- *Billy Elliot* at the Victoria Palace Theatre (p84)
- *Ghost Stories* at the Duke of York's Theatre (p147)
- *Legally Blonde* at the Savoy Theatre (p147)

Best classical venues
- Kings Place (p128)
- Royal Opera House (p147)
- Wigmore Hall (p107)

Best cinemas
- BFI Southbank (p76)
- Curzon Soho (p138)

Best for theatre
- Donmar Warehouse (see box p145)
- National Theatre (p76)
- Royal Court Theatre (p100)

Best for contemporary dance
- Place (p128)
- Sadler's Wells (p172)

Most innovative work
- London Sinfonietta at Kings Place (p128)
- Punchdrunk (p42)
- Royal Court Theatre (p100)

Best festivals
- Greenwich & Docklands International Festival (p51)
- London Film Festival (p45)
- The Proms (p52)

Best bargains
- Half-price West End shows from tkts (p139)
- Prince Charles Cinema (p138)
- Standing tickets at Shakespeare's Globe (p70)
- £10 Monday at the Royal Court Theatre (p100)
- £10 Travelex tickets at the National Theatre (p76)

makes a wonderfully authentic setting for works by the Bard, but also check out the annual London season of the **Royal Shakespeare Company** (www.rsc.org.uk), usually at the **Roundhouse** (p171); the RSC also opens their musical version of Roald Dahl's *Matilda* (www. matildamusical.com) in the West End in autumn 2011.

At the younger, cultier end of the scale, watch out for the masters of immersive theatre, **Punchdrunk** (www.punchdrunk.org.uk), whose masked revels have been sending ecstatically spooked audiences through many-roomed venues in search of spectacular action for several years now. Their success was rewarded by an impressive 141% increase in Arts Council funding. Other theatre companies in favour include **Ockham's Razor** (www.ockhamsrazor.co.uk), who specialise in circus aerialist stunts. Some of the more acrobatic local and international theatre groups get to show off their skills at the always popular annual **Greenwich & Docklands International Festival** and revived **LIFT** (for both, p51).

Classical music & opera

The completion of office block-cum-auditorium **Kings Place** (p128) has been the biggest news in classical music over the last few years. It provides headquarters for the very different Orchestra of the Age of Enlightenment (www.oae.co.uk) and London Sinfonietta (www.londonsinfonietta.org.uk), as well as sculpture galleries and two concert halls with extremely good acoustics.

At the **Barbican** (p164), the London Symphony Orchestra (http://lso.co.uk) continues to play 90 concerts a year (watch out for

their performance of Philip Glass's *Einstein on the Beach* on 4-13 May 2012). The Royal Festival Hall at the **Southbank Centre** (p77) regularly hosts Esa-Pekka Salonen's Philharmonia Orchestra (www.philharmonia.co.uk), whose roster this year includes a live soundtrack for *Ben Hur* (9 June 2012) and Mahler's Resurrection Symphony (28 June 2012), as well as the London Philharmonic Orchestra (www.lpo.org.uk), playing a Prokofiev Festival (18-28 Jan 2012) and Bruckner's Symphony No.1 (30 Nov 2011).

London also has a pair of fine opera houses: Covent Garden's **Royal Opera House** (p147) combines assured crowd-pleasers – Verdi's *La traviata*, Mozart's *Don Giovanni* and *Le nozze di Figaro* – with a developing penchant for rarities: the world première of *Anna Nicole*, Mark-Anthony Turnage's opera about Playmate and celebrity widow Anna Nicole Smith, was an unlikely triumph last year, selling out its entire run. At the **Coliseum** (p146), the English National Opera performs classics (always in English), but also more experimental projects, increasingly film/music collaborations, with variable success.

Much of the city's classical music action happens in superb venues on an intimate scale. The exemplary **Wigmore Hall** (p107), **Cadogan Hall** (p100) and **LSO St Luke's** (p164) are all very atmospheric, and a number of churches host fine concerts: try **St Martin-in-the-Fields** (p80) and **St John's, Smith Square** (p84).

Film

In the death-struggle against increasingly sophisticated home entertainment systems (even mid-brow hotels often have in-room

DVD players now), many London cinemas try to make film-going an event: witness the luxury seats and auditorium alcohol licences. **Secret Cinema** (www.secretcinema.org) has even pioneered film-watching as immersive theatrical experience – strange locations, dressing up and lots of collateral entertainment.

Its been good to see new cinemas open (among them Curzon Millbank, just north of Tate Britain, in spring 2011), but less pleasing is the way mainstream titles creep on to the playbills of even arthouse cinemas, as the likes of the **Curzon Soho** (p138) and Everyman's revamped **Screen on the Green** (p172) struggle to keep audiences. This, plus the **Barbican** (p164) temporarily closing two of three screens and money troubles at the **ICA** (p87) leading to a slimmed down programme there, has meant smaller films find it hard to breathe in the capital. Cinemas committed to foreign and alternative films now amount to few more than the **BFI Southbank** (p76) – where London-obsessives will love the 'Capital Tales' archive strand.

Don't fret. As the multiplexes stuff their screens with bloated blockbusters (many presented in the 3D or IMAX alternative formats), smaller, less formal venues have begun to pick up the slack, and major attractions such as **Tate Modern** (p70) and even **St Paul's Cathedral** (p159) include film screenings on their events rosters. Keep an eye on *Time Out* magazine or www.timeout.com for these various venues, and for details of the city's frequent film festivals.

Dance

Two companies provide the full blocks-and-tutus experience. The **English National Ballet** (at the Coliseum, p146) and the **Royal Ballet** (at the Royal Opera House, p147) oblige with Tchaikovsky's *The Nutcracker* over Christmas. The Royal Ballet's programme is largely classics (*The Sleeping Beauty*, *Romeo & Juliet*), but increasingly throws in more adventurous fare. The company danced their first new commission for 15 years in 2011, selling out Christopher Wheeldon's *Alice in Wonderland* (it returns 17 Mar-3 Apr 2012); Wheeldon also presents his *Polyphonia* with commissions from Liam Scarlett and resident choreographer Wayne McGregor (5-18 Apr 2012); and the season peaks with unique National Gallery (p80) collaboration *Metamorphosis Titian* (14-20 July 2012), part of the London 2012 Festival.

London offers an unmatched range of performers and styles, way beyond the usual choice of classical or contemporary, and – apart from the quieter summer months – there's something worth seeing every night. **Sadler's Wells** (p172) offers a packed programme of top-quality work and hosts must-see festivals: the hip hop of **Breakin' Convention** (p49) is just one highlight. Autumn sees **Dance Umbrella** (p45) unfold with cutting-edge work from around the world. Keep an eye also on the **Barbican** (p164) and **Southbank Centre** (p77), both of which programme fine dance-theatre hybrids.

What's on

We've included long-running musicals we think are likely to survive through 2012. However, a new crop will inevitably open through the year, along with seasons at individual venues. *Time Out* magazine and www.timeout.com have the city's most informed and up-to-date listings.

Calendar

Pride London p51

This is our pick of annual and one-off events. Buy *Time Out* magazine and check www.timeout.com/london for weekly updates, and always confirm dates before making plans. Names of London 2012 events are in pink; dates of public holidays are given in **bold**.

September 2011

until 25 Sept **Road to 2012**
National Portrait Gallery, p80
http://roadto2012.npg.org.uk
Ongoing photography commissions.

4 **London Mela**
Gunnersbury Park, Ealing
www.londonmela.org
South Asian music and street arts.

early Sept **Sky Ride**
www.goskyride.com

Some 50,000 cyclists ride a traffic-free route in a party atmosphere.

8 **International Paralympic Day**
Trafalgar Square, p83
www.paralympic.org
Try out some sports from the London 2012 Paralympic Games; see pp16-17.

10-11 **Mayor's Thames Festival**
Westminster & Tower Bridges
www.thamesfestival.org

17 **Great River Race**
Thames, Richmond to Greenwich
www.greatriverrace.co.uk
Entertaining race of 300 exotic rowing craft from around the world.

17-18 **Open-City London**
www.open-city.org.uk
Free access to 600 amazing buildings normally closed to the public.

18 **Tour of Britain**
Central London
www.tourofbritain.co.uk
Last stage of the eight-day cycle race.

21 **Peace One Day Concert**
O2 Arena, p184
www.peaceoneday.org

24 **Great Gorilla Run**
Mincing Lane, the City
www.greatgorillas.org/london
Fundraising run in gorilla suits.

October 2011

3 Oct-late Nov **Dance Umbrella**
www.danceumbrella.co.uk
The city's headline dance festival.

6 Oct-19 Feb 2012 **Grayson Perry:
Tomb of the Unknown Craftsman**
British Museum, p118
www.britishmuseum.org
Artist's installation using anonymous
craft works from the vast archive.

9 **Pearly Kings & Queens
Harvest Festival**
St Martin-in-the-Fields, p80
www.pearlysociety.co.uk

12-27 **BFI London Film Festival**
BFI Southbank, p76
www.bfi.org.uk/lff

13-16 **Frieze Art Fair**
Regent's Park, p101
www.friezeartfair.com

late Oct-late Apr 2012
**Veolia Environnement Wildlife
Photographer of the Year**
Natural History Museum, p89
www.nhm.ac.uk/wildphoto

26 **Diwali**
Trafalgar Square, p83
www.london.gov.uk

November 2011

Ongoing Dance Umbrella, Grayson
Perry, Wildlife Photographer of the
Year (see Oct)

5 **Bonfire Night**
Firework displays all over town.

6 **London to Brighton
Veteran Car Run**
Serpentine Road in Hyde Park, p95
www.lbvcr.com

9 Nov-5 Feb 2012 **Leonardo
da Vinci: Painter at the Court
of Milan**
National Gallery, p80
www.nationalgallery.org.uk

11-20 **London Jazz Festival**
www.londonjazzfestival.org.uk

12 **Lord Mayor's Show**
The City
www.lordmayorsshow.org
A grand inauguration procession for
the Lord Mayor of the City of London.

13 **Remembrance
Sunday Ceremony**
Cenotaph, Whitehall

Nov-Dec **Christmas Tree & Lights**
Trafalgar Square, p83
www.london.gov.uk
An impressive Norwegian spruce is
mounted and lit in the centre of the city.

December 2011

Ongoing Grayson Perry, Wildlife
Photographer of the Year (see Oct);
Christmas Tree & Lights (see Nov)

mid Dec **Spitalfields Festival**
www.spitalfieldsfestival.org.uk
Biannual festival of classical music.

26 **Christmas Day Bank Holiday**

28 **Boxing Day Bank Holiday**

31 **New Year's Eve Celebrations**
See box p48.

January 2012

Ongoing Grayson Perry, Wildlife
Photographer of the Year (see Oct);
Leonardo da Vinci (see Nov)

Chinese New Year Festival

2 New Year's Day Holiday

10-18 Test Event: Gymnastics
North Greenwich Arena, p207
www.londonpreparesseries.com

29 Chinese New Year Festival
Chinatown, p129, Leicester Square,
p129, & Trafalgar Square, p83
www.londonchinatown.org

**14-29 London International
Mime Festival**
www.mimefest.co.uk

February 2012

Ongoing Grayson Perry, Wildlife
Photographer of the Year (see Oct);
Leonardo da Vinci (see Nov)

9 Feb-27 May
Lucian Freud Portraits
National Portrait Gallery, p80
www.npg.org.uk

17-19 Test Event: Cycling – Track
Velodrome, Olympic Park, p206
www.londonpreparesseries.com

**20-26 Test Event: Aquatics –
Diving**
Aquatics Centre, Olympic Park, p206
www.londonpreparesseries.com

21 Poulters Pancake Day Race
Guildhall Yard, the City
www.poulters.org.uk
Livery companies race while tossing
pancakes; a Shrove Tuesday tradition.

March 2012

Ongoing Wildlife Photographer of
the Year (see Oct); Lucian Freud
(see Feb)

early Mar
Maslenitsa Russian Festival
Trafalgar Square, p83
www.maslenitsa.co.uk

Mar-Aug **British Design 1948-2012**
Victoria & Albert Museum, p93
www.vam.ac.uk

late Mar-early Apr **London Lesbian
& Gay Film Festival**
BFI Southbank, p76
www.llgff.org.uk

April 2012

Ongoing Wildlife Photographer
of the Year (see Oct); Lucian Freud
(see Feb); British Design, Lesbian
& Gay Film Festival (see Mar)

5 Apr-9 Sept **Damien Hirst**
Tate Modern, p70
www.tate.org.uk
Generation-defining British artist.

6 Good Friday

**7 Oxford & Cambridge
Boat Race**
On the Thames, Putney to Mortlake
www.theboatrace.org
The 158th outing for Varsity rowers.

9 Easter Monday

early Apr-early May **Word Festival**
Various East End locations
www.londonwordfestival.com
A month of hip literature events.

early Apr-mid May **Spring Loaded**
Place, p128
www.theplace.org.uk
Contemporary dance festival.

**18-22 Test Event: Aquatics –
Synchronised Swimming**
Aquatics Centre, Olympic Park, p206
www.londonpreparesseries.com

22 London Marathon
Greenwich Park to the Mall
www.virginlondonmarathon.com

23 Apr-9 Sept
World Shakespeare Festival
www.rsc.org.uk
Global season of collaborative plays.

26-29 Sundance London
O2 Arena, p184
www.sundance-london.com
Robert Redford's independent film fest.

Festive Fun

How to get the best out of Christmas and New Year.

London never used to be much fun at the turn of the year. With no public transport on Christmas Day, the centre of the capital feels eerily deserted – a magical transformation for a city usually teeming with people, but not one that's easy to enjoy unless you've got a designated driver happy to forgo the egg nog. And New Year's Eve seemed to involve cramming as many idiots as possible into Trafalgar Square (p83), without so much as a drink to warm them.

Things have changed. There's been an explosion of middle European-style Christmas markets across town. Each has its own approach – from the traditional version in Covent Garden (p139) to the annual fairground of Winter Wonderland in Hyde Park (p95) – but mulled wine, spiced German cake and ice rinks are constants.

For pretty Christmas lights, skip the commercialised ones on Oxford and Regent Streets and try St Christopher's Place, Marylebone High Street and Covent Garden.

The best window displays are usually at old-fashioned Fortnum & Mason (p87) and style-palace Liberty (p136), and Mayor Boris Johnson has declared Oxford Street will close to traffic on 10-11 December in addition to the now traditional Boxing Day closure that facilitates pedestrian access to the crazy sales.

More interested in partying than purchasing? The week after Christmas is when the locals go nuts, and the best advice is to do as they do: forget paying inflated prices for a disappointing New Year's Eve bash and go out instead on New Year's Day. Parties kick off from 5am and attract a cooler crowd, happy in the knowledge they're paying a third of the price for exactly the same DJs as were playing at midnight – check *Time Out* magazine for details. If you do want to join the mob for the trad New Year's Eve bash, head to the South Bank, where a full-on fireworks display is launched from the London Eye and Thames rafts.

late Apr **Camden Crawl**
Camden, p168
www.thecamdencrawl.com
Fun multi-pub music 'microfestival'.

late Apr **Breakin' Convention**
Sadler's Wells, p172
www.breakinconvention.com
Jonzi D's terrific street dance festival.

late Apr **Land of Kings**
Dalston, p172
www.landofkings.co.uk
Trendy music and art mash-up.

May 2012

Ongoing Lucian Freud (see Feb);
British Design (see Mar); Damien
Hirst, World Shakespeare Festival,
Word, Spring Loaded (see Apr)

2-6 **Test Event: Hockey**
Hockey Centre, Olympic Park, p206
www.londonpreparesseries.com

2-6 **Test Event:
Wheelchair Tennis**
Eton Manor, Olympic Park, p206
www.londonpreparesseries.com

3-6 **Test Event: Aquatics –
Water Polo**
Aquatics Centre, Olympic Park, p206
www.londonpreparesseries.com

4-7 **Test Event: Athletics**
Olympic Stadium, p206
www.londonpreparesseries.com

7 Early May Bank Holiday

8 **Test Event: Paralympic
Athletics**
Olympic Stadium, p206
www.londonpreparesseries.com

late May **Chelsea Flower Show**
Royal Hospital Chelsea
www.rhs.org.uk

June 2012

Ongoing British Design (see Mar);
Damien Hirst, World Shakespeare
Festival (see Apr)

2-5 **Diamond Jubilee**
www.thamesdiamondjubileepageant.org
A huge flotilla (2 June) is planned for the
60th anniversary of the coronation.

**4-5 Spring & Queen's Diamond
Jubilee Bank Holidays**

6 June-9 July **Tanztheater
Wuppertal Pina Bausch:
World Cities 2012**
Barbican, p164; Sadler's
Wells, p172
www.pina-bausch.de/en/

DON'T MISS: 2012

Camden Crawl

Superb troupe of the late German choreographer explores ten global cities.

early June **Beating Retreat**
Horse Guards Parade, Whitehall
www.army.mod.uk
A pageant of military music and precision marching, beginning at 7pm.

early June **Little London Fields**
Near Broadway Market, p175
www.littlelondonfields.co.uk
The city's trendiest free music festival.

early June-mid Aug
Opera Holland Park
www.operahollandpark.com

mid-late June **Spitalfields Festival**
See above Dec 2011.

mid June
Open Garden Squares Weekend
www.opensquares.org
Private gardens opened to the public.

mid June **Meltdown**
Southbank Centre, p77
www.southbank.co.uk
Music and culture festival, curated by a different musician every year.

mid June **Trooping the Colour**
Horse Guards Parade, St James's
www.trooping-the-colour.co.uk
The Queen's official birthday parade.

21 June-9 Sept
London 2012 Festival
www.london2012.com
See box p54.

25 June-8 July **Wimbledon Lawn
Tennis Championships**
www.wimbledon.org

28 June-14 Oct **Edvard Munch:
The Modern Eye**
Tate Modern, p70
www.tate.org.uk
Painter of *The Scream* reassessed.

late June-mid Aug **LIFT (London
International Festival of Theatre)**
www.liftfest.org.uk

late June-mid Aug
City of London Festival
The City
www.colf.org
A festival of mostly free music and art, often in historic City venues.

late June-early July **Greenwich &
Docklands International Festival**
www.festival.org
Outdoor theatricals, usually on an impressively large scale.

July 2012

Ongoing British Design (see Mar); Damien Hirst, World Shakespeare Festival (see Apr); World Cities 2012, Opera Holland Park, London 2012 Festival, Wimbledon, Edvard Munch, LIFT, City of London Festival, Greenwich & Docklands International Festival (see June)

early July **Wireless Festival**
Hyde Park, p95
www.wirelessfestival.co.uk
Three nights of rock and dance acts in the lovely Royal Park.

early July **Pride London**
Oxford Street to Victoria
Embankment
www.pridelondon.org
Huge annual gay and lesbian parade.

early July-mid Sept
Watch This Space
National Theatre, p76
www.nationaltheatre.org.uk/wts
Alfresco theatre beside the Thames.

7-15 **Big Dance 2012**
www.bigdance2012.com
Royal Ballet's Wayne McGregor will work with 2,000 dancers in Trafalgar Square, among other highlights.

mid July **Lovebox Weekender**
Victoria Park, Hackney
www.lovebox.net
Top-quality weekend music festival.

mid July **Somerset House Series**
Somerset House, p152

Oxford & Cambridge Boat Race p47

www.somerset-house.org.uk/music
A dozen concerts in the fountain court.

mid July-mid Sept
The Proms (BBC Sir Henry Wood Promenade Concerts)
Royal Albert Hall, p95
www.bbc.co.uk/proms
London's best classical music festival, packed with top-class performers – at bargain prices if you're happy to stand.

late July-late Sept **Road to 2012**
See above Sept 2011.

21-27 **London 2012 Torch Relay**
www.london2012.com
The Olympic Torch arrives in London for the end of its 70-day tour of the UK.

27 July-12 Aug
London 2012 Olympic Games
Venues across the country, p206
www.london2012.com
For schedule, see pp14-15.

27 July-12 Aug **The Olympic Journey: the Story of the Games**
Royal Opera House, p147
www.roh.org.uk/theolympicjourney
Free exhibition of every medal since 1896 and every Torch since 1936.

31 July-16 Sept **Another London**
Tate Britain, p83
www.tate.org.uk
150 snaps of the city, taken by such key 20th-century photographers as Henri Cartier-Bresson and Robert Frank.

August 2012

Ongoing British Design (see Mar); Damien Hirst, World Shakespeare Festival (see Apr); Opera Holland Park, London 2012 Festival, Edvard Munch, LIFT, City of London Festival (see June); Watch This Space, The Proms, London 2012 Olympic Games, The Olympic Journey, Another London (see July)

early Aug
Great British Beer Festival
Earls Court Exhibition Centre
http://gbbf.camra.org.uk
Terrific introduction to proper ale.

25-26 **Notting Hill Carnival**
Notting Hill, p186
www.nottinghillcarnival.biz
Europe's biggest street party brings Caribbean music and dance to town.

27 **Summer Bank Holiday**

29 Aug-9 Sept
London 2012 Paralympic Games
Venues across the country, p206
www.london2012.com
For schedule, see p17.

September 2012

Ongoing Damien Hirst, World
Shakespeare Festival (see Apr);
London 2012 Festival, Edvard
Munch (see June); Watch This
Space, The Proms, Another London
(see July); London 2012 Paralympic
Games (see Aug)

early Sept **London Mela**
See above Sept 2011.

early Sept **Sky Ride**
See above Sept 2011.

from 12 **Pre-Raphaelites:
Victorian Avant-Garde**
Tate Britain, p83
www.tate.org.uk
The first British modern art movement.

mid Sept
Mayor's Thames Festival
See above Sept 2011.

mid Sept **Tour of Britain**
See above Sept 2011.

mid Sept **Open-City London**
See above Sept 2011.

late Sept **Great River Race**
See above Sept 2011.

late Sept **Great Gorilla Run**
See above Sept 2011.

October 2012

Ongoing Edvard Munch (see June);
Dance Umbrella (see Sept)

early Oct **Pearly Kings &
Queens Harvest Festival**
See above Oct 2011.

early Oct-late Nov **Dance Umbrella**
See above Oct 2011.

mid Oct-early Nov
London Film Festival
See above Oct 2011.

mid Oct **Frieze Art Fair**
See above Oct 2011.

from late Oct **Veolia
Environnement Wildlife
Photographer of the Year**
See above Oct 2011.

November 2012

Ongoing Dance Umbrella (see
Sept); London Film Festival,
Wildlife Photographer of the
Year (see Oct)

5 **Bonfire Night**

11 **Remembrance Sunday**
See above Nov 2011.

13 **Diwali**
See above Oct 2011.

early Nov **London to Brighton
Veteran Car Run**
See above Nov 2011.

early Nov **Lord Mayor's Show**
See above Nov 2011.

mid Nov **London Jazz Festival**
See above Nov 2011.

Nov-Dec **Christmas Tree
& Lights**
See above Nov 2011.

December 2012

Ongoing Wildlife Photographer of
the Year (see Oct); Christmas Tree
& Lights (see Nov)

mid Dec **Spitalfields Festival**
See above Dec 2011.

25 **Christmas Day**

26 **Boxing Day**

31 **New Year's Eve Celebrations**

London 2012 Festival

The artiest party of the year.

Culmination of the Cultural Olympiad – £83m of artistic activity right across the country – the **London 2012 Festival** will run from 21 June to 9 September 2012, and the programme for the capital is shaping up nicely.

In east London, BBC Radio 1's Hackney Weekend will host 80 musicians on six stages. Former Blur frontman Damon Albarn and cartoonist Jamie Hewlett have been commissioned to create a new opera, while *Metamorphosis: Titian 2012*, a National Gallery (p80) and Royal Opera House (p147) collaboration, responds to paintings by the Renaissance master. Simon Armitage will host a Poetry Parnassus event at the Southbank Centre (p77). There will also be artefacts on display from the Olympic Museum (p52), an expanded Big Dance 2012 (p51) and city-themed work from ace choreographer Pina Bausch's Tanztheater Wuppertal (p49).

As well as commissions from Olafur Eliasson (with the Serpentine Gallery, p93) and Martin Creed, contemporary art will be represented by high-profile exhibitions of David Hockney (Royal Academy, p107), Rachel Whiteread (Whitechapel Gallery, p174), Lucian Freud (p47) and Damien Hirst (p47).

In theatre, the Barbican (p164) stages *Gross und Klein*, starring Cate Blanchett, and Desdemona Project, a collaboration between author Toni Morrison and Malian singer Rokia Traoré. Theatre Royal Stratford East (p181) is developing new work, while the Bard is represented by the RSC's World Shakespeare Festival (p47) and, at Shakespeare's Globe (p70), each of his plays staged in a different language – Arabic, Urdu, Aboriginal and sign language among them.

On 26 July 2012, the eve of the Opening Ceremony, Rivers of Music will feature free music events at key sites along the Thames for 500,000 spectators.

Tickets for more than 1,000 festival events are due to go on sale in October 2011.

■ *www.london2012.com/festival*

Big Dance 2012

Itineraries

Tower Bridge

The Sights in a Trice

Got a couple of free days after your sessions at the 2012 Games? Fancy ticking off the major sights in double-quick time? This two-day itinerary uses the Thames as its axis. It's mostly on foot, but uses some public transport, so slip on comfy trainers, grab your Oyster travelcard (p216) and get set… go!

Day 1

The **Tower of London** (p161) gets mobbed as the day progresses, so it's a good place to start. Get there for 9am (10am Mon, Sun) and take the travelator past the Crown Jewels before the queue builds up. Then join one of the Yeoman Warder ('Beefeater') tours for an entertaining overview of the place, before checking out the armaments and garderobes in the White Tower and the prisoner graffiti in Beauchamp Tower.

Next, take in the brilliant views as you stroll across **Tower Bridge** (p161); www.towerbridge.org.uk gives bridge lift times. Turn right, down to the Queen's Walk, and head east along the south bank, passing **City Hall** (p62) and **HMS Belfast** (p63). On Thursday, Friday or Saturday have a gourmet refuel at **Borough Market** (p74): perhaps a chocolate brownie from Flour Power City Bakery, seared scallops from Shellseekers Fish & Game, or Kappacasein's toasted cheese sandwiches. If the market's closed, **Roast** (p73) can supply slow-roast Wicks Manor pork belly and grilled calf's liver. Then pep yourself up for the next stint with a latte from Monmouth Coffee.

Continue along the Thames until you hit **Tate Modern** (p70), the world's most-visited modern art gallery. The displayed works are superb, of course, but so is the river vista from the Espresso Bar or Tate Modern Restaurant.

Cross the **Millennium Bridge** and walk up the broad, snaking staircase to **St Paul's Cathedral** (p159), Wren's masterwork. You then have two choices. You could take a nostalgic ride on a red double-decker bus to Aldwych. The **Routemaster** (p80) has been phased out of use (a new version comes into service in 2012), but a few continue to run on Heritage Route 15. Board at Stop SJ, outside St Paul's, for a ride west along Fleet Street, past the Royal Courts of Justice (look right after the griffin statue in the middle of the road) and along the Strand. Get off at Savoy Street (Stop U) for the deco entranceway to the **Savoy Hotel** (p201), then nip across the busy road into Covent Garden for supper – try the **Opera Tavern** (p143), opposite the Drury Lane Theatre – before checking out the buzz and buskers of **Covent Garden Market** (p139).

Otherwise, head north from St Paul's through Paternoster Square, along Little Britain, past Smithfield Market and up St John Street, where you'll find a cluster of London's finest restaurants, including modern British classic **St John** (p156). If you've got more energy, superclub **Fabric** (p157) is open at weekends.

Day 2

Feeling the effects from last night's party? Grab a hot perk-me-up and sandwiches for lunch at **Green Park** tube (Caffè Nero and Pret A Manger, ubiquitous London chains, are both here), then walk across the lawns to **Buckingham Palace** (p85). The Changing of the Guard happens here at 11.30am daily from May to July (alternate days August to April), lasting about half an hour. In summer, you can tour the palace's State Rooms, or the Royal Mews can be visited year-round.

When you're done with the palace, head into lovely **St James's Park** (p85) for your picnic or take the second left at the Queen Victoria

Memorial roundabout on to Spur Road, then along Birdcage Walk, to pop your eyes at Westminster's finest structures. Admire the twin towers and flying buttresses of **Westminster Abbey** (p83), pop into the **Houses of Parliament** (p80) to watch a peppery debate, or just listen to the familiar tune of the tallest four-faced chiming clock in the world – the famous clocktower of **Big Ben**. Parliament Square is another, usually traffic-disturbed, picnic possibility.

Wander north up **Whitehall**, with its war memorials and blank-faced government buildings. On your left, you pass **Downing Street** – home of the Prime Minister (at no.10) and his Chancellor (at no.11), but with no public access – and, at **Horse Guards** (p85), sword-bearing cavalrymen in sentryboxes. **Trafalgar Square** (p83) opens out at the end of Whitehall; behind the black statue of a mounted Charles I, a plaque marks the official centre of London. After a look at the **Fourth Plinth** – now a site for contemporary sculpture commissions – climb the steps on to the pedestrianised northern side of the square.

You're now in front of the **National Gallery** (p80), one of the world's greatest repositories for art. Admission is free, as are ace guided tours that might steer you to masterpieces by Raphael, Rembrandt or Monet. For dinner, the gallery has two options: the **National Dining Rooms** (p84), with a bakery-cafe (open to 5.30pm, or 8.30pm on Fridays) and rather more expensive restaurant, and the darkly handsome **National Café**, open until 11pm (6pm on Sunday).

Head due north. You'll not want to linger in **Leicester Square** (p129), but instead push past **Chinatown** and into **Soho** – for great traditional pubs and hip bars (pp129-135).

ITINERARIES

Olympic Stadium

Olympic Park Ride

The best way to get a sneak preview of the **Olympic Park** (p179) – and a fine way to enjoy some time off between sessions if you've tickets to the 2012 Games – is exploring the banks of the canals, cuts and rivers that surround the Park. Given the scale of the site, a bike is the best mode of transport through what was until recently just an industrial wasteland a few miles east of the centre of town.

Try to do this itinerary on a weekday, when the cafés, pubs and towpaths are all quieter. We've assumed you'll be coming from the centre of town, but the route can be done as a walk from the Olympic Park itself, simply by picking up the instructions at the View Tube. The second half of the itinerary would be a long walk (around two hours, without breaks); you can also do the first half in reverse, taking about an hour to Bethnal Green tube station, with the last 20mins on the pavements of busy

roads. On a bicycle, the itinerary takes a relaxed couple of hours, but hire your bike for four hours to give you time to take breaks.

Board a Central line tube (it has stops at Oxford Circus and other very central locations) to Bethnal Green. Exit on to Cambridge Heath Road, heading south. **Bikeworks** (nos.138-140, E1 5QJ, 8980 7998, www.bikeworks.org.uk) is on your left after about 5mins, shortly after the railway bridge. It opens at 9am (10am Fri, Sat). Four hours' hire costs £10 (with helmet, lock and lights), plus £150 pre-authorised on your credit card. (You can instead leave your passport or driving licence with them.)

Bike ready? Helmet on? This is the least enjoyable section of the itinerary. Pedal back north past Bethnal Green tube station and, just after the **V&A Museum of Childhood** (p172) on your right, turn along Old Ford Road. You'll soon see the fountain lake of

Victoria Park through the fence on your left. Keep going. At a little roundabout, the Park is split by Grove Road. Enter the second section of the park and that's the last you'll see of traffic for a while.

Alongside the park is the **Hertford Union Canal**, which connects Regent's Canal to the River Lea. Take the first bridge exit out of the park and descend to the towpath. It's an easy ride, apart from some steep locks and short bone-rattling sections, but does get tight under bridges. Remember your towpath etiquette: two tings on the bell to alert pedestrians and bikes, and always give way to walkers.

There's usually a cluster of narrowboats under a pedestrian bridge with a big red hoop. If you skipped breakfast, cross for Roach Road's Counter Café (07952 696 388); otherwise, keep on to where the towpath soon makes a sharp left turn at the Lee Navigation. Here you get a first eyeful of the white girders and spotlight stanchions of the **Olympic Stadium**.

The towpath heads steeply up over a bridge. Cross and descend the equally steep far side. Serious students of the 2012 Games might want to venture north to see the IBC/MPC (International Broadcast Centre/Main Press Centre), Handball Arena and Velodrome, but we're going to go straight south.

The stadium grows irresistibly larger on your left as you pedal alongside the Olympic Park. To your right across the river, you'll spot the new premises of venerable fish smokery **Forman's** (p181), in its appropriately salmon-pink hue. Keep going through **Old Ford Lock**, one of the prettiest on the Lea, and straight after a cluster of skewed bridges by some new flats, you'll see a signpost tree. Follow the 'Capital Ring' and 'Link to the Greenway 80 yards' pointers up a gentle slope and you're on a ridge alongside the Olympic Park venues.

The main stadium demands your attention, but off to the right is the swooping glass roof of Zaha Hadid's **Aquatics Centre**, with a lime-green corrugated iron building facing it. This is the **View Tube** (see box p182), with a fine café and several bike stands. The upstairs

Velodrome

balcony has excellent views and information boards that help you figure out what you can see.

Return the way you've come, then double back behind the View Tube on a lower path to come out at Pudding Mill Lane DLR station. Go left, away from the Stadium, and left again on the next bit of towpath. This takes you to Blaker Road. Again head away from the Stadium, then wheel the bike left along the pavement of the busy four-lane High Street (the A118). Take the pedestrian crossing, turn right and remount when you're on the towpath of **Three Mills Wall River**. This is a continuation of the Waterworks River, which runs along the far side of the Olympic Park, past the Olympic Village.

Keeping south, you'll soon come to the narrowboats of **Three Mills Island** (p179), with Canary Wharf on the horizon. Head across the grass to your left to admire the pale concrete and black hydraulic jacks of Three Mills Lock. In the distance is the rust-red, lime-green and grey

View Tube p59

roof of Bazalgette's impressive Abbey Mills Pumping Station, built back in the 1860s.

Back by the narrowboats, head over the cobbles between the mills that give this little river island its name – look for the pair of witch's hat roofs on the Clock Mill. After the cobbles, hop back on the bike and veer left along the easy path between Bow Creek and the last section of the Lee Navigation. The Canary Wharf skyscrapers now cluster large in front of you as you ride past a willow and under a mix of iron railway bridges and concrete, before crossing a steep white bridge over **Bow Locks**.

Limehouse Cut zooms straight south-west from here towards the marina of Limehouse Basin. Stop and look back over your left shoulder just before it begins its final curve: that geometrically spiky white tower is the spire of Hawksmoor's palatial St Anne's Limehouse, consecrated in 1730. Turn left into the little park as soon as you can, veering right to pedal gently past the bandstand on to Narrow Street. Another right brings you to the old **Grapes** pub (76 Narrow Street, E14 8BP, 7987 4396). There are three bike stands opposite. Food is served from noon to about 2pm, but the place closes mid-afternoon on weekdays.

Fortified, it's back to the park and across the Cut on the big black pedestrian bridge you previously cycled beneath. Follow the edge of the basin round to the lock gates under the brick bridge, and head north up the **Regent's Canal**. Not long after the fine traditional Palm Tree pub, the towpath heads steeply up and, from the top, you'll see the start of another canal. It's the Hertford Union again. Exit north on to the proper road: this is Old Ford Road. Turn left to retrace your route back to Bikeworks.

London by Area

The South Bank

Tourists have been coming to the South Bank for centuries, but the entertainments have changed a little. **Shakespeare's Globe** has risen again, but for the associated prostitutes, gamblers and bear-baiting you'd need a time machine. Instead, enjoy a revitalised cultural hub – the **Southbank Centre**, **BFI Southbank** cinema complex and **Hayward** gallery – or join the multitude strolling the broad riverside walkway that takes you between Tower Bridge (p161) and Westminster Bridge. This strings together fine views and must-see attractions such as **Tate Modern**, and the **London Eye**. **Borough Market** typifies the South Bank's appeal: visitors find it charming, but locals love it too.

Until late 2011 (when a cross-river station should be complete), the South Bank walk is subject to an irritating inland diversion just after Blackfriars Bridge.

Sights & museums

City Hall

Queen's Walk, SE1 2AA (www.london.gov.uk). London Bridge tube/rail. **Open** 8.30am-6pm Mon-Thur; 8.30am-5.30pm Fri. **Admission** free. **Map** p65 F2 ❶
Designed by Foster & Partners, this 45m-tall, eco-friendly rotund glass structure leans 31° away from the river. Home to London's metropolitan government, it has a huge aerial photo of the city you can walk on in the lower ground floor Visitor Centre and a café. Next door, Potters Fields Park and outdoor amphitheatre the Scoop host events through the summer.

Design Museum

Shad Thames, SE1 2YD (7403 6933, www.designmuseum.org). Tower Hill tube or London Bridge tube/rail. **Open** 10am-5.45pm daily. **Admission** £8.50; free-£6.50 reductions. **Map** p65 F2 ❷
The temporary exhibitions in this white 1930s building (previously a banana

warehouse) focus on modern and contemporary industrial and fashion design, architecture, graphics and multimedia developments. The smart Blueprint Café has a fine balcony overlooking the river. **Event highlights** 'Designers in Residence' (until 22 Jan 2012).

Fashion & Textile Museum

83 Bermondsey Street, SE1 3XF (7407 8664, www.ftmlondon.org). London Bridge tube/rail. **Open** 11am-6pm Wed-Sun. **Admission** £6.50; free-£3.50 reductions. **Map** p65 F4 ❸

Flamboyant as its founder, fashion designer Zandra Rhodes, this pink and orange museum holds 3,000 of Rhodes' garments, some on permanent display, along with her archive of paper designs, sketchbooks, silk screens and show videos. There are also a shop, a little café and changing exhibitions. **Event highlights** 'Tommy Nutter: The Rebel on the Row' (until 22 Oct 2011); 'From Catwalk to Cover' (18 Nov 2011-26 Feb 2012).

Florence Nightingale Museum

St Thomas's Hospital, 2 Lambeth Palace Road, SE1 7EW (7620 0374, www.florence-nightingale.co.uk). Westminster tube or Waterloo tube/rail. **Open** 10am-5pm daily. **Admission** £5.80; free-£4.80 reductions; £16 family. **Map** p64 A3 ❹

The nursing skill and zeal that made Nightingale a Victorian legend are honoured here. Reopened for the centenary of her death in 1910, the museum is now a chronological tour through her family life, the Crimean War and health reforms. Among the period mementoes are her slate and her pet owl, Athena.

Garden Museum

Lambeth Palace Road, SE1 7LB (7401 8865, www.gardenmuseum.org.uk). Lambeth North tube or Waterloo tube/rail. **Open** 10.30am-5pm Mon-Fri; 10.30am-4pm Sat. **Admission** £6; free-£5 reductions. **Map** p64 A4 ❺

The world's first horticulture museum fits neatly into the old church of St Mary's. A 'belvedere' gallery, built out of eco-friendly wood sheeting, contains the permanent collection of art, antique tools and horticultural memorabilia, while the ground floor hosts temporary exhibitions. In the small back garden, a replica 17th-century knot garden was created in honour of John Tradescant, intrepid plant-hunter and gardener to Charles I. Tradescant is buried here.

Golden Hinde

St Mary Overie Dock, Cathedral Street, SE1 9DE (7403 0123, www.golden hinde.com). London Bridge tube/rail. **Open** 10am-5.30pm daily. **Admission** £6; £4.50 reductions; £18 family. **Map** p65 E2 ❻

This replica of Drake's 16th-century flagship is so meticulous it was able to reprise the privateer's circumnavigatory voyage. On weekends, it swarms with junior pirates. **Event highlights** 'Living History Experiences'; book well in advance.

Hayward

Southbank Centre, Belvedere Road, SE1 8XX (0844 875 0073, www.south bankcentre.co.uk). Waterloo tube/rail or Embankment tube. **Open** 10am-6pm Mon-Thur, Sat, Sun; 10am-10pm Fri. **Admission** varies. **Map** p64 A2 ❼

This versatile art gallery continues its excellent programme of contemporary exhibitions, often with a strong interactive element. Casual visitors can hang out in the industrial-look café-bar downstairs, or visit free contemporary exhibitions in the inspired Project Space – take the stairs up from the glass foyer extension.

HMS Belfast

Morgan's Lane, Tooley Street, SE1 2JH (7940 6300, www.iwm.org.uk). London Bridge tube/rail. **Open** *Mar-Oct* 10am-6pm daily. *Nov-Feb* 10am-5pm daily. **Admission** £12.95; free-£10.40 reductions. **Map** p65 F2 ❽

LONDON BY AREA

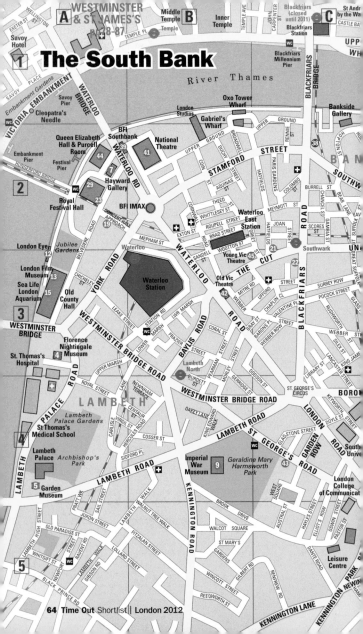

The South Bank

WESTMINSTER & ST JAMES'S pp78-87

A

Savoy Hotel

1

Middle Temple Temple PL Temple

B

Inner Temple

TEMPLE AVE
JOHN CARPENTER ST

Blackfriars (closed until 2011)

St Andr by the Wa

C

CASTLE BA

Blackfriars Station

UPP
WH

Blackfriars Millennium Pier

River Thames

VICTORIA EMBANKMENT
Embankment Gardens

WELLINGTON
EXETER ST
SAVOY PLACE

Savoy Pier

Cleopatra's Needle

TEMPLE PL.

BLACKFRIARS BRIDGE

Oxo Tower Wharf

London Studios

Gabriel's Wharf

Bankside Gallery

UPPER GROUND

RENNIE ST

38

HOPTON ST

BAN

Embankment Pier

WATERLOO BRIDGE

Queen Elizabeth Hall & Purcell Room **39**

National Theatre

UPPER GROUND

BROADWALL

DUCHY ST

DUCHY

CORN

STAMFORD

HATFIELDS

PARIS GARDENS

COLOMBO

BURRELL ST

CHANCEL ST

BEAR LANE

GAMBIA ST

STREET

SOUTHW

2

Festival Pier

44

HUNGERFORD BRIDGE

41

WATERLOO RD

Hayward Gallery

29

23

BELVEDERE ROAD

CONCERT HALL APPROACH
19

Royal Festival Hall

BFI IMAX

AQUINAS
THEED
WHITTLESEY ST
EXTON ST
ROUPELL STREET
BRAD STREET
CORNWALL

Waterloo East Station

MEYMOTT

SCORES ST

LONDON ROAD

LIBRARY SUFFOR

GLASS

London Eye

Jubilee Gardens

CHICHELEY ST

YORK ROAD

Waterloo

MEPHAM ST

SANDELL ST

WATERLOO ROAD

WOOTTON ST

Young Vic Theatre **45**

JOAN STREET

21

Southwark

UN

London Film Museum **13**

Sea Life London Aquarium **15**

Old County Hall

3

WESTMINSTER BRIDGE

St. Thomas's Hospital

4

Florence Nightingale Museum

STATION RD

Waterloo Station

LOWER MARSH

LEAKE STREET

LWR MARSH

FRAZIER ST

THE CUT

MITRE RD

Old Vic Theatre

WEBBER ROW

42

GRAY ST

BARONS PL

CHAPLIN CL

UPFORD ST

VALENTINE PLACE

22

SURREY ROW

POCOCK STREET

RUSHWORTH ST

WEBBER ST

SILEX ST

KING JAMES

LANCASTER ST

BAYLIS ROAD

CORAL ST

PEARMAN STREET

MORLEY ST

GERRIDGE ST

DODSON ST

WESTMINSTER BRIDGE ROAD

LAMBETH

4

PALACE ROAD

St Thomas's Medical School

Lambeth Palace Gardens

UPPER MARSH

ROYAL STREET

NEWNHAM TERRACE

CENTAUR ST

Lambeth North

BURDETT ST

ST. GEORGE'S CIRCUS

BORO

KEYWORTH STREET

GLADSTONE STREET

DOYLE ST

South Unive

Lambeth Palace

Archbishop's Park

CARLISLE LANE

HERCULES ROAD

VIRGIL ST

COSSER ST

SIDFORD PL

KING EDWARD WALK

LAMBETH ROAD

ST GEORGE'S ROAD

GARDEN ROW

LONDON ROAD

London College of Communicat

5

Garden Museum

LAMBETH ROAD

JUXON STREET

SAIL STREET

PRATT WK

LAMBETH WALK

WALNUT TREE WALK

FITZALAN STREET

LOLLARD STREET

Imperial War Museum

BROOK DRIVE

WALCOT SQUARE

ST MARY'S GARDENS

Geraldine Mary Harmsworth Park **9**

WEST SQUARE

AUSTRAL ST

HAYLES STREET

ELLIOT'S ROW

OSWIN ST

PASTOR ST

43

Leisure Centre

DANTE RD

LAMBETH HIGH ST

WHITGIFT ST

OLD PARADISE ST

NEWPORT ST

SAUNDEY RD

LAMBETH WALK

GIBSON RD

BLACK PRINCE RD

FITZALAN STREET

WINCOTT STREET

GILBERT ST

RENFREW RD

REEDWORTH STREET

KENNINGTON ROAD

KENNINGTON LANE

KENNINGTON PARK NEWM

Shard p70

This large light cruiser is the last surviving big gun World War II warship in Europe. Built in 1938, the Belfast provided cover for convoys to Russia, and was instrumental in the Normandy Landings. It now makes an unlikely playground for kids, who tear round its guns, bridge and engine room. An interactive display in the Operations Room has a radar simulation and you can play at controlling the Fleet.

Imperial War Museum

Lambeth Road, SE1 6HZ (7416 5320, www.iwm.org.uk). Lambeth North tube or Elephant & Castle tube/rail. **Open** 10am-6pm daily. **Admission** free. *Special exhibitions* prices vary. **Map** p64 B4 **9**

Antique guns, tanks, aircraft and artillery are parked up in the main hall of this imposing edifice, which illustrates the history of armed conflict from World War I to the present day. The tone of the museum darkens as you ascend: the third-floor Holocaust Exhibition is not recommended for under-14s; Crimes against Humanity – a minimalist space in which a film exploring contemporary genocide and ethnic violence rolls relentlessly – is unsuitable for under-16s. Since autumn 2010, the museum has also displayed the world's largest collection of Victoria Crosses.

Event highlights 'Women War Artists' (until 8 Jan 2012); 'The Children's War' (until 29 Feb 2012).

London Bridge Experience

2-4 Tooley Street, SE1 2SY (0844 847 2287, www.thelondonbridgeexperience. com). London Bridge tube/rail. **Open** 10am-5pm Mon-Fri; 10am-6pm Sat, Sun. **Admission** £21.95; £16.95-£17.95 reductions; £64.95 family. **Map** p65 E2 **10**

Old London Bridge, finished in 1209, was the first Thames crossing made of stone – and London's only Thames bridge until Westminster Bridge was finished in 1750. This kitsch, family-focused exhibition is a costumed tour of the crossing's past, as well as a scary adventure into the haunted foundations: dank, pestilential catacombs peopled by animatronic torture victims. There's also a museum section, which contains Peter Jackson's numerous bridge-related artefacts.

London Dungeon

28-34 Tooley Street, SE1 2SZ (0871 423 2240, www.thedungeons.com). London Bridge tube/rail. **Open** Nov-Mar 10am-5pm daily. Apr, Aug 9.30am-7pm daily. May-July, Sept, Oct 10am-5.30pm daily. These opening times are for guidance only; phone or check the website for a detailed breakdown. **Admission** £23; £17-£21 reductions. **Map** p65 F2 **11**

These railway arches contain a jokey celebration of torture, death and disease. Visitors are led through dry-ice past graves and corpses to experience nasty symptoms in the Great Plague exhibition: an actor-led medley of boils, projectile vomiting and worm-filled skulls. The Great Fire gets the treatment too, and Bloody Mary has joined the Ripper and Sweeney Todd in the rogues' gallery of infamy.

London Eye

Jubilee Gardens, SE1 7PB (0870 500 0600, www.londoneye.com). Waterloo tube/rail or Westminster tube. **Open** Oct-May 10am-8pm daily. June-Sept 10am-9pm daily. **Admission** £17.50; free-£14 reductions. **Map** p64 A3 **12**

It's hard to believe this giant wheel was intended to turn for only five years: it has proved so popular that no one wants it to come down, and pod-by-pod refurbishment to fit it for another two decades should be complete in time for the 2012 Games. A 'flight' takes half an hour, allowing plenty of time to get your snaps of the landmarks. Some people book in advance (taking a gamble with the weather), but you can turn up and queue for a ticket on the day – there can be long waits in summer.

LONDON BY AREA

Team GB pin badges
Official Product of London 2012

For the London 2012 Olympic and Paralympic Games, we are creating 2,012 pin badge designs. These designs will represent London, the UK, and every part of the London 2012 Games — from culture to sport, from the environment to education.

Wear your pin with pride and show your support for the Great Britain team competing at the London 2012 Olympic Games.

Team GB Lion's head logo TM c BOA 2009

Available at official London 2012 shops & other good retailers.
London2012.com/shop

London Film Museum

*County Hall, Riverside Building, SE1
7PB (7202 7040, www.londonfilm
museum.com). Westminster tube or
Waterloo tube/rail.* **Open** 10am-5pm
Mon-Fri; 10am-6pm Sat, Sun.
Admission £12; free-£10 reductions.
Map p64 A3 ⑬

The London Film Museum celebrates
the silver screen with props from *Star
Wars*, *Superman* and *The Italian Job*,
as well as the Rank gong. There's a
gallery dedicated to animation, and
you can watch interviews with the
stars and clips from TV series that
made it into film. A permanent exhibition, 'Charles Chaplin: The Great
Londoner', focuses on the silent film
star, who was born nearby.

Old Operating Theatre, Museum & Herb Garret

*9A St Thomas's Street, SE1 9RY
(7188 2679, www.thegarret.org.uk).
London Bridge tube/rail.* **Open**
10.30am-5pm daily. **Admission**
£5.80; £3.25-£4.80 reductions; £13.75
family. No credit cards. **Map** p65 E2 ⑭

The atmospheric tower that houses
this salutary reminder of antique sur-
gical practice used to be part of the
chapel of St Thomas's Hospital.
Visitors enter by a vertiginous wooden
spiral staircase to view an operating
theatre dating from 1822 (before the
advent of anaesthetics), with tiered
viewing seats for students. As fascinat-
ingly gruesome are the operating tools,
which look like torture implements.

Sea Life London Aquarium

*County Hall, Riverside Building,
Westminster Bridge Road, SE1 7PB
(0871 663 1678, www.sealife.co.uk).
Westminster tube or Waterloo tube/rail.*
Open *July, Aug* 10am-8pm daily. *Sept-
June* 10am-7pm Mon-Thur, Sun; 10am-
8pm Fri, Sat. **Admission** £18;
free-£16.50 reductions; £55 family.
Map p64 A3 ⑮

This is one of Europe's largest aquari-
ums and a hit with kids. Inhabitants

Sky-high Hideaway

Sleep up on the roof.

A unique artistic/architectural
collaboration, *A Room for London*
enables guests to spend the
night in boat-shaped, timber-built
accommodation on the roof of
the **Southbank Centre**'s Queen
Elizabeth Hall (p77).

This boat-cum-bedroom will
perch on the very edge of the
concert hall, offering guests and
invited artists a place of refuge
and 'self-reflection' above the
continuous flow of people along
the popular riverfront walk, as
well as an incredible panorama
that takes in London landmarks
including Big Ben and St Paul's.
The designers hope occupants
will keep a 'logbook' of their
experiences; during their stay,
a flag will be raised to indicate
the boat has been 'boarded'.

Out of the more than 500
designs submitted for *A Room
for London*, the installation by
David Kohn (Young Architect of
the Year in 2009) and artist
Fiona Banner (perhaps most
famous for her 2010 Duveens
Commission: she suspended a
Sea Harrier jump-jet, nose down,
from the ceiling of Tate Britain,
p83) was chosen for this part of
the **London 2012 Festival** (p54).

Members of the public will
be able to spend their night in
A Room for London between
January and December 2012.
Guests are allowed to board for
only a single night; bookings for
the room are due to open from
8 September 2011.
■ www.living-architecture.co.uk

are grouped by geographical origin, beginning with the Atlantic, where blacktail bream swim alongside the Thames Embankment. There are poison arrow frogs, crocodiles and piranha in the 'Rainforests of the World' exhibit. The Ray Lagoon is still popular, though touching the friendly flatfish is no longer allowed (it's bad for their health). Starfish, crabs and anenomes can be handled in special open rock pools instead, and the clown fish still draw crowds. There's a mesmerising Seahorse Temple and a tank full of turtles. The centrepieces, though, are the two massive Pacific and Indian Ocean tanks, with menacing sharks quietly circling fallen Easter Island statues and dinosaur bones.

Shakespeare's Globe

21 New Globe Walk, SE1 9DT (7401 9919, www.shakespeares-globe.org). Southwark tube or London Bridge tube/rail. **Open** *Exhibition* 10am-5pm daily. *Globe tours* Oct-Apr 10am-5pm daily. May-Sept 9.30am-12.30pm Mon-Sat; 9.30-11.30am Sun. *Rose Theatre tours* May-Sept 1-5pm Mon-Sat; noon-5pm Sun. **Admission** £10.50; £6.50-£8.50 reductions; £28 family. **Map** p65 D2 ⑯

The original Globe Theatre, co-owned by Shakespeare and where many of his plays were first staged, burned down in 1613 during a performance of Henry VIII. Nearly 400 years later (it celebrates its 15th birthday in 2012), the Globe was rebuilt not far from its original site, using construction methods and materials as close to the originals as possible. It's a fully operational theatre, with historically authentic performances mixed with brand-new plays in a season running from the Bard's birthday (23 Apr) through to autumn. There's an exhibition on the reconstruction and Renaissance London in the UnderGlobe, and guided tours (lasting an hour and a half) run all year, visiting the nearby site of the Rose Theatre during Globe matinées.

Event highlights For the London 2012 Festival (see box p54), all Shakespeare's plays will be staged in 38 languages.

Shard

NEW *32 London Bridge Street, SE1 9SS (www.the-shard.com). London Bridge tube/rail.* **Map** p65 E2 ⑰

In late 2010, while it was just concrete core, the Shard overtook One Canada Square (p178) as London's tallest building. Work on it should be complete by May 2012, when Renzo Piano's elongated glass pyramid is due to open restaurants and a 205-room, five-star Shangri-La hotel to the public. By then it will be the tallest building in Western Europe, stretching 1,016ft into the sky.

Tate Modern

Bankside, SE1 9TG (7887 8888, www.tate.org.uk). Southwark tube or London Bridge tube/rail. **Open** 10am-6pm Mon-Thur, Sun; 10am-10pm Fri, Sat. *Tours* hourly, 11am-3pm daily. **Admission** free. *Special exhibitions* prices vary. **Map** p65 D2 ⑱

Thanks to its industrial architecture, this powerhouse of modern art is awe-inspiring even before you enter. It shut down as Bankside Power Station in 1981, then opened as a spectacularly popular museum in 2000. The huge turbine hall houses the Unilever Series of temporary, large-scale installations (Tacita Dean has the space from Oct 2011 to Apr 2012; Tino Sehgal from July 2012), while the permanent collection draws from the Tate's magnificent collection of international modern art to display Matisse, Rothko, Bacon, Twombly and Beuys. Since spring 2011, you've also been able to see Picasso's *Nude, Green Leaves & Bust* in a new room dedicated to the artist. The gallery attracts five million visitors a year to a building intended for half that number; work is well under way on a dramatic, origami-like pyramid extension on the south side of the main gallery, due for completion in 2012; the work won't interfere with the opening of main galleries. The Tate-to-Tate boat service (£5 adult) – polka-dot decor by Damien Hirst, bar on board – links with the London Eye (p67) and Tate Britain (p83) every 20mins. **Event highlights** Damien Hirst retrospective (5 Apr-9 Sept 2012); 'A Bigger Splash: Painting after Performance Art' (from 7 Nov 2012).

Topolski Century

150-152 Hungerford Arches, SE1 8XU (7620 1275, www.topolskicentury.org. uk). Waterloo tube/rail. **Open** 11am-7pm Mon-Sat; noon-6pm Sun. **Admission** free. **Map** p64 A2 ⑲
Just inland from the Royal Festival Hall, this expansive mural depicts the extraordinary jumble of 20th-century events through the roughly painted faces of Bob Dylan, Winston Churchill and many, many others. It's the work of Polish-born expressionist Feliks Topolski, who made his name as a war artist in World War II – he was an eye witness to the horrors of Belsen.

Winston Churchill's Britain at War Experience

64-66 Tooley Street, SE1 2TF (7403 3171, www.britainatwar.co.uk). London Bridge tube/rail. **Open** Apr-Oct 10am-5pm daily. Nov-Mar 10am-4.30pm daily. **Admission** £12.95; free-£6.50 reductions; £29 family. **Map** p65 F3 ⑳
This old-fashioned exhibition recalls the privations endured by the British during World War II. Visitors descend from street level in an ancient lift to a reconstructed tube station shelter. The experience continues with Blitz-time London: real bombs, rare documents, photos and reconstructed shopfronts. Displays on rationing and food production are fascinating, and the set-piece bombsite quite disturbing.

Eating & drinking

Borough Market (p74) is great for gourmet snackers, while the cluster of chain eateries beside

and beneath the Royal Festival Hall, includes Wagamama, Strada and, our pick, **Canteen** (below).

Anchor & Hope

36 The Cut, SE1 8LP (7928 9898). Southwark or Waterloo tube/rail. **Open** 5-11pm Mon; noon-11pm Tue-Sat; noon-5pm Sun. **££**. **Gastropub**. **Map** p64 C2 ㉑
This monument to all things meaty, seasonal and British put Waterloo on the gastronomic map a few years back, and it still offers a lively dining experience – serving large cuts of beef, lamb or game in a plain but relaxed setting. It's a very popular place, but doesn't take evening bookings – so you'll often have to wait an hour at the noisy bar; weekday lunches are quieter. Sundays have a single 2pm sitting.

Baltic

74 Blackfriars Road, SE1 8HA (7928 1111, www.balticrestaurant.co.uk). Southwark tube. **Open** noon-3pm, 5.30-11.15pm Mon-Sat; noon-10.30pm Sun. **£££**. **Eastern European**. **Map** p64 C3 ㉒
This stylish spot (in the high-ceiling restaurant, a stunning chandelier is made of hundreds of amber shards) remains London's brightest star for east European food. The menu gives the best of eastern Europe – from Georgian-style lamb with aubergines to Romanian sour cream *mamaliga* (polenta) – a light, modern twist. Great cocktails, many vodkas, eclectic wines and friendly service add to the appeal.

Canteen

Royal Festival Hall, Belvedere Road, SE1 8XX (0845 686 1122, www. canteen.co.uk). Waterloo tube/rail. **Open** 8am-11pm Mon-Fri; 9am-11pm Sat, Sun. **££**. **British**. **Map** p64 A2 ㉓
Busy Canteen is furnished with utilitarian oak tables and benches. Dishes range from a bacon sandwich and afternoon jam scones to full roasts. Classic breakfasts (eggs benedict,

LONDON BY AREA

Grouse
Partridge
Pigeon
Wild ducks
Lakeland rabbits
Lakeland hares
Lakeland pheasants

Hendersons
award-winning
blackpudding

Wild lakeland
rabbit

Wild lakeland
venison

SUNSET ORANGE
Cauliflower
OR GRAFFITI purple
£1·80
EACH

Borough Market p74

welsh rarebit) are served all day, joined by the likes of macaroni cheese or sausage and mash from lunchtime.

Gladstone Arms
64 Lant Street, SE1 1QN (7407 3962). Borough tube. **Open** noon-11pm Mon-Fri; noon-midnight Sat; noon-10.30pm Sun. **Map** p65 D3 ㉔
While the Victorian prime minister still glares from the massive mural on the outer wall, inside is funky, freaky and candlelit. Gigs (blues, folk, acoustic) take place at one end of a tiny space; opposite, a bar dispenses ales and lagers. Retro touches include an old 'On Air' studio sign and pies as bar snacks.

Magdalen
152 Tooley Street, SE1 2TU (7403 1342, www.magdalenrestaurant.co.uk). London Bridge tube/rail. **Open** noon-2.30pm, 6.30-10pm Mon-Fri; 6.30-10pm Sat. **£££**. **British**. **Map** p65 F3 ㉕
Magdalen makes the most of somewhat unprepossessing surroundings with friendly and efficient staff. A la carte prices are just about reasonable (£17.50 for flavoursome Middle White belly with veg and good gravy, £16.50 for a beautifully presented fish stew), but portions aren't huge; opt instead for the set lunch, a steal at £15.50 for two courses or £18.50 for three. Poached rhubarb with shortbread and crème anglaise is the best pud.

M Manze
87 Tower Bridge Road, SE1 4TW (7407 2985, www.manze.co.uk). Bus 1, 42, 188. **Open** 11am-2pm Mon; 10.30am-2pm Tue-Thur; 10am-2.15pm Fri; 10am-2.45pm Sat. **£**. No credit cards. **Pie & mash**. **Map** p65 F4 ㉖
The finest remaining purveyor of the dirt-cheap traditional food of London's working classes. This Manze is not only the city's oldest pie shop, established back in 1902, but also in its own functional way the most beautiful, with marble-top tables and spick-and-span tiles. Expect scoops of mash, beef pies

and liquor (a thin parsley sauce); for the brave, the stewed eels are a must.

Rake
14 Winchester Walk, SE1 9AG (7407 0557). London Bridge tube/rail. **Open** noon-11pm Mon-Fri; 10am-11pm Sat. **Pub**. **Map** p65 E2 ㉗
The Veltins lager and Maisels Weiße taps stay in place at this blue-fronted cubicle of a bar, but the likes of Aechte Schlenkerle Rauchbier (a rare smoked variety from Bamberg) and Grisette Fruits des Bois probably won't be when you arrive. No matter: everything served here is good – as the sign above the bar says, there's 'No crap on tap'.

Roast
Floral Hall, Borough Market, Stoney Street, SE1 1TL (7940 1300, www.roast-restaurant.com). London Bridge tube/rail. **Open** 7-11am, noon-3pm, 5.30-11pm Mon-Fri; 8-11.30am, noon-4pm, 6-11pm Sat; 11.30am-6pm Sun. **£££**. **British**. **Map** p65 E2 ㉘
Perched above the market, Roast celebrates its location with a menu inspired by British produce, much of it sourced from stallholders below. Seasonality and freshness are the buzzwords and there's no doubting the quality of the ingredients; enjoy them for less from the bar menu after 3pm, or sample the fine roster of teas.

Skylon
Royal Festival Hall, Belvedere Road, SE1 8XX (7654 7800, www.danddlondon.com). Waterloo tube/rail. **Open** 11am-midnight daily. **£££**. **Brasserie/bar**. **Map** p64 A2 ㉙
For London connoisseurs, there aren't many better views than from the huge riverside windows. Sit near the bar counter (between two restaurant areas) to watch buses, bridges and boats while supping finely crafted cocktails. Despite the room's aircraft-hangar proportions, screens and bronze accents keep the feel intimate. Prices are high, and the food not always impressive.

Tapas Brindisa

*18-20 Southwark Street, SE1 1TJ
(7357 8880, www.brindisa.com).
London Bridge tube/rail.* **Open**
11am-11pm Mon-Sat. **£££. Tapas.**
Map p65 E2 ③

Top-quality ingredients have always
been the key at Brindisa, but its genius
lies in the ability to assemble them into
delicious and deceptively simple tapas.
The set-up here is as basic as the food:
there's a bar area dotted with high
tables, and a close-packed, concrete-
floored dining room at the other end.
Both are generally thronged.

Wine Wharf

*Stoney Street, Borough Market, SE1
9AD (7940 8335, www.winewharf.
com). London Bridge tube/rail.* **Open**
4-11.30pm Mon-Wed; noon-11.30pm
Thur-Sat. Wine bar. **Map** p65 E2 ③

An extension of the wine-tasting
attraction Vinopolis (7940 8300, www.
vinopolis.co.uk), Wine Wharf inhabits
two industrial-chic storeys of a
reclaimed Victorian warehouse. The
250-bin list stretches to 1953 d'Yquem
and serious champagne but, with
nearly half the wines by the glass, you
can probably afford to experiment a little. For a similar take on beer, try
neighbouring Brew Wharf (7378 6601,
www.brewwharf.com).

Zucca

NEW *184 Bermondsey Street, SE1 3TQ
(7378 6809, www.zuccalondon.com).
London Bridge tube/rail or Bermondsey
tube.* **Open** noon-3pm, 6.30-10pm Tue-
Sat; noon-3pm Sun. **££. Italian. Map**
p65 F4 ③

If only more restaurants had Zucca's
approach: good food at great prices,
served by interested staff with a genuine regard for diners. It sounds simple, yet it's pretty rare. The modern
Italian menu is partnered by an all-
Italian wine list, and the staff are
happy to enlarge on both. The restaurant is open-plan, with the kitchen completely exposed to view, and the decor

runs to shiny white surfaces with occasional splashes of intense orange.

Shopping

London's *bouquinistes* sell second-
hand books and old prints from
trestles by the **BFI** (p76), and the
Fashion & Textile Museum
(p63) presides over a few boutiques
on Bermondsey Street.

Borough Market

*Southwark Street, SE1 1TL (7407
1002, www.boroughmarket.org.uk).
London Bridge tube/rail.* **Open** 11am-
5pm Thur; noon-6pm Fri; 8am-5pm Sat.
Map p65 E2 ③

Despite demolitions to make way for a
rail viaduct overhead, London's busiest
foodie market remains a major tourist
attraction. Gourmet goodies – rare-
breed meats, fruit and veg, cakes and
preserves, oils and teas – run the
gamut from Flour Power City Bakery's
organic loaves to Neal's Yard Dairy's
speciality British cheese; none of it
comes cheap, but quality is high. The
market opens on Thursday, which is
quieter than the always-mobbed weekends – Saturday is monstrously busy.

Maltby Street

NEW *London Bridge tube/rail.*
Map p65 F3 ③
See box right.

Nightlife

As well as classical music and
dance, the **Southbank Centre**
(p77) programmes terrific rock,
jazz and world music gigs.

Cable

*33A Bermondsey Street, SE1 2EG
(7403 7730, www.cable-london.com).
London Bridge tube/rail.* **Open** 10pm-
6am Fri, Sat; 10pm-5am Sun. **Map** p65
F3 ③

All old-style brickwork and industrial
air-con ducts, Cable has two dance are-

The Next Borough Market?

The place to be when you're bored of the foodie throng.

Maltby Street (left) is an unlikely place to find food retailers, but there's been a buzz about the Saturday openings here since they began in late 2010. It's emphatically not a street market – merely a collection of rented railway arches where Borough Market stalwarts had set up storage. The cool, damp vaults were perfect for grinding machines, brewing vats and ovens, and provided the ideal conditions for maturing cheese. When the traders decided to experiment with opening to the public, London's foodies had a new shopping destination.

Monmouth Coffee in Arch 34 marks the caffeine-fuelled starting point of a greedy amble. Pick your way through the rubble of Rope Walk to find, grouped in one arch, the Ham & Cheese company and the production sites of the Kernel Brewery and Kappacasein Dairy.

Across Millstream Road, Fern Verrow biodynamic vegetables can be found next to the Borough Cheese Company. In a further arch is a collection of matured cheese from Neal's Yard Dairy, joined once a month by Aubert & Mascoli natural wines. On the Druid Street side, Arch 104 is home to a warehouse collective, with Swiss cheeses (Käse Suisse), cured meats (Topolski) and the only hot bite in the area – hot oatcakes with Leicestershire cheese.

The venerable Booth's greengrocers (now Tayshaw Ltd) is at the other end of the street (Arch 60). Between them, in Arch 72, the St John Bakery was a significant arrival, bringing oven-hot loaves to the trestle table at the front of a cavernous space.

If you're expecting lots of snacks and jolly stallholders to snap, you'll be disappointed – this is just a row of railway arches in a former industrial quarter. But you get the space and time to find out about provenance directly from producers who really care about sourcing.

Most traders open 9am-2pm Sat (some a little later); the website has updates of who's where.
■ www.maltbystreet.com

nas, a bar with a spot-and-be-spotted mezzanine, plenty of seats and a great covered smoking area. The programming was taken over in 2010 by We Fear Silence, who put together a fizzing mix of quality nights from across the eclectronic music spectrum: favourites include Buzzin' Fly, Chew the Fat! and the bass-heavy Deviation parties (Metalheadz, Dirty Canvas).

Corsica Studios

Units 4/5, Elephant Road, SE17 1LB (7703 4760, www.corsicastudios.com). Elephant & Castle tube/rail. No credit cards. **Map** p65 D5 ③

This flexible performance space is increasingly used as one of London's more adventurous live music venues and clubs, supplementing the bands and DJs with sundry poets, live painters and wigged-out projectionists. **Event highlights** The Boiler Room (Tue) – hip underground electronic music, streamed at www.boilerroom.tv.

Ministry of Sound

103 Gaunt Street, SE1 6DP (7740 8600, www.ministryofsound.com). Elephant & Castle tube/rail. **Map** p65 D4 ③

This refurbished clubbing powerhouse left the most important aspect of its success intact: the killer sound system. Playing on it across the Ministry's five rooms are guests that tend towards the stellar: on a Friday and Saturday night you might find such household names as Basement Jaxx, Groove Armada, Paul Van Dyk, Judge Jules and Armin Van Buuren playing out, with styles ranging from Richie Hawtin's minimal techno to Sasha's progressive trance.

Pulse

NEW *1 Invicta Plaza, SE1 9UF (www. pulse-club.info). Southwark tube.* **Map** p64 C2 ③

With room for 6,000 groovers, Pulse is not only London's newest club, but its biggest too. It opened in spring 2011 with Erick Morillo's Voodoo Nights –

and a few complaints about heat, condensation and general lack of organisation. It seemed to be settling into its stride as the year progressed.

Arts & leisure

Free-standing Pit tickets are superb value at the **Globe** (p70).

BFI Southbank

South Bank, SE1 8XT (7928 3535, 7928 3232 tickets, www.bfi.org.uk). Embankment tube or Waterloo tube/rail. **Map** p64 A2 ③

An esteemed London institution, with an unrivalled programme of retrospective seasons and previews, as well as regular director and actor Q&As. The riverside seating outside the underpowered main café is hugely popular, but the handsome cocktail bar/restaurant alongside the terrific Mediatheque (a free archive-viewing room) is better.

Made-for-IMAX kiddie pics and wow-factor documentaries are the usual fare at the nearby BFI IMAX (1 Charlie Chaplin Walk, 0870 787 2525), the biggest screen in the country, but there's a robust programme of monster-sized mainstream films too, including ace all-night screenings of film trilogies and tetralogies.

Event highlights 'Capital Tales' – fine strand screening archive London films.

Menier Chocolate Factory

51-53 Southwark Street, SE1 1RU (7907 7060, www.menierchocolate factory.com). Southwark tube or London Bridge tube/rail. **Map** p65 D2 ④

This fringe theatre, which has a fine bar-restaurant on the premises, has had a bit of a golden touch for West End musical transfers.

National Theatre

South Bank, SE1 9PX (7452 3400, 7452 3000 tickets, www.national theatre.org.uk). Embankment or Southwark tube, or Waterloo tube/rail. **Map** p64 B2 ④

This concrete monster is the flagship venue of British theatre. Three auditoriums allow for different kinds of performance: in-the-round, promenade, even classic proscenium arch. Nicholas Hytner's artistic directorship, with landmark successes such as Alan Bennett's *The History Boys*, has shown that the state-subsidised home of British theatre can turn out quality drama at a profit. The Travelex season ensures a widening audience by offering two-thirds of the seats for £10 (they get snapped up fast) and there's free outdoor performances on the Watch This Space stage all summer.
Event highlights Dominic Cooke directs *The Comedy of Errors* (Nov 2011); Tori Amos musical (Apr 2012); Zoe Wanamaker in Chekhov's *Cherry Orchard*, (May 2012); free summer theatre outdoors for Watch This Space.

Old Vic
The Cut, SE1 8NB (0844 871 7628, www.oldvictheatre.com). Southwark tube or Waterloo tube/rail. **Map** p64 B3 ㊷
The combination of Oscar-winner Kevin Spacey and top producer David Liddiment at this grand, boxy 200-year-old theatre continues to be a commercial success, if not always a critical one. Programming runs from grown-up Christmas pantomimes to the Bridge Project, transatlantic collaborations on serious plays (Chekhov, Shakespeare) directed by Sam Mendes.
Event highlights The Old Vic Tunnels – under Waterloo station – host superb immersive/experimental theatre, music and other performance.

Siobhan Davies Dance Studios
85 St George's Road, SE1 6ER (7091 9650, www.siobhandavies. com). Elephant & Castle tube/rail. **Map** p64 C4 ㊸
This award-winning venue, designed in consultation with dancers, not only meets their needs but looks amazing.

Davies, who founded the company in 1988, often explores spaces outside her theatre, so check with the venue for performance details before setting out.

Southbank Centre
Belvedere Road, SE1 8XX (7960 4200 information, 0844 875 0073 tickets, www.southbankcentre.co.uk). Embankment tube or Waterloo tube/rail. **Map** p64 A2 ㊹
In addition to the Hayward (p63), there are three main venues here: the Royal Festival Hall, with nearly 3,000 seats and the Philharmonia and the Orchestra of the Age of Enlightenment as residents; the Queen Elizabeth Hall, which can seat around 900; and the 365-capacity Purcell Room, for recitals. A £90m renovation a few years back improved the RFH, externally and acoustically, and since Jude Kelly took over as artistic director the programming has been rich in variety, with music and performance of all types, often appealingly themed into festivals. The RFH foyer stage hosts hundreds of free concerts each year, and the river terrace is thronged in good weather.
Event highlights Meltdown Festival (early June 2012); *Ben Hur* with live soundtrack (9 June 2012); Mahler's Resurrection Symphony (28 June 2012).

Young Vic
66 The Cut, SE1 8LZ (7922 2922, www.youngvic.org). Southwark tube or Waterloo tube/rail. **Map** p64 B3 ㊺
This Vic (which is actually well into middle age – it opened in 1970) has more youthful bravura than its sister up the road, packing out the open-air balcony at its popular bar-restaurant with a young crowd at weekends. They come to see European classics with a distinctly modern edge, new writing with an international flavour and the usually superb annual collaboration with the English National Opera (p42).
Event highlights Michael Sheen as *Hamlet* (18 Oct 2011-21 Jan 2012); *Bingo* (16 Feb-31 Mar 2012).

Westminster Abbey p83

Westminster & St James's

Westminster

For many the heart of London – if not the heart of Britain – this area is more formal than inviting. It is home to the **Houses of Parliament**, the seat of government power for 1,000 years, with its **Big Ben** clocktower starring in many holiday snaps; Britain's very first Parliament met in **Westminster Abbey**, the site of almost every British coronation. Here too are **Nelson's Column** and **Trafalgar Square** – another photo-op by day, but often host of festivals by night.

Sights & museums

Banqueting House

Whitehall, SW1A 2ER (0844 482 7777, www.hrp.org.uk). Westminster tube or Charing Cross tube/rail. **Open** 10am-5pm Mon-Sat. **Admission** £4.80; free-£4 reductions. **Map** p79 C2 ❶

This Italianate mansion was built in 1620 and is the sole surviving part of the Tudor and Stuart kings' Whitehall Palace. It features a lavish ceiling by Rubens that glorifies James I, 'the wisest fool in Christendom'. The hall is sometimes closed to host corporate dos. **Event highlights** Songs of Robert Burns (28 Nov 2011).

Churchill War Rooms

Clive Steps, King Charles Street, SW1A 2AQ (7930 6961, www.iwm.org.uk). St James's Park or Westminster tube. **Open** 9.30am-6pm daily. **Admission** £14.95; free-£12 reductions. **Map** p79 C2 ❷

Beneath Whitehall, the cramped and spartan bunker where Sir Winston Churchill planned the Allied victory in World War II remains exactly as he left it on 16 August 1945. The sense of wartime hardship is reinforced by wailing sirens and the great man's wartime speeches on the free audio guide.

LONDON BY AREA

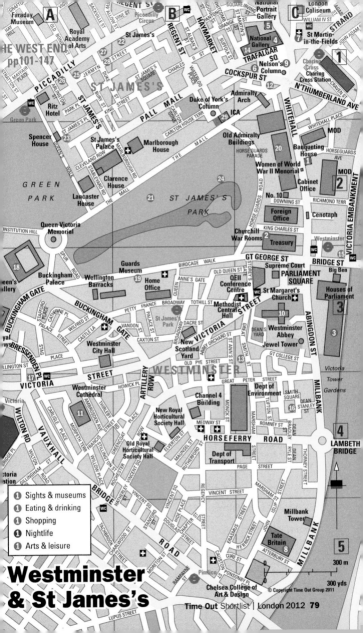

Westminster & St James's

Houses of Parliament

Parliament Square, SW1A 0AA (0844 847 1672 tours, www.parliament.uk). Westminster tube. **Open** phone or check website for details of Sat and summer tours. **Admission** *Visitors' Gallery* free. *Tours* £14; free-£9 reductions. **Map** p79 C3 ❸

Visitors are welcome to observe the debates at the House of Lords and House of Commons – at noon on Wednesday Prime Minister's Question Time is reliably peppery – but tickets must be arranged in advance through your MP or embassy. The best times to visit are Saturdays or in summer recess, when tours – taking in ancient Westminster Hall – are organised (book ahead). The original Parliament buildings burnt down in 1834; the current neo-Gothic extravaganza was completed in 1860.

National Gallery

Trafalgar Square, WC2N 5DN (7747 2885, www.nationalgallery.org.uk). Leicester Square tube or Charing Cross tube/rail. **Open** 10am-6pm Mon-Thur, Sat, Sun; 10am-9pm Fri. *Tours* 11.30am, 2.30pm daily. **Admission** free. *Special exhibitions* prices vary. **Map** p79 C1 ❹

Founded in 1824 to display a collection of just 36 paintings, today the National Gallery is home to more than 2,000 works. There are masterpieces from virtually every European school of art, from austere 13th-century religious paintings to the visceral delights of Van Gogh. Straight ahead on entry, in the North Wing, are 17th-century Dutch, Flemish, Italian and Spanish Old Masters, including Velázquez's Rokeby Venus, while the East Wing contains hugely popular French Impressionist and Post-Impressionist paintings by Monet, Renoir and Seurat. You can't see everything in one visit, but free guided tours, audio guides and the Art Start computer system (helping you navigate between your own must-sees) can point you to the highlights.

Event highlights 'Leonardo da Vinci' (9 Nov 2011-5 Feb 2012).

National Portrait Gallery

St Martin's Place, WC2H 0HE (7306 0055, www.npg.org.uk). Leicester Square tube or Charing Cross tube/rail. **Open** 10am-6pm Mon-Wed, Sat, Sun; 10am-9pm Thur, Fri. **Admission** free. *Special exhibitions* prices vary. **Map** p79 C1 ❺

Portraits don't have to be stuffy. The NPG has everything from oil paintings of stiff-backed royals to photos of soccer stars and gloriously unflattering political caricatures. The portraits of musicians, scientists, artists, philanthropists and celebrities are arranged in chronological order from the top to the bottom of the building.

Event highlights 'Glamour of the Gods: Hollywood Portraits' (until 23 Oct 2011); BP Portrait Award 2012 (mid June-mid Sept 2012).

Routemaster buses

Cockspur Street, Stops B & (opposite) S. **Map** p79 C1 ❻

The iconic red double-deckers were withdrawn from service in 2005, but refurbished Routemasters run Routes 9 (Stop B) and 15 (Stop S) every 15mins, 9.30am to 6.30pm. No.9 goes west to the Royal Albert Hall, no.15 east via St Paul's to Tower Hill. Unless you're already in possession of an Oyster or Travelcard (p216), you must buy a ticket before boarding, but you can board at any stop along each route.

St Martin-in-the-Fields

Trafalgar Square, WC2N 4JJ (7766 1122, www.smitf.org). Leicester Square tube or Charing Cross tube/rail. **Open** 8am-7pm daily. *Brass Rubbing Centre* 10am-7pm Mon-Wed; 10am-9pm Thur-Sat; 11am-6pm Sun. **Admission** free. *Brass rubbing* £4.50. **Map** p79 C1 ❼

Built in 1726, St Martin's bright interior was recently restored, with Victorian furbelows removed and the addition of a strikingly plain altar window of the Cross, stylised as if rippling on water. In the crypt are a decent café and the London Brass Rubbing Centre.

LONDON BY AREA

Boris Bikes

The two-wheel takeover is under way.

Since public transport at rush hour can become a sweaty mosh pit, it's perhaps no surprise that cycling is undergoing a boom in London. In summer 2010, Mayor Boris Johnson opened a scheme first mooted by his predecessor, Ken Livingstone, and thus the Boris Bike was born.

The idea, modelled on similar schemes in Paris and Montreal, is to provide bikes for people to use as an alternative to public transport for short trips around town. In an area equivalent to Zone 1 of the tube map, there are 6,000 bikes available from some 400 docking stations – one station roughly every 300m. (A useful map showing the location of every docking station is at https://web.barclayscyclehire.tfl.gov.uk/maps.)

The self-service scheme operates 24 hours a day and is open to anyone over 14 who has a valid credit or debit card. You pay an access fee (£1 for 24 hours or £5 a week), after which trips under half an hour are free, those up to an hour cost £1 and so on up.

There have been teething problems. As in Paris, some docking stations are more popular for taking a bike and thus often empty (near stations, say), while others are more popular for leaving a bike (at the bottom of a hill rather than the top, for example) and so are full when you try to deposit your bike. The redistribution vans set up to deal with this problem were initially a specially green, specially quiet all-electric fleet, but the number of vans required was heavily underestimated – operators Serco almost immediately had to hire ordinary, non-eco-friendly white vans to supplement them. There have also been isolated incidents of overcharging or malfunctions, and the first Boris Bike accident was reported in September 2010 – no helmets are supplied.

TfL is already planning to extend the hire scheme, sensibly focusing the extra bikes on Stratford and the vicinity of the Olympic Park (p179). At the time of writing, the most easterly docking station is near Whitechapel tube station.

LONDON BY AREA

National Dining Rooms p84

Event highlights Candlelit evening concerts of Mozart and Vivaldi; free lunchtime recitals (Mon, Tue, Fri).

Tate Britain

Millbank, SW1P 4RG (7887 8888, www.tate.org.uk). Pimlico tube. **Open** 10am-6pm daily; 10am-10pm 1st Fri of mth. *Tours* 11am, noon, 2pm, 3pm Mon-Fri; noon, 3pm Sat, Sun. **Admission** free. *Special exhibitions* prices vary. **Map** p79 C5 ❽

Tate Modern (p70) gets all the attention, but the original Tate Gallery has a broader and more inclusive brief. Housed in a stately Portland stone building on the riverside, it's second only to the National (p80) for historical art in London. A £45m interior revamp began in February 2011 (it should be finished in 2013), but the superb collection of British art remains accessible – Hogarth, Gainsborough, Reynolds, Constable, and Turner (in the Clore Gallery), modern Brits Stanley Spencer, Lucian Freud and Francis Bacon, and Art Now installations that showcase up-and-comers. The handy Tate-to-Tate boat service (p71) zips east along the river to Tate Modern every 40mins. Event highlights 'Picasso and Britain' (15 Feb-15 July 2012); 'Pre-Raphaelites' (from 12 Sept 2012).

Trafalgar Square

Leicester Square tube or Charing Cross tube/rail. **Map** p79 C1 ❾

Trafalgar Square was conceived in the 1820s as a homage to Britain's naval power. Always been a natural gathering point – semi-pedestrianisation in 2003 made it more so – the square now regularly hosts celebrations, festivals and protests. The focus is Nelson's Column, a Corinthian pillar topped by a statue of naval hero Horatio Nelson, but the contemporary sculpture on the Fourth Plinth brings fresh colour (Elmgreen & Dragset's golden rocking horse will appear in 2012) and a 21ft countdown clock ticks off the seconds to the start of the 2012 Games.

Westminster Abbey

20 Dean's Yard, SW1P 3PA (7222 5152 information, 7654 4900 tours, www.westminster-abbey.org). St James's Park or Westminster tube. **Open** 9.30am-4.30pm Mon, Tue, Thur, Fri; 9.30am-7pm Wed; 9.30am-4.30pm Sat. *Abbey Museum, Chapter House & College Gardens* 10am-4pm daily. **Admission** £15; free-£12 reductions; £36 family. *Abbey Museum* free. *Tours* £3. **Map** p79 C3 ❿

The cultural significance of the Abbey is hard to overstate. Edward the Confessor commissioned it, but it was only consecrated on 28 December 1065, eight days before he died. William the Conqueror had himself crowned here on Christmas Day 1066, followed by every British king and queen since – bar two. This is also where, in spring 2011, HRH Prince William married Kate Middleton, and many notables are interred in the abbey – Poets' Corner is always a draw. The Abbey Museum occupies one of the oldest parts of the Abbey: you'll find effigies of British monarchs, among them Edward II and Henry VII, wearing the robes they donned in life.

Westminster Cathedral

42 Francis Street, SW1P 1QW (7798 9055, www.westminstercathedral.org. uk). Victoria tube/rail. **Open** 7am-6pm Mon-Fri; 8am-6.30pm Sat; 8am-7pm Sun. *Bell tower & exhibition* 9.30am-4.30pm daily. **Admission** free; donations appreciated. *Bell tower & exhibition* £8; free-£4 reductions. **Map** p79 A4 ⓫

With domes, arches and a soaring tower, the architecture of England's most important Catholic church (built 1895-1903) was heavily influenced by Hagia Sophia. A brooding, dark ceiling sets off mosaics and marble columns with Eric Gill's savage Stations of the Cross at their head. A lift runs up the 273ft bell tower, for great views, and an exhibition shows off a Tudor chalice and the architect's original model.

Eating & drinking

Albannach

*66 Trafalgar Square, WC2N 5DS
(7930 0066, www.albannach.co.uk).
Charing Cross tube/rail.* **Open** noon-
1am Mon-Sat. **Cocktail bar.** Map
p79 C1 ⑫

Albannach specialises in Scotch
whiskies and cocktails based on
Scotch, and the impressive location –
facing right on to Trafalgar Square –
will help you overlook the loud office
groups and the kitsch of kilted staff
and an illuminated reindeer.

Cinnamon Club

*Old Westminster Library, 30-32 Great
Smith Street, SW1P 3BU (7222 2555,
www.cinnamonclub.com). St James's
Park or Westminster tube.* **Open** 7.30-
9.30am, noon-2.30pm, 6-10.45pm Mon-
Fri; noon-2.30pm, 6-10.45pm Sat.
££££. Indian. Map p79 C3 ⑬

Aiming to create a complete Indian
fine-dining experience, Cinnamon Club
provides cocktails, fine wines, tasting
menus, breakfasts (Indian, Anglo-
Indian, British), private dining-rooms
and all attendant flummery in an
impressive, wood-lined space. Even the
well-priced set meal (£20 for two
courses) is invitingly unusual.

National Dining Rooms

*Sainsbury Wing, National Gallery,
Trafalgar Square, WC2N 5DN (7747
2525, www.thenationaldiningrooms.
co.uk). Charing Cross tube/rail.* **Open**
Bakery 10am-5.30pm Mon-Thur, Sat,
Sun; 10am-8.30pm Fri; 10am-7.30pm
Sat. *Restaurant* noon-3.30pm Mon-
Thur, Sat, Sun; noon-3.30pm, 5-7.15pm
Fri. Bakery **£**. Restaurant **£££**.
British. Map p79 C1 ⑭

Oliver Peyton's finest restaurant is still
in great shape, although prices have
been rising. Cultured afternoon teas
can be taken, but the real attraction is
the main menu of British staples,
immaculately cooked and presented in
a nicely relaxed atmosphere. The East

Wing's darkly romantic National Café
bar-restaurant (7747 5942, www.the
nationalcafe.com) is rarely busy, and
opens to 11pm every day but Sunday.

St Stephen's Tavern

*10 Bridge Street, SW1A 2JR (7925
2286). Westminster tube.* **Open** 10am-
11.30pm Mon-Sat; 10.30am-11pm Sun.
Map p79 C3 ⑮

Done out with dark woods, etched mirrors and lovely Arts and Crafts-style
wallpaper, this is a handsome pub. The
food is reasonably priced and the ales
are excellent, but expensive. Brilliantly
located by Big Ben, it's neither too
touristy nor as busy as you might fear.

Arts & leisure

St John's, Smith Square

*Smith Square, SW1P 3HA (7222
1061, www.sjss.org.uk). Westminster
tube.* Map p79 C4 ⑯

With its distinctive four towers, this
elegant church was finished in 1728. It
now hosts orchestral and chamber concerts more or less every night, along
with occasional recitals on its magnificent Klais organ. In the crypt is the
Footstool restaurant.

Victoria Palace Theatre

*Victoria Street, SW1E 5EA (0844 248
5000, www.victoriapalacetheatre.co.uk).
Victoria tube/rail.* Map p79 A4 ⑰

Billy Elliot, scored by Elton John, is set
during the 1984 coal miners' strike. A
working-class lad loves ballet – to the
consternation of his salt-of-the-earth
dad. Production subject to change.

St James's

Traditional, quiet and exclusive,
St James's is where **Buckingham
Palace** presides over lovely **St
James's Park**. Everything is
dignified and unhurried, whether
you're shopping at **Fortnum's** and
on **Jermyn Street**, or entertaining
in **Dukes** or the **Wolseley**.

Sights & museums

Buckingham Palace & Royal Mews

The Mall, SW1A 1AA (7766 7300 Palace, 7766 7301 Queen's Gallery, 7766 7302 Royal Mews, www.royal collection.org.uk). Green Park tube or Victoria tube/rail. **Open** *State Rooms mid July-Sept 9.45am-6pm (last entry 3.45pm) daily. Queen's Gallery 10am-5.30pm daily. Royal Mews Mar-July, Oct 11am-4pm Mon-Thur, Sat, Sun; Aug, Sept 10am-5pm daily. Nov, Dec 11am-4pm Mon-Fri.* **Admission** *Palace £17; free-£15.50 reductions. Gallery £8.75; free-£7.75 reductions. Mews £7.75; free-£7 reductions.* **Map** p79 A3 ⑲

The present home of the British royals is open to the public each year while the family Windsor are away on their summer holidays; you'll be able to see the State Apartments, which are still used to entertain dignitaries and guests of state. At other times of year, visit the Queen's Gallery to see the Queen's personal collection of treasures. Further along Buckingham Palace Road, the Royal Mews is the home of the royal Rolls-Royces, the splendid royal carriages and the horses that pull them.

Event highlights The Changing of the Guard (except in rain: 11.30am alternate days, daily Apr-July).

Guards Museum

Wellington Barracks, Birdcage Walk, SW1E 6HQ (7414 3428, www.the guardsmuseum.com). St James's Park tube. **Open** *10am-4pm daily.* **Admission** *£4; free-£2 reductions.* **Map** p79 B3 ⑲

This small museum tells the 350-year story of the Foot Guards, using flamboyant uniforms, medals, period paintings and memorabilia, such as stuffed Victorian mascot, Jacob the Goose.

Household Cavalry Museum

Horse Guards, Whitehall, SW1A 2AX (7930 3070, www.householdcavalry.co.

uk). Westminster tube or Charing Cross tube/rail. **Open** *Apr-Oct 10am-6pm daily. Nov-Mar 10am-5pm daily.* **Admission** *£6; free-£4 reductions; £15 family.* **Map** p79 C2 ⑳

The Household Cavalry, the Queen's official guard, tell their stories through video diaries at this small but entertaining museum. Separated from the stables by a mere pane of glass, you'll also get a peek – and sniff – of the huge horses that parade outside daily.

Event highlights Changing of the Guard (except in rain: 11am Mon-Fri; 10am Sat). The parade ground will host Beach Volleyball for the 2012 Games.

St James's Park

St James's Park or Westminster tube. **Map** p79 B2 ㉑

St James's Park, founded as a deer park, was remodelled on the orders of George IV – and it's lovely. The central lake is home to numerous species of wildfowl, including pelicans that are fed at 3pm daily, and the bridge across gives glimpses west of Buckingham Palace. Just across the Mall, Green Park is featureless by comparison, but will in May 2012 gain a new memorial – to World War II Bomber Command.

St James's Piccadilly

197 Piccadilly, W1J 9LL (7734 4511, www.st-james-piccadilly.org). Piccadilly Circus tube. **Open** *8am-6.30pm daily.* **Admission** *free.* **Map** p79 B1 ㉒

Consecrated in 1684, St James's is the only church Sir Christopher Wren built on a new site. A calming place with few frills, it is home to the William Blake Society (he was baptised here) and hosts a churchyard market (antiques, Tue; arts and crafts, Wed-Sat).

Event highlights Free classical recitals (1.10pm Mon, Wed, Fri).

Eating & drinking

Dukes Bar

35 St James's Place, SW1A 1NY (7491 4840, www.dukeshotel.co.uk). Green

READING ROOM EVENTS — OCTOBER.

14th OCT 7pm TALK: ART AND RESISTANCE - KENNAR...

16th OCT 12pm FAMILY WORKSHOP: NO TO BAD TH...

21st OCT 7pm TALK: FANZINES, ART AND POLITICS FROM...
                    — STEWART HOME IN CONVERSATION ...

23 OCT 8pm — STUDENT FORUM PRESENTS... EVE...

ICA

Park tube. **Open** from 2pm Mon-Thur; from noon Fri, Sat; from 4pm Sun.

Cocktail bar. Map p79 A2 ㉓

In 2007, this centenarian hotel transformed its discreet, highly regarded but old-fashioned bar into a landmark destination. Dukes' dry martinis are flamboyantly made at guests' tables – and you pay plenty for the privilege – but this is one of London's most soothing, most elegant drinking experiences.

Inn The Park

St James's Park, SW1A 2BJ (7451 9999, www.innthepark.com). St James's Park tube. **Open** 8am-9pm Mon-Fri; 9am-9pm Sat, Sun. **££-£££**. **British café-restaurant. Map** p79 B2 ㉔

Self-service customers fight over tables at the back, while the front terrace by the lake is reserved for the fatter of wallet. The restaurant is open from (build your own) breakfast to dinner, with the accent on in-season, British ingredients. While the food quality sometimes disappoints, the location never does.

Wiltons

55 Jermyn Street, SW1Y 6LX (7629 9955). Green Park or Piccadilly Circus tube. **Open** noon-2.30pm, 6-10.30pm Mon-Fri. **££££**. **British**. **Map** p79 A1 ㉕

If you want to glimpse a vanishing way of life (and have deep pockets), head for Wiltons: 'noted since 1742 for the finest oysters, fish and game'. The cossetting service, the muted decor and the sense of calm are perfect for anyone who finds the 21st century a bit much. It hardly matters what the food's like, but it's better than you might think.

Wolseley

160 Piccadilly, W1J 9EB (7499 6996, www.thewolseley.com). Green Park tube. **Open** 7am-midnight Mon-Fri; 8am-midnight Sat; 8am-11pm Sun. **££££**. **Brasserie. Map** p79 A1 ㉖

In a gorgeous room, the Wolseley shimmers with 1920s glamour, its dining room filled with lively social energy

and battalions of waiters. It's a sought-after venue at all times of day: breakfast, brunch, lunch, tea or dinner.

Shopping

Fortnum & Mason

181 Piccadilly, W1A 1ER (7734 8040, www.fortnumandmason.co.uk). Green Park or Piccadilly Circus tube. **Open** 10am-8pm Mon-Sat; noon-6pm Sun. **Map** p79 A1 ㉗

Revamped for its tercentenary in 2007, F&M is stunning: a spiral staircase sweeps through the five-storey building, light flooding down from a central glass dome. The classic eau de nil blue and gold colour scheme with flashes of rose pink is everywhere, both as decor and on the packaging of the fabulous ground-floor treats – chocolates, biscuits, preserves and, of course, tea.

Jermyn Street

Green Park or Piccadilly Circus tube. **Map** p79 A1 ㉘

Hilditch & Key (nos.37 & 73), Emma Willis (no.66) and Turnbull & Asser (nos.71-72) continue this street's proud bespoke tradition, but even on Jermyn Street things change. Bates the Hatter had to move its wonderful topper-shaped sign to join H&K at no.73, and Charles Tyrwhitt (nos.98-100) has opened a smart new store.

Arts & leisure

ICA

The Mall, SW1Y 5AH (7930 0493, 7930 3647 box office, www.ica.org.uk). Piccadilly Circus tube or Charing Cross tube/rail. **Open** noon-11pm Wed; noon-1am Thur-Sat; noon-9pm Sun. **Admission** free. **Map** p79 B1 ㉙

Founded in 1947 by an arts collective, the Institute for Contemporary Arts hosts arthouse cinema, performance art, exhibitions and edgy club nights. After management changes, the programme is shaping up – but public funding was cut by 37% for 2012/13.

Royal Albert Hall p95

South Kensington & Chelsea

South Kensington

Once known as 'Albertopolis' in honour of the prince behind its superb museums and concert hall, built out of profits from the 1851 Great Exhibition, this area is home to the **Natural History Museum**, **Science Museum** and **V&A**; such is the wealth of exhibits in each you'd be foolish to try to 'do' more than one in any single day. The grandiose **Royal Albert Hall** and overblown, splendidly restored **Albert Memorial** also pay homage to the man behind it all, with **Kensington Gardens** a refreshing green backdrop.

Sights & museums

Albert Memorial

Kensington Gardens, SW7 (7495 0916). South Kensington tube. Map p90 B1 ❶

An extraordinary memorial, with 180ft spire, unveiled 15 years after Prince Albert's death. Created by Sir George Gilbert Scott, it centres on a gilded, seated Albert holding a catalogue of the Great Exhibition. A tour guide points out the highlights (2pm, 3pm 1st Sun of mth; £5, £4.50 reductions).

Brompton Oratory

Thurloe Place, SW7 2RP (7808 0900, www.bromptonoratory.com). South Kensington tube. **Open** 6.30am-8pm daily. **Admission** free; donations appreciated. Map p90 C3 ❷

The second largest Catholic church in the country (after Westminster Cathedral, p83) was completed in 1884, but it feels older – partly because of its baroque Italianate style, partly because much of the decoration pre-dates the structure: such as Mazzuoli's late 17th-century apostle statues are from Siena cathedral. The Cardinal Newman Chapel opened in 2010.

Kensington Palace & Gardens

NEW *Kensington Gardens, W8 4PX (0844 482 7777, 0844 482 7799 reservations, www.hrp.org.uk). High Street Kensington or Queensway tube.* **Open** *Nov-Feb* 10am-5pm daily. *Mar-Oct* 10am-6pm daily. **Admission** £12.50; free-£11 reductions; £34 family. **Map** p90 A1 ❸

At the end of the 1600s, Sir Christopher Wren extended this Jacobean mansion to palatial proportions on the instructions of William III. Kensington Palace has been home to royals minor and major ever since. Enchanted Palace – which uses fashion installations and participatory theatre to tell the stories of seven tragic princesses who lived here – has been running during a £12m refurbishment. It finishes on 9 Jan 2012, and the palace reopens on 26 Mar. Tickets will then (check the website for changes) give you access to the new 'Victoria Revealed' and 'Princess Diana' exhibits, the latter featuring frocks from the Royal Ceremonial Dress Collection. There's free entrance to a central foyer for shops and the café.

The palace's new visitor entrance will open directly into Kensington Gardens, a park only delineated from Hyde Park (p95) by the Serpentine boating lake and Long Water. Diana's presence is also strong here: paddle in the ring-shaped Princess Diana Memorial Fountain or make the kids happy by taking them to the pirate-ship climbing frame in the brilliant Diana, Princess of Wales Playground.

Natural History Museum

Cromwell Road, SW7 5BD (7942 5000, www.nhm.ac.uk). South Kensington tube. **Open** 10am-5.50pm daily. **Admission** free. *Special exhibitions prices vary.* **Map** p90 B3 ❹

The NHM opened in a magnificent, purpose-built, Romanesque palazzo in 1881. Now, the vast entrance hall is taken up by a cast of a diplodocus skeleton, and to the left the Blue Zone

Air Scares

The new climate gallery at the Science Museum.

The floor of the strikingly futuristic new Atmosphere gallery at the **Science Museum** (p93) represents the land and water masses on Earth, while the installation hanging from the ceiling plays the part of the sky. The blue-hued design isn't just decorative: floor and ceiling form a giant board for Interconnected Earth, an interactive game hub that introduces visitors to the subject of climate change.

Exhibits include interpretation of data from tree rings and stalagmite slices, a time-travel game and details of pioneering scientists, such as Joseph Fourier (1768-1830), who suggested the atmosphere could regulate the Earth's surface temperature, and Guy Callendar (1898-1964), who linked fossil fuel energy and rising carbon dioxide levels. Zone C has the most exciting exhibit: a metre-long ice core from Antarctica (the only one on display in the UK) that tells us exactly what the air was like 1410, thanks to the bubbles trapped inside the ice. Quite apart from its scientific usefulness, it's beautiful.

The Atmosphere gallery isn't all doom and gloom. It provokes serious thought about the sort of energy we use in our cars and homes, but also explains radical new solutions to unprecedented changes in temperature and CO_2 levels: a hydrogen-powered urban car, for instance, or paving slabs that generate energy as you walk across them.

LONDON BY AREA

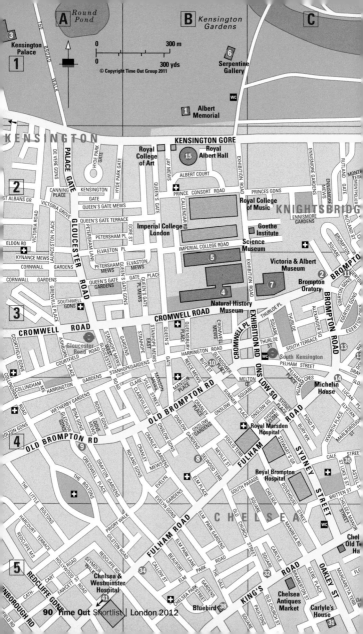

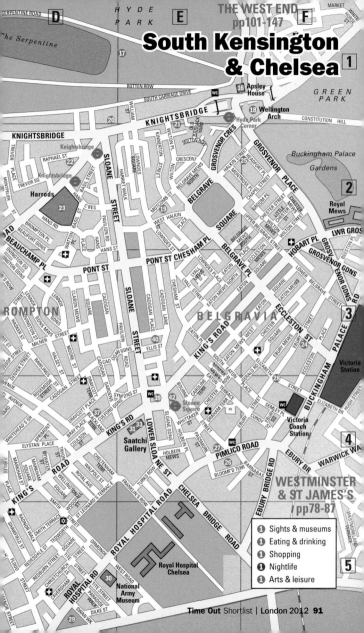

South Kensington
& Chelsea

HYDE PARK

The Serpentine

SERPENTINE ROAD

D

E

F

MARKET

GREEN PARK

1

ROTTEN ROW

SOUTH CARRIAGE DRIVE

WC

16 Apsley House

18 Wellington Arch

Hyde Park Corner

CONSTITUTION HILL

Buckingham Palace Gardens

KNIGHTSBRIDGE

WILLIAM

20

KNIGHTSBRIDGE

KINNERTON STREET

WILTON PL

WILTON ROW

21

HALKIN STREET

HEADFORT PL

MONTROSE PL

GROSVENOR CRES

GROSVENOR PLACE

2

Royal Mews

Knightsbridge

RAPHAEL ST

22

Knightsbridge

TREVOR PLACE

TREVOR SQ

BASIL STREET

SLOANE

STREET

HARRIET WALK

LOWNDES SQUARE

MOTCOMB ST

CADOGAN PLACE

CRESCENT

BELGRAVE MEWS NORTH

CHAPEL PL

BROOM PL

CHESTER STREET

LITTLE CHESTER

WILTON

CHESTER STREET

LWR GROS

Harrods

23

HANS C RES

PAVILION RD

WEST HALKIN ST

19

BELGRAVE

SQUARE

UPPER BELGRAVE STREET

WILTON STREET

HOBART PL

GROSVENOR GDNS

BEAUCHAMP PL

BROMPTON RD

BEAUFORT PL

OVINGTON GDNS

HANS RD

WATSON PLACE

HANS PLACE

HANS ST

LOWNDES ST

CHESHAM ST

LYALL STREET

LOWNDES PLACE

WALL STREET

BELGRAVE MEWS

EATON MEWS NORTH

ECCLESTON MEWS

EATON

SQUARE

LOWER BELGRAVE ST

GROSVENOR GDNS

BEESTON PL

PONT ST

CHESHAM PL

PONT ST

SLOANE

STREET

CADOGAN LANE

CADOGAN PLACE

EATON MEWS WEST

CHESTER

BELGRAVIA

EATON

EATON MEWS

ECCLESTON ST

BUCKINGHAM PALACE RD

3

BROMPTON

KENNOX

GONS MWS

SQUARE

CLARON MEWS

CADOGAN

MILNER

PAVILION

ELLIS ST

KING'S ROAD

EATON MEWS WEST

EATON

CHESTER

ELIZABETH

ECCLESTON

EBURY MEWS

Victoria Station

40

CADOGAN GARDENS

SYMONS ST

BOURNE

CAROLINE

EATON TERRACE

28

STREET

ROSEMOOR

MOORE ST

CADOGAN

39

42

WC

Sloane Square

GRAHAM TERRACE

CUNDY ST

Victoria Coach Station

SEMLEY PL

WC

AVENUE

WHITEHEAD'S GR

DENYER STREET

RAWLINGS ST

HALSEY ST

BRAY PL

BLACKLAND TERR

DRAYCOTT PL

CULFORD GDNS

COULSON ST

KING'S RD

37 38

LOWER SLOANE ST

WHITTAKER

HOLBEIN PL

CHESTER ROW

PASSMORE

WC

PIMLICO ROAD

EBURY BR

WARWICK WA

4

ELYSTAN PLACE

SPIRMONT PLACE

MARKHAM SQUARE

BYWATER ST

MARKHAM STREET

WELLINGTON SQUARE

ROYAL AVE

CHELTENHAM TERRACE

WALPOLE ST

ST LEONARD'S TERRACE

SMITH

WOODFALL

FRANKLIN'S ROW

TURKS ROW

Saatchi Gallery

HOLBEIN MEWS

BLOOMF'D TERR

ST BARNABAS ST

27

EBURY BRIDGE RD

WESTMINSTER & ST JAMES'S
pp78-87

5

RADNOR WALK

SMITH TERRACE

TEDWORTH SQ

REDESDALE ST

TITE STREET

CHRISTCHURCH

REDBURN STREET

CHELTENHAM TCE

ORMONDE

WEST ROAD

Royal Hospital Chelsea

FLOOD

SWAN WK

CAVERSHAM

ROYAL HOSPITAL RD

TITE STREET

PARADISE WK

DILKE ST

29

30

National Army Museum

CHELSEA BRIDGE ROAD

RADNOR

JUBILEE PLACE

KING'S ROAD

Time Out Shortlist | London 2012 **91**

1	Sights & museums
1	Eating & drinking
1	Shopping
1	Nightlife
1	Arts & leisure

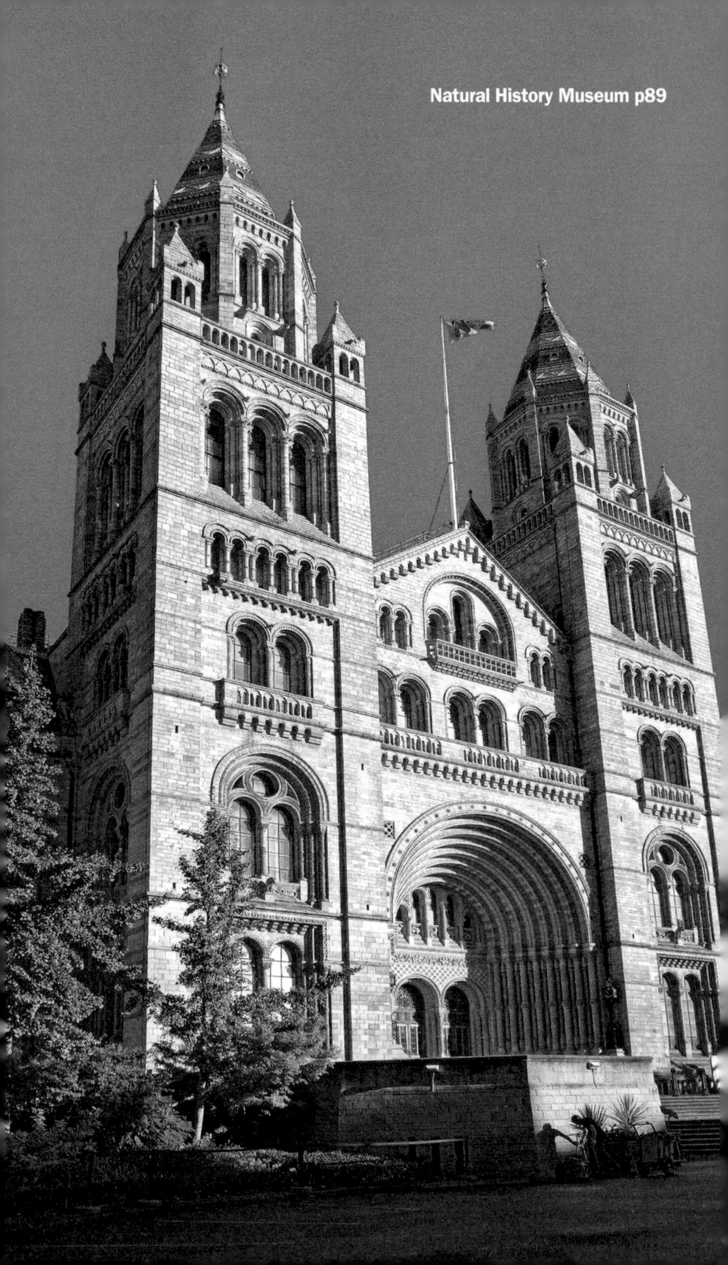

Natural History Museum p89

has a 90ft model of a blue whale and often queues as long to see the animatronic *T Rex*. The Green Zone displays a cross-section through a giant sequoia tree – as well as an amazing array of stuffed birds, among which you can compare the fingernail-sized egg of a hummingbird with an elephant bird egg as big as a football – and another 22 million insect and plant specimens are housed (with the research scientists working on them) in the eight-storey, white Cocoon of the Darwin Centre. 'Images of Nature', a new permanent gallery of the NHM's art collection, opened in early 2011.

Event highlights 'Sexual Nature' (until 2 Oct 2011); Veolia Environnement Wildlife Photographer of the Year (Oct 2011-Mar 2012); 'Scott's Last Expedition' (Jan-Oct 2012); 'Sensational Butterflies' (Apr-Sept 2012).

Science Museum
Exhibition Road, SW7 2DD (7942 4000, 0870 870 4868 information, www.sciencemuseum.org.uk). South Kensington tube. **Open** 10am-6pm daily. **Admission** free. *Special exhibitions* prices vary. **Map** p90 B3 ❺
Only marginally less popular with the kids than its natural historical neighbour, the Science Museum celebrates technology in the service of daily life: from Puffing Billy, the world's oldest steam locomotive (built in 1815), via classic cars, to the Apollo 10 command module and (new this year) a reconstruction of pioneering engineer James Watts' attic workshop. In the Wellcome Wing, the revamped Who Am I? gallery explores genetics, brain science and psychology, and the brand-new, highly interactive Atmosphere (see box p89), which looks at the history of the science of climate change. Back in the main body of the museum, the third floor is dedicated to flight (with stunning new simulators) and the Launchpad gallery features levers, pulleys, explosions and all manner of experiments for kids.

South Kensington & Chelsea

Serpentine Gallery
Kensington Gardens, W2 3XA (7402 6075, www.serpentinegallery.org). Lancaster Gate or South Kensington tube. **Open** 10am-6pm daily. **Admission** free; donations appreciated. **Map** p90 B1 ❻
This secluded, small and airy gallery mounts rolling, two-monthly exhibitions by up-to-the-minute artists, along with the annual Serpentine Pavilion project (June-Sept), a temporary structure specially commissioned from an internationally renowned architect.
Event highlights The Serpentine Sackler Gallery opens in 2012 in the nearby Grade II-listed Magazine – redesigned by starchitect Zaha Hadid.

Victoria & Albert Museum
Cromwell Road, SW7 2RL (7942 2000, www.vam.ac.uk). South Kensington tube. **Open** 10am-5.45pm Mon-Thur, Sat, Sun; 10am-10pm Fri. *Tours* hourly, 10.30am-3.30pm daily. **Admission** free. *Special exhibitions* prices vary. **Map** p90 C3 ❼
The V&A is a superb showcase for applied arts from around the world, and its brilliant FuturePlan programme has revealed some stunning new galleries – not least the wonderfully visual Medieval & Renaissance Galleries. Among the unmissable highlights of the collection are the seven Raphael Cartoons (painted in 1515 as Sistine Chapel tapestry designs), the Great Bed of Ware and the splendid Ardabil carpet, the world's oldest floor covering. On the first floor are the Theatre and Performance Galleries, the William & Judith Bollinger Gallery of European jewellery (including diamonds that belonged to Catherine the Great) and the Gilbert Collection of gold snuffboxes and urns. There are also some superb architecture models.
Event highlights 'The House of Annie Lennox' (15 Sept 2011-26 Feb 2012); 'Postmodernism: Style & Subversion' (24 Sept 2011-8 Jan 2012); 'British Design 1948-2012' (Mar-Aug 2012).

LONDON BY AREA

Eating & drinking

The fabled trio of tea rooms at the **V&A** (p93) are just a chandelier or two different from how they were in the 19th century. They're self-service. Expect to queue.

Anglesea Arms

15 Selwood Terrace, SW7 3QG (7373 7960, www.capitalpubcompany.com). South Kensington tube. **Open** 11am-11pm Mon-Sat; noon-10.30pm Sun. **Pub**. Map p90 B4 ❽

Nearly 200 years old, the Anglesea was a local for Dickens and DH Lawrence. Aristocratic etchings and 19th-century London photographs adorn the dark, panelled wood walls, adding to the feel of a place lost in time. Real ales are the speciality: Brakspear Oxford Gold, Hogs Back and Adnams among them. Food, served in a dining area with hearth fire, is traditional English; there's an outdoor terrace for summer.

Cambio de Tercio

163 Old Brompton Road, SW5 0LJ (7244 8970, www.cambiodetercio. co.uk). Gloucester Road or South Kensington tube. **Open** noon-3pm, 7-11.30pm Mon-Sat; noon-3pm, 7-11pm Sun. **£££. Tapas**. Map p90 A4 ❾

Pared down, discreet, smart and decorated with colourful art, Cambio de Tercio attracts sophisticates and – thanks to the location – Latino ambassadors with their familias. The cooking verges on the extraordinary, with the cured ham and the bread as good as you'd find in Madrid. Waiting staff are knowledgeable and friendly. At no.174, the same owner's Tendido Cero (7370 3685) is a cheaper, but still excellent, version of Cambio.

Oddono's

14 Bute Street, SW7 3EX (7052 0732, www.oddonos.co.uk). South Kensington tube. **Open** 11am-11pm Mon-Thur, Sun; 11am-midnight Fri, Sat. **£. Ice-cream**. Map p90 B3 ❿

With a plain interior, this place is all about premium ingredients and classic flavours. Even on a grey day, regulars troop in for a fix of vaniglia made from Madagascan vanilla pods. The pistachio is some of the best anywhere, with generous sprinkles of the rich green nut.

Racine

239 Brompton Road, SW3 2EP (7584 4477). Knightsbridge or South Kensington tube, or bus 14, 74. **Open** noon-3pm, 6-10.30pm Mon-Fri; noon-3.30pm, 6-10.30pm Sat; noon-3.30pm, 6-10pm Sun. **£££. French**. Map p90 C3 ⓫

Heavy curtains inside the door allow diners to make a grand entrance into Racine's warm 1930s retro atmosphere. The clientele seems to have become less varied, feeling more male and monied than before, but there's plenty to enjoy from the menu: try a starter such as garlic and saffron mousse with mussels, or, for dessert, a clafoutis with morello cherries in kirsch.

Tini

87-89 Walton Street, SW3 2HP (7589 8558, www.tinibar.com). Knightsbridge or South Kensington tube. **Open** 6pm-midnight Mon-Thur; 6pm-1am Fri, Sat; 6pm-12.30am Sun. **Bar**. Map p90 C3 ⓬

Tini is a cocktail lounge hangout for haves and have-yachts, proper posh and a bit ridiculous. Serviced by genteel Gianfrancos in suits and spread under low ceilings, it's laced with traces of pink neon and fancy fleshiness courtesy of Italian-leaning drinks and Pirelli calendars from yesteryear.

Shopping

Caramel Baby & Child

291 Brompton Road, SW3 2DY (7589 7001, www.caramel-shop.co.uk). South Kensington tube. **Open** 10am-6pm Mon-Sat; noon-5pm Sun. Map p90 C3 ⓭

Now more than a decade old, this is a great place to head to for tasteful togs for children, from baby to 12-year-old.

The look is relaxed, but the clothes are well finished in modern, muted colour schemes. The styles have been inspired by the sturdy clothes of the past, but never submit to full-blown nostalgia.

Conran Shop

Michelin House, 81 Fulham Road, SW3 6RD (7589 7401, www.conran.co.uk). South Kensington tube. **Open** 10am-6pm Mon, Tue, Fri; 10am-7pm Wed, Thur; 10am-6.30pm Sat; noon-6pm Sun. **Map** p90 C4 ⑭

Sir Terence Conran's flagship store in this lovely 1909 building showcases furniture and design for every room in the house, and the garden. Portable accessories, gadgets, books, stationery and toiletries make great gifts.

Arts & leisure

Royal Albert Hall

Kensington Gore, SW7 2AP (7589 3203 information, 7589 8212 box office, www.royalalberthall.com). South Kensington tube or bus 9, 10, 52, 452. **Map** p90 B2 ⑮

Another memorial to Queen Victoria's husband, this vast rotunda is best approached for the annual BBC Proms, despite acoustics that do orchestras few favours. Look out for recitals on the great Willis pipe organ and grand ballet extravaganzas at Christmas. **Event highlights** The Proms (mid July-mid Sept 2012).

Knightsbridge

Knightsbridge is about be-seen-in restaurants and designer shops, but that doesn't mean it's particularly stylish. There are terrific people-watching opportunities, though.

Sights & museums

Apsley House

149 Piccadilly, W1J 7NT (7499 5676, www.english-heritage.org.uk). Hyde Park Corner tube. **Open** Nov-Mar

11am-4pm Wed-Sun. *Apr-Oct* 11am-5pm Wed-Sun. **Admission** £6; £3-£5.10 reductions. **Map** p91 E1 ⑯

Called No.1 London because it was the first London building encountered on the road to the City from Kensington village, Apsley House was the Duke of Wellington's residence for 35 years. His descendants still live here, but several rooms are open to the public and give a superb feel for the man and his era.

Hyde Park

7298 2000, www.royalparks.gov.uk. Hyde Park Corner, Lancaster Gate or Marble Arch tube. **Map** p91 E1 ⑰

At 1.5 miles long and a mile wide, Hyde Park is one of the largest Royal Parks. It was a hotspot for demonstrations in the 19th century and remains so today – a march against war in Iraq in 2003 was the largest in British history. The legalisation of public assembly in the park led to the creation of Speakers' Corner in 1872 (close to Marble Arch tube), where political and religious ranters still have the floor, and Marx, Lenin, Orwell and the Pankhursts have previously spoken. Rowing boats and pedalos can be hired to venture among the ducks, swans and grebes on the Serpentine – venue for the Swimming 10km Marathon and the Triathlon's swimming element for London 2012.

Wellington Arch

Hyde Park Corner, W1J 7JZ (7930 2726, www.english-heritage.org.uk). Hyde Park Corner tube. **Open** Apr-Oct 10am-5pm Wed-Sun. *Nov-Mar* 10am-4pm Wed-Sun. **Admission** £3.70; free-£3.10 reductions. **Map** p91 F1 ⑱

Built in the 1820s and initially topped by a vast statue of Wellington, since 1912 the bronze Peace Descending on the Quadriga of War has finished the Arch with a flourish. Three floors of displays cover its history and that of the Blue Plaques scheme (which puts their biographical details on the houses where famous people lived); the third floor has great views from its balcony.

Eating & drinking

Amaya

19 Motcomb Street, 15 Halkin Arcade, SW1X 8JT (7823 1166, www.amaya. biz). Knightsbridge tube. **Open** 12.30-2.15pm, 6.30-11.30pm Mon-Sat; 12.45-2.45pm, 6.30-10.30pm Sun. **£££**. **Indian**. Map p91 E2 ⑲

Glamorous, stylish and seductive, Amaya is sleekly appointed with sparkly chandeliers, splashes of modern art and a groovy bar. The restaurant's calling card is its sophisticated Indian creations, chosen from a menu that cleverly links dressed-up street food with regal specialities.

Bar Boulud

NEW *Mandarin Oriental Hyde Park, 66 Knightsbridge, SW1X 7LA (7201 3899, www.barboulud.com). Knightsbridge tube.* **Open** noon-2.30pm, 5.30-10.30pm daily. **£££**. **French bistro**. Map p91 D1 ⑳

In the same hotel as Heston's heavily hyped Dinner, Bar Boulud is our preferred restaurant. See box right.

Blue Bar

The Berkeley, Wilton Place, SW1X 7RL (7235 6000, www.the-berkeley.co.uk). Hyde Park Corner tube. **Open** 4pm-1am Mon-Sat; 4-11pm Sun. **Cocktail bar**. Map p91 E2 ㉑

This bar has sky-blue armchairs, deep-blue ornate plasterwork and navy-blue leather-bound menus, combined with discreet lighting to striking effect. It's a see-and-be-seen place, but staff treat all-comers like royalty, and the cocktails are masterful.

Zuma

5 Raphael Street, SW7 1DL (7584 1010, www.zumarestaurant.com). Knightsbridge tube. **Open** noon-11pm Mon-Fri; 12.30-11pm Sat; 12.30-10.30pm Sun. **££££**. **Japanese fusion/bar**. Map p91 D2 ㉒

One of London's smartest restaurants, there's more to this buzzy 'contemporary izakaya' (Japanese tapas bar, in effect) than its striking wood-and-stone interior. The surprise is that the mix of Japanese and fusion food on the long menu fully justifies high prices.

Shopping

Harrods

87-135 Brompton Road, SW1X 7XL (7730 1234, www.harrods. com). Knightsbridge tube. **Open** 10am-8pm Mon-Sat; noon-6pm Sun. Map p91 D2 ㉓

All the glitz and marble can be a bit much, but in the store that boasts of selling everything, it's hard not to leave with at least one thing you like. In fact, it even sold itself in 2010: former owner Mohammed Al Fayed got a reported £1.5bn from Qatar Holdings for the place. The food halls are legendary, but it's on the fashion floors that Harrods comes into its own, with well-edited collections from the heavyweights – and a rather impressive new shoe department (see box p106).

Belgravia & Pimlico

This area is characterised by a host of embassies and the fact that everyone living here is very rich. Enjoy strolling through tiny mews, then settle into some plush dining, drinking or shopping.

Eating & drinking

Boisdale of Belgravia

13-15 Eccleston Street, SW1W 9LX (7730 6922, www.boisdale.co.uk). Victoria tube/rail. **Open** noon-1am Mon-Fri; 6pm-1am Sat. **Whisky bar**. Map p91 F3 ㉔

From the labyrinthine bar and restaurant spaces and heated cigar terrace to overstated tartan accents, there's something brilliantly preposterous about Boisdale. It's hard not to love a posh, Scottish-themed enterprise that specialises in superb single-malt whiskies.

Excellence without Excess

Bar Boulud gets our nod over Heston Blumenthal's Dinner.

Bar Boulud

On 31 January 2011, the circus came to town. The opening of **Dinner by Heston** (7201 3833, www.dinnerbyheston.com) at the Mandarin Oriental Hyde Park was accompanied by an extravaganza of twirling pineapples, puffs of nitrogen mist, table-hopping chefs, camera flashes, former pop stars and tabloid clowns jumping through hoops. Roll on up, folks, it's the show of the year – seats instantly sold out until (we were told) May.

Celebrity chef-scientist Heston Blumenthal's menu is an odd read, inspired by his passion for historic British dishes: there's the startling 'meat fruit' – chicken liver pâté that looks exactly like a mandarin – and any number of revived techniques, among them 18th-century hay-smoking. Many of the dishes are fascinating. But Dinner is hugely oversubscribed and as hugely expensive (a meal for two with wine and service costs £180).

Oddly enough, the Mandarin Oriental hotel already contained a new restaurant that had – with much less fanfare – become one

of our favourites. The basement setting of French-born, US-based star chef Daniel Boulud's **Bar Boulud** (left) has low-key decor with nods to classic brasserie styling. Casual wear, small children and happily boisterous groups are cheerfully embraced, resulting in a buzzing place where everyone feels at home. The menu has a few American dishes (small burgers with exquisite french fries), but is mainly inspired by Lyon, where Boulud was born. Terrines, pâtés, hams and sausages take centre stage, served with delightfully tangy 'hors d'oeuvres' such as carrots with coriander or celery and apple remoulade. Mains run from croque monsieur to coq au vin, along with specials such as wild halibut with ratatouille and tapenade, but our highlight was *lapin de la garrigue* (Provençal pulled rabbit with carrot, courgette and herbs) – a hefty slice of jewelled jelly. Staff are charm itself, whether serving a bottle from the serious wine list or a fresh fruit juice, and prices for this first-class performance are most reasonable.

Nahm

Halkin, Halkin Street, SW1X 7DJ
(7333 1234, www.halkin.como.bz).
Hyde Park Corner tube. **Open** noon-
2.30pm, 7-10.45pm Mon-Fri; 7-10.45pm
Sat; 7-9.45pm Sun. **££££. Thai. Map**
p91 F2 ㉕

Done out in gold and bronze tones, this
elegant hotel dining room feels opulent
yet unfussy. Tables for two – perfect
for a date – look out over a manicured
garden, and the chance to share rare
dishes of startling flavour combinations from David Thompson's kitchen
makes for a memorable meal. Smoky
beef stir-fried with oyster sauce, onions
and basil was a recent stand-out dish.

Orange Public House

NEW *37-39 Pimlico Road, SW1W 8NE*
(7881 9844, www.theorange.co.uk).
Sloane Square tube. **Open** 8am-11.30pm
Mon-Thur; 8am-midnight Fri, Sat; 8am-
10.30pm Sun. **£££. Gastropub. Map**
p91 E4 ㉖

An elegant, airy conversion of a former
brewery, the Orange is all stripped
wood and potted orange trees. The
'pub' part – is a single, ground-floor
room – is a bit too civilised, but the
'gastro' aspect – a dining room beside
the bar (no bookings) and first-floor
restaurant – is fully justified, from
creamily rich chicken liver parfait in a
little kilner jar to crispy, salt-crusted
sea bream with a minty pea sauce.

Shopping

Daylesford Organic

44B Pimlico Road, SW1W 8LJ
(7881 8060, www.daylesfordorganic.
com). Sloane Square tube. **Open**
8am-8pm Mon-Sat; 10am-4pm Sun.
Map p91 E4 ㉗

Part of a new wave of chic purveyors
of health food, this impressive offshoot
of Lady Carole Bamford's Cotswold-
based farm shop is set over three floors,
and includes a café. Goods include
ready-made dishes, and such store-
cupboard staples as pulses and pasta.

Elizabeth Street

Sloane Square tube. **Map** p91 F4 ㉘
The Victoria Coach Station location
doesn't inspire confidence, but
Elizabeth Street sells show-stopping
jewellery (Erickson Beamon, no.38),
gorgeous invitations and correspon-
dence cards (Grosvenor Stationery
Company, no.47), quality cigars
(Tomtom, no.63) and fine perfumes
(Les Senteurs, no.71). There's also the
only British outpost of French bakery
Poilâne (no.46).

Chelsea

It's been more than four decades
since *Time* magazine declared that
London – they meant the **King's
Road** – was 'swinging'. These days
you're more likely to find suburban
swingers wondering where it went
than the next Jean Shrimpton, but
places like **Anthropologie** have
improved the retail opportunities
and the **Saatchi Gallery** has put
it back on the tourist map. Chelsea
proper starts at **Sloane Square**,
spoiled by traffic but redeemed by
the edgy **Royal Court Theatre**.

Sights & museums

Chelsea Physic Garden

66 Royal Hospital Road, SW3 4HS
(7352 5646, www.chelseaphysicgarden.
co.uk). Sloane Square tube or bus 11,
19, 239. **Open** *Apr-Oct* noon-5pm
Wed-Fri; noon-6pm Sun. **Admission**
£8; free-£5 reductions. **Map** p91 D5 ㉙
The 165,000sq ft grounds of this gorgeous botanic garden are filled with
healing herbs and vegetables, rare
trees and dye plants. The garden was
founded in 1673 by Sir Hans Sloane
with the purpose of cultivating and
studying plants for medical purposes.

National Army Museum

Royal Hospital Road, SW3 4HT (7730
0717, www.national-army-museum.
ac.uk). Sloane Square tube or bus 11,

137, 170. **Open** 10am-5.30pm daily. **Admission** free. **Map** p91 D5 ③⓪
More entertaining than its rather dull exterior suggests, this museum of the history of the British Army kicks off with 'Redcoats', a gallery that starts at Agincourt in 1415 and ends with the American War of Independence. You'll also find some fingertips, frostbitten on Everest, and Dame Kelly Holmes' gold medals from Athens 2004.

Saatchi Gallery

Duke of York's HQ, SW3 4SQ (7823 2363, www.saatchi-gallery.co.uk). Sloane Square tube. **Open** 10am-6pm daily. **Admission** free. **Map** p91 E4 ③①
Charles Saatchi's gallery has three floors, providing more than 50,000sq ft of space for temporary exhibitions that generally show Saatchi's taste is broader than his reputation as a champion of Brit Art suggests. Still, some of his famous British acquisitions – notably Richard Wilson's brilliant sump-oil installation *20:50* – remain.

Eating & drinking

The art deco former garage **Bluebird** (350 King's Road, 7559 1000, www.danddlondon.com) has a fine modern European restaurant.

Cadogan Arms

298 King's Road, SW3 5UG (7352 6500, www.thecadoganarmschelsea. com). Sloane Square tube. **Open** 11am-11pm Mon-Sat; 11am-10.30pm Sun. **££**. **Gastropub**. **Map** p90 C5 ③②
This 19th-century pub was given a rebuild by the Martin brothers, the men behind the Botanist (7 Sloane Square, 7730 0077, www.thebotanistonsloane square.com) up the road. It now has a countrified air, complete with antlers, a stuffed rabbit and fly-fishing paraphernalia, and a smoothly run dining area, but it's a proper boozer with a bar built for drinking. Dishes are expertly cooked and attractively presented; there's also a good cheeseboard.

Gallery Mess

Saatchi Gallery, Duke of York's HQ, King's Road, SW3 4LY (7730 8135, www.saatchigallery.co.uk). Sloane Square tube. **Open** 10am-9.30pm Mon-Sat; 10am-7pm Sun. **££**. **Brasserie**. **Map** p91 E4 ③③
The Saatchi Gallery (left) is home to a fabulous brasserie. There's a simple breakfast menu (pastries, eggs and toast or fry-up) to 11.30am, then lunch and dinner take over, with salads, pastas and burgers joined by daily specials: perhaps steamed salmon served in a yellow 'curry' broth or saddle of lamb drizzled with yoghurt. You can sit inside surrounded by modern art, but the grounds outside – littered with portable tables until 6pm in fair weather – are an attractive option.

Haché

329-331 Fulham Road, SW10 9QL (7823 3515, www.hacheburgers.com). South Kensington tube. **Open** noon-10.30pm Mon-Thur, Sun; noon-11pm Fri, Sat. **£**. **Burgers**. **Map** p90 B5 ③④
Haché is French for 'chopped', but the only Gallic twist on the great American burger here is attention to detail. Rather than underpinning them with skewers, Haché's toasted ciabattas are left ajar so that you can admire the ingredients – they're worth admiring.

Tom's Kitchen

27 Cale Street, SW3 3QP (7349 0202, www.tomskitchen.co.uk). South Kensington or Sloane Square tube. **Open** 8-11am, noon-3pm, 6-11pm Mon-Fri; 10am-4pm, 6-11pm Sat, Sun. **££**. **Brasserie**. **Map** p90 C4 ③⑤
Home from home for Chelsea's super-rich, but don't let that put you off. The warm, welcoming room, framed in gleaming white tiles and homespun prints, feels as if it was set up just to make everybody happy. The menu is superb, covering much of what you'd want to eat at any time of day, from macaroni cheese through moules and steak and chips to a fine Sunday lunch.

LONDON BY AREA

Shopping

Anthropologie Decor

NEW *131-141 King's Road, SW3 5PW (7349 3110, www.anthropologie.eu). Sloane Square tube then bus 11, 19, 22, 319, 211.* **Open** 10am-7pm Mon-Sat; noon-6pm Sun. **Map** p91 D5 ❸❻

This American shop, vintage-inspired and stylishly bohemian, has refocused to concentrate on homeware, with a bumper stock of haberdashery, wallpapers and design books. Fashion is at the other branch on Regent's Street.

John Sandoe

10 Blacklands Terrace, SW3 2SR (7589 9473, www.johnsandoe.com). Sloane Square tube. **Open** 9.30am-5.30pm Mon, Tue, Thur-Sat; 9.30am-7.30pm Wed; noon-6pm Sun. **Map** p91 D4 ❸❼

Tucked away on a Chelsea side street, this 50-year-old independent looks just as a bookshop should. The stock is literally packed to the rafters, and of the 25,000 books here, 24,000 are a single copy – so there's serious breadth.

Shop at Bluebird

350 King's Road, SW3 5UU (7351 3873, www.theshopatbluebird.com). Sloane Square tube. **Open** 10am-7pm Mon-Sat; noon-6pm Sun. **Map** p90 B5 ❸❽

Part lifestyle boutique and part design gallery, the Shop at Bluebird offers a shifting showcase of clothing for men, women and children (exclusive and sophisticated labels such as Ossie Clark, Peter Jensen, Marc Jacobs), accessories, books, furniture and gadgets. The shop has a bit of a retro feel, all vintage furniture, reupholstered seats and hand-printed fabrics.

Sloane Square

Sloane Square tube. **Map** p91 E4 ❸❾

The shaded benches and fountain in the middle of the square provide a lovely counterpoint to the looming façades of Tiffany & Co and the enormous 1930s Peter Jones department store, as well as the grinding traffic. Come summer, the brasserie terraces teem with stereotypical blonde Sloane Rangers sipping rosé; an artier crop of whatever's stylishly edgy will have taken up residence outside the Royal Court Theatre.

Arts & leisure

Cadogan Hall

5 Sloane Terrace, SW1X 9DQ (7730 4500, www.cadoganhall.com). Sloane Square tube. **Map** p91 E3 ❹⓿

Built a century ago as a Christian Science church, this austere building was transformed into a light and airy auditorium. It's hard to imagine how the renovations could have been bettered: the 905-capacity hall is comfy and the acoustics excellent.

Chelsea Football Club

Stamford Bridge, Fulham Road, SW6 1HS (0871 984 1905, www.chelseafc.com). Fulham Broadway tube. **Map** p90 A5 ❹❶

The capital's most recent Premiership winners are eager to rejoin battle with key rivals Manchester United in the 2011/2012 season. You're unlikely to get tickets to see any league action, but you can check out the museum or seek tickets for European matches or cup ties against lower league opposition.

Royal Court Theatre

Sloane Square, SW1W 8AS (7565 5000, www.royalcourttheatre.com). Sloane Square tube. **Map** p91 E4 ❹❷

A hard-hitting theatre in a well-heeled location, the emphasis here has always been on new voices in British theatre – since John Osborne's *Look Back in Anger* in the theatre's inaugural year, 1956, there have been innumerable discoveries made here: *Jerusalem*, *Enron* and *Clybourne Park* are only the most recent successful West End transfers from the Royal Court. On a Monday, all tickets cost just £10, one of London's best theatrical bargains.

Covent Garden p139

The West End

Marylebone

There is relentless trade on Oxford Street, home to hip **Selfridges**, doughty **John Lewis** and chain flagships for **Uniqlo** and **Topshop**, but few locals esteem the historic thoroughfare. Despite the new Shibuya-style diagonal crossing at Oxford Circus, perhaps an inkling of future improvements, clogged pavements make for unpleasant shopping. Escape the crowds among the pretty boutiques on **Marylebone High Street** to the north. Among the sights, the **Wallace** is too often overlooked, and **Regent's Park** is one of London's finest green spaces.

Sights & museums

Madame Tussauds
Marylebone Road, NW1 5LR (0870 400 3000, www.madametussauds.com). Baker Street tube. **Open** 9.30am-6pm

daily. **Admission** £28; £24 reductions; £99 family. Map p103 A1 ❶
Madame Tussaud brought her show to London in 1802, 32 years after it was founded in Paris, and it's been here since 1884. There are 300 figures in the collection now, under various themes: 'A-list Party' (Brad, Keira, Kate Moss), 'Première Night' (Monroe, Chaplin, Arnie), 'By Royal Appointment' and so on. In the Chamber of Horrors in 'Scream', only teens claim to enjoy the floor drops and scary special effects; they're similarly keen on the Iron Man, Spiderman and an 18ft Hulk in Marvel Super Heroes 4D. Get here before 10am to avoid huge queues, and book ahead online to make prices more palatable.

Regent's Park
Baker Street or Regent's Park tube. Map p103 B1 ❷
Regent's Park (open 5am-dusk daily) is one of London's most popular open spaces. Attractions run from the animal noises and odours of London Zoo

(p169) to enchanting Open Air Theatre versions of *A Midsummer Night's Dream* that are an integral part of a London summer. Hire a rowing boat on the lake or just walk among the roses.

Wallace Collection

Hertford House, Manchester Square, W1U 3BN (7935 0687, www.wallace collection.org). Bond Street tube. **Open** 10am-5pm daily. **Admission** free. Map p103 A2 ❸

This handsome house, built in 1776 and being steadily returned to its original state after 'improvements' in previous generations, has an exceptional collection of 18th-century French paintings and objets d'art, as well as armour and weapons. Open to the public since 1900, room after room contains Louis XIV and XV furnishings and Sèvres porcelain, while the galleries are hung with work by Titian, Velázquez, Fragonard and Gainsborough.

Eating & drinking

Artesian

Langham Hotel, 1C Portland Place, W1B 1JA (7636 1000, www.artesian-bar.co.uk). Oxford Circus tube. **Open** 4pm-midnight Mon-Fri; noon-midnight Sat, Sun. **££££**. **Bar**. Map p103 C2 ❹

Order any three of the extraordinary cocktails here, add service, and you won't get much change from a £50 note. But you'll be drinking them in style: David Collins has done a fine job on the decor, the back bar theatrically lit by huge hanging lamps.

L'Autre Pied

5-7 Blandford Street, W1U 3DB (7486 9696, www.lautrepied.co.uk). Baker Street tube. **Open** noon-2.30pm, 6-10.30pm Mon-Sat; noon-3pm, 6.30-9.30pm Sun. **£££**. **Modern European**. Map p103 A2 ❺

L'Autre Pied offers nuanced cooking in handsome rooms. Despite the trappings of somewhere that takes food very seriously, it's an accessible and relaxing place to eat, and the kitchen rarely puts a foot wrong, displaying a light touch and subtle use of herbs.

Comptoir Libanais

65 Wigmore Street, W1U 1PZ (7935 1110, www.lecomptoir.co.uk). Bond Street tube. **Open** 8am-10pm Mon-Fri; 10am-10pm Sat, Sun. **£**. **Lebanese**. Map p103 B3 ❻

Part canteen, part deli, Libanais stores cutlery in harissa cans on its communal bar and is decorated with kitsch murals. Pick up a wrap (falafel, say, or chicken kofta) for lunch, pop by for mint tea and a rosewater macaron in the afternoon, or linger over an informal dinner of moussaka or tagine with organic couscous or rice. Breads (baked in-house) and sweets are a key draw.

Fairuz

3 Blandford Street, W1U 3DA (7486 8108, www.fairuz.uk.com). Baker Street or Bond Street tube. **Open** noon-11.30pm Mon-Sat; noon-11pm Sun. **££**. **Middle Eastern**. Map p103 B2 ❼

Fairuz is a rough-hewn one-off. A youngish crowd are attracted by the relatively low prices at this singularly rustic and well-regarded Lebanese. Check out the makloobeh, which is a terrific stew made of aubergine, rice, lamb and almonds.

La Fromagerie

2-6 Moxon Street, W1U 4EW (7935 0341, www.lafromagerie.co.uk). Baker Street or Bond Street tube. **Open** 8am-7.30pm Mon-Fri; 9am-7pm Sat; 10am-6pm Sun. **£**. **Café**. Map p103 A2 ❽

Famed with foodies for its dedicated cheese room, Patricia Michelson's high-end deli also dishes out freshly cooked café food. Its communal tables are often packed with devotees.

Golden Hind

73 Marylebone Lane, W1U 2PN (7486 3644). Bond Street tube. **Open** noon-3pm, 6-10pm Mon-Fri; 6-10pm Sat. **£**. **Fish & chips**. Map p103 B2 ❾

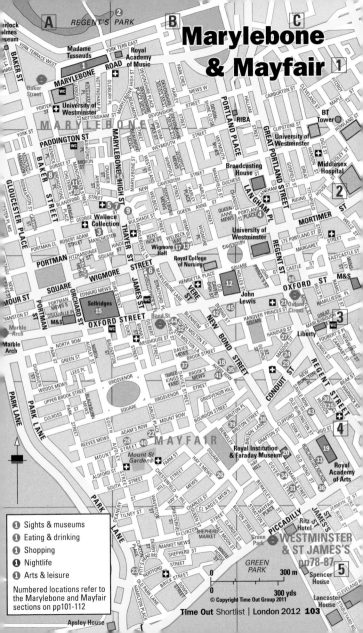

Marylebone & Mayfair

REGENT'S PARK

Madame Tussauds

Royal Academy of Music

RIBA

University of Westminster

BT Tower

Broadcasting House

Middlesex Hospital

Wallace Collection

University of Westminster

Wigmore Hall

Royal College of Nursing

John Lewis

Liberty

Selfridges

Marble Arch

Marble Arch

MAYFAIR

Mount St Gardens

Royal Institution & Faraday Museum

Royal Academy of Arts

PICCADILLY

Ritz Hotel

Green Park

WESTMINSTER & ST JAMES'S pp78-87

GREEN PARK

Spencer House

Lancaster House

Apsley House

❶ Sights & museums
❶ Eating & drinking
❶ Shopping
❶ Nightlife
❶ Arts & leisure

Numbered locations refer to the Marylebone and Mayfair sections on pp101-112

300 m

300 yds

© Copyright Time Out Group 2011

The pastel-hued art deco fryer at this chip shop is only used to store menus these days (the cooking's done in a back kitchen), but the Golden Hind still oozes local character, entirely in keeping with its Marylebone Lane location. Big portions hit the spot, and the Greek staff really make a fuss of customers.

Purl

50 Blandford Street, W1U 7HX (7935 0835, www.purl-london.com). Bond Street tube. **Open** 5pm-11.30pm Mon-Thur; 5pm-midnight Fri, Sat. **Map** p103 A2 ⑩

The four young chaps behind this new speakeasy-style cocktail bar claim inspiration from the golden age of bartending. Accordingly, a lot of effort goes into each drink: for Mr Hyde's Fixer Upper, a hand-held food smoker pipes applewood smoke into a flask of rum, cola reduction and orange bitters. The flask is then sealed with candlewax before being served with a goblet.

Shopping

Held at St Marylebone Parish Church on Saturdays, **Cabbages & Frocks** market (7794 1636, www.cabbagesandfrocks.co.uk) sells vintage clothing and snacks. On Sunday morning, **Marylebone Farmers' Market** is in Cramer Street carpark at Moxton Street.

Cadenhead's Whisky Shop & Tasting Room

26 Chiltern Street, W1U 7QF (7935 6999, www.whiskytastingroom.com). Baker Street tube. **Open** 10.30am-6.30pm Mon-Sat. **Map** p103 A2 ⑪

Cadenhead's is a rarity: an independent whisky bottler. The firm selects barrels from distilleries all over Scotland and bottles them without filtration or any other intervention. One of a kind.

John Lewis

278-306 Oxford Street, W1A 1EX (7629 7711, www.johnlewis.co.uk).

Bond Street or Oxford Circus tube. **Open** 9.30am-8pm Mon-Wed, Fri; 9.30am-9pm Thur; 9.30am-7pm Sat; noon-6pm Sun. **Map** p103 B3 ⑫

Recently renovated – transparent-sided escalators and a partly glazed roof allow in plenty of natural light – and renowned for solid reliability and the courtesy of its staff, John Lewis also deserves a medal for breadth of stock. The ground-floor cosmetics hall, for example, has glamorous Crème de la Mer and Eve Lom, but also natural brands like Neal's Yard and Burt's Bees. There's a London 2012 Shop on the fifth floor for souvenirs.

Margaret Howell

34 Wigmore Street, W1U 2RS (7009 9009, www.margarethowell.co.uk). Bond Street tube. **Open** 10am-6pm Mon-Wed, Fri, Sat; 10am-7pm Thur. **Map** p103 B2 ⑬

Howell's wonderfully wearable outfits are made in Britain and with an old-fashioned attitude to quality. These principles combine to create the best 'simple' clothes in London. Her pared-down approach means prices seem steep, but these are clothes that will get better with time.

Marylebone High Street

Bond Street or Baker Street tube. **Map** p103 B2 ⑭

With tube stations at its top and bottom, this is one of the most accessible shopping streets in town. Browse the likes of elegant lifestyle store Brissi (no.22), inspirational Daunt Books (no.83), the Scandinavian design classics at Skandium (no.86), Kabiri's avant-garde jewellery (no.37) or concept lingerie store Apartment C (no.70). Need a snack? Detour to Marylebone Lane for 1950s timewarp café Paul Rothe & Son (no.35), via high-fashion artisan shoes at Tracey Neuls (no.29).

Selfridges

400 Oxford Street, W1A 1AB (0800 123 400, www.selfridges.com). Bond

Topshop p107

Sole City

Selfridges and Harrods open huge new shoe departments.

Selfridges Shoe Galleries

The world's first temple to wedge heels, platforms, slingbacks and flip-flops, the supersized Shoe Galleries at **Selfridges** (p104) opened last year. Having taken over a massive chunk of the department store's second floor, the Galleries are said to be larger than Tate Modern's Turbine Hall, displaying 120 brands in a series of 'apartments' and open spaces.

More importantly, the Galleries are gorgeous. Hushed dark areas give way to wooden floors and natural light, and clever details include vintage cinema seating and bespoke designer areas. Pricing is surprisingly democratic – luxury labels like Nicholas Kirkwood and Christian Louboutin share the space with high-street classics, while über-cool Sino-French brand Feiyue has set up a concept shop where you can get your hands on its unisex range of sneakers in original canvas, leather and suede, as well as customise your own pair.

How do you approach such a huge space? Start at the 'Left & Right' sites, near the central escalator. They're dedicated conceptual, interactive sites that change every six to eight weeks – accommodating shoe-inspired temporary shops, mini-exhibitions and art installations.

Hot on the Shoe Galleries', ahem, heels, **Harrods** (p196) opened its art deco Shoe Salon in spring 2011. The Salon is decked out in champagne-coloured marble, with bespoke furnishings and shiny brass swirls. The list of brands reads like a wanton shoe dream: Balenciaga, Chanel, YSL, smoking-hot satin Charlotte Olympias, super-cute Miu Mius and trendy Opening Ceremony numbers. Unlike at the Shoe Galleries, there's barely a whiff of high street: the focus here is on the upper edge of luxury, and what it lacks in affordability, it makes up for in pure fantasy. Harrods bosses explain that they are trying to 'capture the essence of the glamorous Golden Era', and here statement pieces such as Christian Louboutin crystal-embellished stilettos and Brian Atwood's floral sandals glisten side by side.

Street or Marble Arch tube. **Open** 9.30am-9pm Mon-Sat; noon-6pm Sun. **Map** p103 A3 ⑮

Selfridges' hyper-energised atmosphere seems recession-proof. The department store remains the first port-of-call for stylish one-stop shopping, and useful floor plans make navigating easy-peasy. On the ground floor, the Wonder Room – 19,000sq ft of luxury brands – goes from strength to strength, the fashion selections are superb and the new Shoe Galleries (see box left) might make you weak at the knees. As well as a slew of events and celeb appearances, there's been a major reworking of the third floor ('3rd Central') and fab new concessions from b store and Alexander Wang. World-class, inventive and contemporary.

Topshop

214 Oxford Street, W1W 8LG (0844 848 7487, www.topshop.com). Oxford Circus tube. **Open** 9am-9pm Mon-Sat; 11.30am-6pm Sun. **Map** p103 C3 ⑯

Topshop's massive, throbbing flagship is a teenage Hades at weekends, but there's nowhere on the high street that's more on-trend. You'll find a boutique of high-fashion designer capsule ranges, vintage clothes, even a Hersheson hairstylist among cheap and well-cut jeans, the Kate Moss range and all manner of other temptations. Topman is catching up with its sister, with a whole new floor.

Arts & leisure

Wigmore Hall

36 Wigmore Street, W1U 2BP (7935 2141, www.wigmore-hall.org.uk). Bond Street tube. **Map** p103 B2 ⑰

Built in 1901 as the display hall for Bechstein Pianos, but now boasting perfect acoustics, art nouveau decor and an excellent basement restaurant, the Wiggy is one of the world's top chamber-music venues. The Monday-lunch recitals and Sunday morning coffee concerts are great value.

Mayfair

Mayfair still means money, but these days not necessarily stuffy exclusivity, with even the tailors of **Savile Row** loosening their ties a little. Even so, there's enough old-world decorum to satisfy the most fastidious visitor, from elegant shopping arcades to five-star hotels. **Piccadilly Circus** remains its unloveable self.

Sights & museums

Handel House Museum

25 Brook Street (entrance Lancashire Court), W1K 4HB (7399 1953, www.handelhouse.org). Bond Street tube. **Open** 10am-6pm Tue, Wed, Fri, Sat; 10am-8pm Thur; noon-6pm Sun. **Admission** £5; free-£4.50 reductions. **Map** p103 B3 ⑱

George Frideric Handel settled in this Mayfair house aged 37, remaining here until his death in 1759. The house has been beautifully restored with original and recreated furnishings, paintings and a welter of the composer's scores (in the same room as photos of Jimi Hendrix, who lived next door). There are recitals every Thursday.

Royal Academy of Arts

Burlington House, Piccadilly, W1J 0BD (7300 8000, www.royalacademy.org.uk). Green Park or Piccadilly Circus tube. **Open** 10am-6pm Mon-Thur, Sat, Sun; 10am-10pm Fri. **Admission** free. *Special exhibitions* prices vary. **Map** p103 C4 ⑲

Britain's first art school, founded in 1768, moved to the extravagantly Palladian Burlington House a century later. You'll have to pay for blockbuster exhibitions in the Sackler Wing or main galleries, but shows in the John Madejski Fine Rooms – drawn from the RA's holdings (which range from Constable to Hockney) – are free. **Event highlights** Summer Exhibition (June-Aug 2012).

Royal Institution & Faraday Museum

21 Albemarle Street, W1S 4BS (7409 2992, www.rigb.org). Green Park tube. **Open** 9am-6pm Mon-Fri. **Admission** free. **Map** p103 C4 ⓴

The Royal Institution has been at the forefront of scientific achievements for more than 200 years. Following a complete rebuild, you can enjoy the Michael Faraday Laboratory (a replica of the electromagnetic pioneer's workspace) and a fun new events programme.

Eating & drinking

Wild Honey (12 St George Street, W1S 2FB, 7758 9160, www.wild honeyrestaurant.co.uk) is a similarly affordable sister restaurant to the always excellent Arbutus (p132).

Chisou

4 Princes Street, W1B 2LE (7629 3931, www.chisou.co.uk). Oxford Circus tube. **Open** noon-2.30pm, 6-10.15pm Mon-Sat. **££**. **Japanese**. **Map** p103 C3 ㉑

Chisou looks quiet, but inside it hums with activity. Salted belly pork, and the pure ume cha (rice in a hot broth with pickled plum) are highlights, and there's a serious saké and shochu list. Pop next door for noodles and donburi.

Connaught Bar

16 Carlos Place, W1K 2AL (7499 7070, www.theconnaught.com). Bond Street tube. **Open** 4pm-1am Mon-Sat. **££££**. **Cocktail bar**. **Map** p103 B4 ㉒

The Connaught is one of London's most properly old-fashioned luxury hotels (p197) – but this is one hell of a sexy bar, with a sleek, black-and-chrome, cruise-liner style interior, and well-crafted cocktails to match. Across the corridor, the equally impressive Coburg Bar specialises in more traditional mixed drinks.

Galvin at Windows

Hilton, 22 Park Lane, W1K 1BE (7208 4021, www.galvinatwindows.com).

Green Park or Hyde Park Corner tube. **Open** 11am-1am Mon-Wed; 11am-3am Thur, Fri; 3pm-3am Sat; 11am-10.30pm Sun. **Bar**. **Map** p103 B5 ㉓

Despite London's several new options for sky-high sipping (see box p160), this remains a remarkable site for a bar: 28 floors up, with a panoramic view of the capital, and a sleek interior that mixes art deco glamour with a hint of 1970s petrodollar kitsch.

Hibiscus

29 Maddox Street, W1S 2PA (7629 2999, www.hibiscusrestaurant.co.uk). Oxford Circus tube. **Open** noon-2.30pm, 6.30-10pm Tue-Fri; 6-10pm Sat. **£££**. **Haute cuisine**. **Map** p103 C3 ㉔

Small and intimate, Hibiscus is one of the capital's most exciting places to eat. Chef-patron Claude Bosi is a kitchen magician, playing with texture and flavour in ways that challenge and excite, without making diners feel they're in some weird experiment.

Momo

25 Heddon Street, W1B 4BH (7434 4040, www.momoresto.com). Piccadilly Circus tube. **Open** noon-2.30pm, 6.30-11.30pm Mon-Sat; 6.30-11pm Sun. **£££**. **North African**. **Map** p103 C4 ㉕

A big reputation, cool Marrakech-style decor, great Maghrebi soundtrack and some of the best North African food in London keep punters pouring in to Momo for an experience to savour.

Only Running Footman

5 Charles Street, W1J 5DF (7499 2988, www.therunningfootman.biz). Green Park tube. **Open** 7.30am-11pm daily. **Pub**. **Map** p103 B4 ㉖

Reopening a few years back after a huge refurb, this place looks as if it's been here forever. On the ground floor, jolly chaps prop up the mahogany bar, enjoying three decent ales on draught and an extensive menu: anything from a bacon buttie takeaway to Welsh rarebit with watercress, or £7.50 eggs benedict for breakfast.

Connaught Bar

Pollen Street Social

NEW *8-10 Pollen Street, W1S 1NG (7290 7600, www.pollenstreetsocial. com). Oxford Circus tube.* **Open** noon-1am Mon-Sat. **££££. Modern European**. Map p103 C3 ㉗

Owner Jason Atherton earned plaudits for his innovative small dishes at Gordon Ramsay's Maze. Here dishes remain tiny, but they are also pretty, daring and always a delightful surprise. Choose a selection of savoury dishes (seafood is a strength) and then move to the dessert bar, where you can chat to the chefs as they prepare moreish sweets such as 'PBJ' (peanut butter and jelly as a frozen dessert).

Scott's

20 Mount Street, W1K 2HE (7495 7309, www.caprice-holdings.co.uk). Bond Street or Green Park tube. **Open** noon-10.30pm Mon-Sat; noon-10pm Sun. **££££. Fish & seafood**. Map p103 B4 ㉓

Of the celebrity hangouts in the capital, Scott's is the one that most justifies the hype: from the greeting by doorman to the look-at-me contemporary British art on the walls and the glossy Rich List crowd. The food – perhaps tiny boar sausages with chilled rock oysters – gets better and better.

Sketch: The Parlour

9 Conduit Street, W1S 2XJ (0870 777 4488, www.sketch.uk.com). Oxford Circus tube. **Open** 8am-9pm Mon-Fri; 10am-9pm Sat. **£££. Café**. Map p103 C3 ㉙

Of the three parts of Pierre Gagnaire's legendarily expensive Sketch, which also include Gallery's destination dining and Lecture Room's haute-beyond-haute cuisine, Parlour appeals the most for its tongue-in-cheek sexiness. Saucy nudes illustrate the chairs, and the chandelier appears to be covered with red fishnet tights. The menu includes simple hearty dishes and quirky high-concept creations, such as the club sandwich with red-and-green bread.

Tibits

12-14 Heddon Street, W1B 4DA (7758 4110, www.tibits.ch). Oxford Circus tube. **Open** 9am-10.30pm Mon-Wed; 9am-midnight Thur-Sat; 10am-10.30pm Sun. **££. Vegetarian**. Map p103 C4 ㉚

It's all California-cool in this groovy vegetarian export from Switzerland. The buffet-cum-pay-per-100g concept left us sceptical at first, but the global offerings have proven to be notches above the usual all-you-can-eat gaff.

Shopping

Acne Studio

NEW *13 Dover Street, W1S 4LN (7629 9374, www.acne-studios.com). Green Park tube.* **Open** 10am-7pm Mon-Sat. Map p103 C4 ㉛

This lovely shop from the Stockholm conceptual fashion and design brand is as clipped and clean as its collections. The skinny, four-storey ex-gallery has artfully placed accessories, men's and women's clothing, Acne's optical illusion furniture and denim in all manner of clever washes.

Browns

23-27 South Molton Street, W1K 5RD (7514 0000, www.brownsfashion.com). Bond Street tube. **Open** 10am-6.30pm Mon-Wed, Fri, Sat; 10am-7pm Thur. Map p103 B3 ㉜

Among the 100-odd designers jostling for attention in Joan Burstein's five interconnecting shops (menswear is at no.23) you might find Chloé and Marc Jacobs, labels such as Felipe Oliveira Baptista, with oversized blazers and print leggings, or exclusives from Balenciaga and James Perse. Browns Focus (nos.38-39, 7514 0063) is younger and more casual; Labels for Less (no.50, 7514 0052) sells last season's leftovers. Shop 24 (p112) is her latest initiative.

Burlington Arcade

Piccadilly, W1 (7630 1411, www. burlington-arcade.co.uk). Green Park tube. **Open** 8am-6.30pm Mon-Wed, Fri;

8am-7pm Thur; 9am-6.30pm Sat; 11am-5pm Sun. **Map** p103 C4 ㉝
The Royal Arcades in the vicinity of Piccadilly are a throwback to shopping past: Burlington is the largest and, commissioned by Lord Cavendish in 1819, oldest of them. Highlights include collections of classic watches, Luponde Teas, iconic British brands Globe-Trotter and Mackintosh... and the top-hatted beadles who keep order.

Dover Street Market

17-18 Dover Street, W1S 4LT (7518 0680, www.doverstreetmarket.com). Green Park tube. **Open** 11am-6pm Mon-Wed; 11am-7pm Thur-Sat. **Map** p103 C4 ㉞
Comme des Garçons designer Rei Kawakubo's six-storey space combines the edgy energy of London's indoor markets – concrete floors, Portaloo dressing-rooms – with rarefied labels. Recent additions include the store's own relaxed menswear label, DSM, and Gitman & Co's 1980s-style oxford and gingham check shirts.

Elemis Day Spa

2-3 Lancashire Court, W1S 1EX (7499 4995, www.elemis.com). Bond Street tube. **Open** 9am-9pm Mon-Sat; 10am-6pm Sun. **Map** p103 B3 ㉟
This leading British spa brand's exotic, unisex retreat is tucked away down a cobbled lane off Bond Street. The elegantly ethnic treatment rooms are a lovely setting in which to relax and enjoy a spot of pampering, from wraps to results-driven facials.

Georgina Goodman

44 Old Bond Street, W1F 4GD (7493 7673, www.georginagoodman.com). Green Park tube. **Open** 10am-6pm Mon-Wed, Fri, Sat; 10am-7pm Thur. **Map** p103 C4 ㊱
Goodman started her business crafting sculptural, made-to-measure footwear from a single piece of untreated vegetan leather, and a couture service is still available at her airy, gallery-like shop.

The ready-to-wear range (you'll pay from £165 for her popular slippers) brings Goodman's individualistic approach to a wider customer base.

Grays Antique Market & Grays in the Mews

58 Davies Street, W1K 5LP; 1-7 Davies Mews, W1K 5AB (7629 7034, www.graysantiques.com). Bond Street tube. **Open** 10.30am-6.30pm Mon-Wed, Fri; 10.30am-7.30pm Thur; 11am-5pm Sat; noon-5pm Sun. No credit cards. **Map** p103 B3 ㊲
More than 200 dealers run stalls in this smart covered market – housed in a Victorian lavatory showroom – selling everything from antiques, fine art and jewellery to vintage fashion.

Louis Vuitton Maison

NEW *17-20 New Bond Street, W1S 2UE (7399 3856, www.louisvuitton.com). Bond Street tube.* **Open** 10am-7pm Mon-Sat; noon-6pm Sun. **Map** p103 C4 ㊳
The palatial Louis Vuitton Maison, designed by New York's Peter Marino, stocks only rare and exclusive Vuitton pieces. Complete with a Men's Club Area, gigantic changing rooms and a chic 'Librairie' that sells Brit art books, this shop encompasses every aspect of the jet-set lifestyle. We like gawking at the sumptuous shop interior, complete with Takashi Murakami installations, stacked monogrammed cases and well-coiffed customers.

Miller Harris

21 Bruton Street, W1J 6QD (7629 7750, www.millerharris.com). Bond Street or Green Park tube. **Open** 10am-6pm Mon-Sat. **Map** p103 B4 ㊴
Grasse-trained British perfumer Lyn Harris's distinctive, long-lasting scents are made with quality natural extracts and oils, and delightfully packaged.

Mount Street

Bond Street or Green Park tube. **Map** p103 B4 ㊵

LONDON BY AREA

Mount Street, with its dignified Victorian terracotta façades and by-appointment art galleries, master butcher Allens (no.117) and cigar shop Sautter (no.106), has taken on a new, cutting-edge persona. At no.12, near the Connaught's cool cocktail bars (p108), Balenciaga has set its super-chic clothes in a glowing sci-fi interior. Here too are Britain's first Marc by Marc Jacobs (nos.24-25), revered shoe-designer Christian Louboutin (no.17) and a five-floor Lanvin (no.128). Further delights (such as Rick Owens) are on South Audley Street.

Paul Smith Sale Shop

23 Avery Row, W1X 9HB (7493 1287, www.paulsmith.co.uk). Bond Street tube. **Open** 10.30am-6.30pm Mon-Wed, Fri, Sat; 10.30am-7pm Thur; 1-5.30pm Sun. **Map** p103 B3 ❸

Samples and last season's stock can be found at a 30-50% discount. You'll find clothes for men, women and children, as well as a range of accessories.

Postcard Teas

9 Dering Street, W1S 1AG (7629 3654, www.postcardteas.com). Bond Street or Oxford Circus tube. **Open** 10.30am-6.30pm Tue-Sat. **Map** p103 B3 ❷

The range in this exquisite little shop isn't huge, but it is selected with care – usually from single estates. There's a central table for those who want to try a pot. Tea-ware and accessories are also sold, and there are tastings on a Saturday morning.

Savile Row

Oxford Circus or Piccadilly Circus tube. **Map** p103 C4 ❸

Even Savile Row is moving with the times. US import Abercrombie & Fitch has been ensconced here for a few years, not far from the cutting-edge and iconoclastic designers (Ute Ploier, Opening Ceremony, Peter Jensen) of b store at no.24A. Be reassured: expensive bespoke tailoring remains the principal activity, with the workaday

task of shopping for a suit transformed into an almost otherworldly experience at such emporia as Gieves & Hawkes (no.1) or, erstwhile tailor to Sir Winston Churchill, Henry Poole (no.15).

Shop 24

NEW *24 South Molton Street, W1K 5RD (7514 0032, www.brownsfashion. com). Bond Street tube.* **Open** 10am-6.30pm Mon-Wed, Fri, Sat; 10am-7pm Thur. **Map** p103 B3 ❷

Proving that simple ideas are the best, Browns (p110) has opened a boutique selling 'the staple items you can't live without'. The idea is that you can come here for all your wardrobe essentials, albeit luxurious ones. Looking for the ultimate Breton top? How about the melt-in-the-hands cashmere version by Vince, at £140. Or the perfect cotton T-shirt? Try a James Pearse, from £55.

Uniqlo

311 Oxford Street, W1C 2HP (7290 7701, www.uniqlo.co.uk). Bond Street or Oxford Circus tube. **Open** 10am-9pm Mon-Sat; 11.30am-6pm Sun. **Map** p103 B3 ❹

There are three outposts of Uniqlo, Japan's biggest clothes retailer, on Oxford Street alone – but this one is 25,000sq ft and three storeys of flag-ship. Not as cheap as Primark but more stylish, Uniqlo sells simple, single-colour staples for men and women.

Fitzrovia

West of Tottenham Court Road and north of Oxford Street, Fitzrovia – once a gathering point for radicals, writers and boozers, mostly in reverse order – retains sufficient traces of bohemianism to appeal to the media types that now frequent it. Some of the capital's best hotels and restaurants cluster at Charlotte Street, but these days **Bradley's** or the **Long Bar** are more satisfying places to have a drink than the Fitzroy Tavern or Wheatsheaf.

breakfast, brunch and lunch.
serving beer, wine, tea, coffee
cakes, tarts, muffins, friands ...

Lantana p115

TART OF THE DAY
3.-

FIG WITH PROSCIUTTO
STILTON, PECANS &
RASPBERRY VINAIGRETTE

Sights & museums

All Saints

7 Margaret Street, W1W 8JG (7636 1788, www.allsaintsmargaretstreet. org.uk). Oxford Circus tube. **Open** 7am-7pm daily. **Admission** free. **Map** p116 B4 ❶

Respite from the tumult of Oxford Street, this 1850s church was designed by William Butterfield, one of the great Gothic Revivalists. Behind the polychromatic brick façade, the shadowy, lavish interior is one of the capital's ecclesiastical triumphs.

BBC Broadcasting House

Portland Place, Upper Regent Street, W1A 1AA (0370 901 1227, www.bbc. co.uk/showsandtours/tours). Oxford Circus tube. **Admission** *Tours* £9.95; £7.75-£9.25 reductions; £30 family. **Map** p116 A4 ❷

Each Sunday there are nine tours of the various radio stations in the BBC's HQ. Completed in 1932, it was Britain's first purpose-built broadcast centre. Booking ahead is essential. Tours are also available at west London's BBC Television Centre (Wood Lane, Shepherd's Bush, W12 7RJ, 0370 901 1227), taking in the news desk, studios and Weather Centre.

BT Tower

60 Cleveland Street, W1. Goodge Street tube. **Map** p116 B3 ❸

The BT Tower (formerly the Post Office Tower) was designed to provide support for radio, TV and telephone aerials. It was opened in 1964 and its crowning glory was a revolving restaurant, closed to the public in 1971 after a bomb attack by the Angry Brigade. The building was Grade II-listed in 2003, but remains accessible only for private functions.

Pollock's Toy Museum

1 Scala Street (entrance Whitfield Street), W1T 2HL (7636 3452, www.pollockstoymuseum.com). Goodge Street tube. **Open** 10am-5pm Mon-Sat.

Admission £5; free-£4 reductions. **Map** p116 C4 ❹

Housed in a creaky Georgian townhouse, Pollock's is named after one of the last Victorian toy theatre printers. By turns beguiling and creepy, the museum is a nostalgia-fest of old board games, tin trains, porcelain dolls and Robertson's gollies.

Royal Institute of British Architects

66 Portland Place, W1B 1AD (7580 5533, www.architecture.com). Great Portland Street tube. **Map** p116 A3 ❺

Temporary exhibitions are held in RIBA's Grade II-listed HQ, which houses a bookshop, café and library, and hosts an excellent lecture series.

Eating & drinking

Benito's Hat

56 Goodge Street, W1T 4NB (7637 3732, www.benitos-hat.com). Goodge Street tube. **Open** 11.30am-10pm Mon-Wed, Sun; 11.30am-11pm Thur-Sat. **£**. **Burritos**. **Map** p116 B4 ❻

London's TexMex eateries are ten a peso at the moment, but Benito's Hat is one of the best – no wonder its expanded into Covent Garden and on to Oxford Street. The production line compiles some of the best burritos in town, and a few cocktails or Mexican beer are served if you choose to eat in.

Bradley's Spanish Bar

42-44 Hanway Street, W1T 1UT (7636 0359). Tottenham Court Road tube. **Open** noon-11pm Mon-Sat; noon-10pm Sun. **Pub**. **Map** p116 C5 ❼

There's a touch of the Barcelona dive bar about this pub and San Miguel on tap, but it ain't really Spanish. Not that the hotchpotch of local workers, shoppers and exchange students who fill the cramped two-floor space care.

Hakkasan

8 Hanway Place, W1T 1HD (7927 7000). Tottenham Court Road tube.

Open noon-3pm, 6-11pm Mon-Wed;
noon-3pm, 6pm-midnight Thur, Fri;
noon-4pm, 6pm-midnight Sat; noon-
4pm, 6-11pm Sun. **££££**. **Chinese**.
Map p116 C4 **❽**
The moody, nightclub feel of this glam
take on the Shanghai teahouse still
pulls a lively, monied crowd for high-
ticket dining. Enjoy the experience for
less by visiting for the lunchtime dim
sum. The bar (which opens later than
the restaurant) is also very chic.

Lantana

*13 Charlotte Place, W1T 1SN (7637
3347, www.lantanacafe.co.uk). Goodge
Street tube.* **Open** 8am-3pm Mon-Wed;
8am-3pm, 5-9pm Thur, Fri; 9am-3pm
Sat, Sun. **£**. **Café**. **Map** p116 B4 **❾**
The super salads (smoky aubergine or
a crunchy sugar snap and red cabbage
combo, for example), cakes and sunny
breakfasts have drawn throngs of regulars to this Antipodean-style eaterie
ever since it opened. The espresso
machine is the coffee connoisseur's
choice – La Marzocco – and the beans
come from the excellent Monmouth.

Long Bar

*Sanderson, 50 Berners Street, W1T
3NG (7300 1400, www.sanderson
london.com). Oxford Circus or Goodge
Street tube.* **Open** 11am-midnight
Mon-Wed; 11am-1am Thur-Sat; noon-
10.30pm Sun. **Bar**. **Map** p116 B4 **❿**
The Long Bar's early noughties glory
days may be a faded memory, but
there's still easy glamour for the taking. The bar is indeed long – a thin
onyx affair – but nabbing one of the
eyeball-backed stools is unlikely. Try
the lovely courtyard instead, where
table service, candlelight and watery
features make a much nicer setting.

Match Bar

*37-38 Margaret Street, W1G 0JF
(7499 3443, www.matchbar.com).
Oxford Circus tube.* **Open** 11am-
midnight Mon-Sat; 4pm-midnight Sun.
Cocktail bar. **Map** p116 B4 **⓫**

London's Match cocktail bars celebrate
the craft of the bartender with a selection of authentic concoctions, such as
juleps and fizzes, made from high-end
liquor. DJs spin from 7.30pm Thur-Sat.

Newman Arms

*23 Rathbone Street, W1T 1NG (7636
1127, www.newmanarms.co.uk).
Goodge Street or Tottenham Court
Road tube.* **Open** noon-12.30am Mon-
Fri. **Pub**. **Map** p116 C4 **⓬**
The cabin-like Newman Arms has had
the decorators in, but is still in touch
with its history: a poster for Michael
Powell's *Peeping Tom*, filmed here in
1960, faces a black-and-white portrait
of former regular George Orwell. In the
Famous Pie Room upstairs (you may
have to book), pies with a variety of fill-
ings cost around a tenner, and there are
good beers on tap downstairs.

Salt Yard

*54 Goodge Street, W1T 4NA (7637
0657, www.saltyard.co.uk). Goodge
Street tube.* **Open** noon-11pm Mon-Fri;
5-11pm Sat. **££**. **Spanish-Italian
tapas**. **Map** p116 B4 **⓭**
The artful menu of Iberian and Italian
tapas standards served at this dark,
calm and classy joint is aimed at diners
in search of a slow lunch or lightish
dinner. Fine selections of charcuterie
and cheese front the frequently changing menu, which features the likes of
tuna carpaccio with baby broad beans,
and ham croquettes with manchego. A
top choice for fuss-free tapas.

Yalla Yalla

NEW *12 Winsley Street, W1W 8HQ
(7637 4748, www.yalla-yalla.co.uk).
Oxford Circus tube.* **Open** 10am-
midnight Mon-Sat; 10am-10pm Sun.
£. **Lebanese**. **Map** p116 B5 **⓮**
Yalla Yalla offers a delectable selection
of mezze (each presented wonderfully,
with slick garnishes of olive oil, herbs
and pomegranate seeds where appropriate) and heartier main courses based
around the grill. The sticky chicken

LONDON BY AREA

Fitzrovia & Bloomsbury

1 Sights & museums

1 Eating & drinking

1 Shopping

1 Nightlife

1 Arts & leisure

Numbered locations refer to the Fitzrovia and Bloomsbury sections on pp112-128

rockers such as Nine Below Zero and the Blockheads continues.

Social

5 Little Portland Street, W1W 7JD (7636 4992, www.thesocial.com). Oxford Circus tube. **Map** p116 B4 ⑱
A discreet, opaque front hides this daytime diner and DJ bar of supreme quality, a place that still feels, a decade after Heavenly Records opened it, more like a displaced bit of Soho than a resident of boutiquey Marylebone.

Bloomsbury

In bookish circles, Bloomsbury is a name to conjure with: it is the HQ of London University and home to the superb British Museum. The name was famously attached to a group of early 20th-century artists and intellectuals (Virginia Woolf and John Maynard Keynes among them), and more recently to the (Soho-based) publishing company that gave us Harry Potter. It is an area that demands an idle browse: perhaps the bookshops of Great Russell Street, Marchmont Street or Woburn Walk, maybe along lovely Lamb's Conduit Street.

Sights & museums

British Museum

Great Russell Street, WC1B 3DG (7323 8299, www.britishmuseum.org). Russell Square or Tottenham Court Road tube. **Open** 10am-5.30pm Mon-Wed, Sat, Sun; 10am-8.30pm Thur, Fri. *Great Court* 9am-6pm Mon-Wed, Sun; 9am-11pm Thur-Sat. **Admission** free; donations appreciated. *Special exhibitions* prices vary. **Map** p117 D4 ⑲
The British Museum is a neoclassical marvel that was built in 1847, and topped off 153 years later with the magnificent glass-roofed Great Court. The £100m roof surrounds the domed Reading Room, where Marx, Lenin,

2... ... ...) (7436 2344, www.caa.org... ... ... Street or Tottenham Court Road tube. **Open** 10am-6pm Mon-Sat. **Map** p116 C4 ⑮
This airy gallery, run by the charitable arts organisation, represents more than 300 makers. Work embraces both the functional (jewellery, textiles, tableware) and unique decorative pieces.

HMV

150 Oxford Street, W1D 1DJ (0843 221 0289, www.hmv.co.uk). Oxford Street or Tottenham Court Road tube. **Open** 9am-8.30pm Mon-Wed, Fri, Sat; 9am-9pm Thur; 11.30am-6pm Sun. **Map** p116 B5 ⑯
With the departure of Zavvi back in 2009, HMV became the last of the mammoth music stores on Oxford Street. Plenty of space is given over to DVDs and games upstairs, but world, jazz and classical have a whole floor in the basement – and the ground floor is packed with pop, rock and dance music, including some vinyl.

Nightlife

100 Club

100 Oxford Street, W1D 1LL (7636 0933, www.the100club.co.uk). Oxford Circus or Tottenham Court Road tube. **Map** p116 C5 ⑰
Perhaps the most adaptable venue in London, this wide, 350-capacity basement room has provided a home for trad jazz, pub blues, northern soul and punk. It was nearly forced to close last year, but Converse trainers jumped in with sponsorship that ensures its programme of jazz, indie acts and ageing

Dickens, Darwin, Hardy and Yeats once worked. Star exhibits include ancient Egyptian artefacts – the Rosetta Stone on the ground floor, mummies upstairs – and Greek antiquities that include the stunning marble friezes from the Parthenon. The King's Library is a calm home to a 5,000-piece collection devoted to the formative period of the museum during the Enlightenment (a replica Rosetta Stone is here, if the real one's too crowded). You won't be able to see everything in one day, so buy a guide and pick some showstoppers, or plan several visits. Free eyeOpener tours offer introductions to particular world cultures. The museum is undergoing extension work in its north-west corner, which should create new temporary galleries and education spaces for 2013.
Event highlights 'Treasures of Heaven: saints, relics & devotion in medieval Europe' (until 9 Oct 2011); 'Creative Beginnings: European Art in the Ice Age' (27 Oct 2011-Feb 2012).

Cartoon Museum
35 Little Russell Street, WC1A 2HH (7580 8155, www.cartoonmuseum.org). Tottenham Court Road tube. **Open** 10.30am-5.30pm Tue-Sat; noon-5.30pm Sun. **Admission** £5.50; free-£4 reductions. **Map** p117 D4 ⑳
On the ground floor of this former dairy, a brief chronology of British cartoon art is displayed, from Hogarth via Britain's cartooning 'golden age' (1770-1830) to examples of wartime cartoons, ending up with modern satirists such as Ralph Steadman and the Guardian's Steve Bell, alongside fine temporary exhibitions. Upstairs is a celebration of UK comics and graphic novels.

Charles Dickens Museum
48 Doughty Street, WC1N 2LX (7405 2127, www.dickensmuseum.com). Chancery Lane or Russell Square tube. **Open** 10am-5pm daily. **Admission** £6; £3-£4.50 reductions; £15 family. **Map** p117 E3 ㉑

London is scattered with plaques marking addresses where the peripatetic Charles Dickens lived, but this is the only one of them still standing. He lived here from 1837 to 1840, during which time he wrote Nicholas Nickleby and Oliver Twist. Ring the doorbell to gain access to four floors of Dickensiana, collected over the years from various other of his residences. 2012 is the 200th anniversary of Dickens' birth, so there will be lively programme of events here – some held jointly with the Foundling Museum.

Foundling Museum
40 Brunswick Square, WC1N 1AZ (7841 3600, www.foundlingmuseum. org.uk). Russell Square tube. **Open** 10am-5pm Tue-Sat; 11am-5pm Sun. **Admission** £7.50; free-£5 reductions. **Map** p117 D3 ㉒
Returning to England from America in 1720, Captain Thomas Coram was appalled by the number of abandoned children on the streets and persuaded artist William Hogarth and composer GF Handel to become governors of a new hospital for them. Hogarth decreed the hospital should also be Britain's first public art gallery, and work by Gainsborough and Reynolds is shown upstairs. The most heart-rending display is a tiny case of mementoes that were all mothers were allowed to leave the children they abandoned here.

Grant Museum of Zoology
NEW *Rockefeller Building, University College London, University Street, WC1E 6DE (3108 2052, www.ucl. ac.uk/museums/zoology). Euston tube/ rail or Goodge Street tube.* **Open** 1-5pm Mon-Fri. **Map** p117 C3 ㉓
Reopened in 2011 in an Edwardian former library, the much-loved Grant Museum of animal skeletons, taxidermy specimens and creatures preserved in fluid retains the air of the house of an avid Victorian collector. The collection includes remains of many rare and extinct animals, such as

LONDON BY AREA

British Museum p118

a dodo and a full skeleton of the zebra-like quagga, hunted out of existence in the 1880s, as well as bisected heads and a jar full of moles.

Petrie Museum of Egyptian Archaeology

University College London, Malet Place, WC1E 6BT (7679 2884, www.petrie. ucl.ac.uk). Goodge Street or Warren Street tube. **Open** 1-5pm Tue-Sat. **Admission** free; donations appreciated. **Map** p116 C3 ㉔

Where the Egyptology collection at the the British Museum (p118) is strong on the big stuff, this fabulous hidden museum is dim case after dim case of minutiae. Among the oddities are a 4,000-year-old skeleton of a man ritually buried in a pot. Wind-up torches help you peer into the gloomy corners.

St George's Bloomsbury

Bloomsbury Way, WC1A 2HR (7242 1979, www.stgeorgesbloomsbury. org.uk). Holborn or Tottenham Court Road tube. **Open** times vary; phone for details. **Admission** free. **Map** p117 D4 ㉕

Consecrated in 1730, St George's is a grand and typically disturbing work by Nicholas Hawksmoor, with an off-set, stepped spire that was inspired by Pliny's account of the Mausoleum at Halicarnassus. Highlights include the mahogany reredos, and 10ft-high sculptures of lions and unicorns clawing at the base of the steeple. There are guided tours and regular concerts.

Eating & drinking

Right opposite the front gates of the British Museum (p118), the Grade II-listed **Museum Tavern** (49 Great Russell Street, WC1B 3BA, 7242 8987) has a good range of ales.

All Star Lanes

Victoria House, Bloomsbury Place, WC1B 4DA (7025 2676, www.allstar lanes.co.uk). Holborn tube. **Open**

5-11.30pm Mon-Wed; 5pm-midnight Thur; noon-2am Fri, Sat; noon-11pm Sun. **Bar & bowling**. **Map** p117 D4 ㉖

Walk past the lanes and smart, diner-style seating, and you'll find yourself in a comfortable, subdued side bar with chilled glasses, classy red furnishings, an unusual mix of bottled lagers and impressive cocktails. There's an American menu and, at weekends, DJs.

Espresso Room

31-35 Great Ormond Street, WC1N 3HZ (07760 714883 mobile, www.the espressoroom.com). Holborn tube or bus 19, 38. **Open** 7.30am-5pm Mon-Fri. **£**. **Coffee bar**. **Map** p117 E3 ㉗

We're big fans of this minuscule coffee bar, which serves excellent espressos, faultless flat whites and a few snacks. Carefully selected and roasted beans, top-notch execution – come here for one of London's finest brews.

Hummus Bros

37-63 Southampton Row, WC1B 4DA (7404 7079, www.hbros.co.uk). Holborn tube. **Open** 11am-9pm Mon-Fri. **£**. **Café**. **Map** p117 D4 ㉘

The simple and successful formula at this café/takeaway is to serve houmous as a base for a selection of toppings, which you scoop up with excellent pitta bread. The food is nutritious and good value. There's a second branch in Soho (88 Wardour Street, 7734 1311) and a third in the City (128 Cheapside, 7726 8011) – handy for St Paul's (p159), but only open weekday lunchtimes.

Lamb

94 Lamb's Conduit Street, WC1N 3LZ (7405 0713, www.youngs.co.uk). Holborn or Russell Square tube. **Open** noon-11.30pm Mon-Wed; noon-12.30am Thur-Sat; noon-10.30pm Sun. **Pub**. **Map** p117 E3 ㉙

Founded in 1729, this Young's pub is the sort of place that makes you misty-eyed for a vanishing era. The Lamb found fame as a theatrical haunt when the A-list included Sir Henry Irving

LONDON BY AREA

and sundry stars of music hall; they're commemorated in vintage photos, surrounded by well-worn seats, polished wood and vintage knick-knacks.

Wagamama

4 Streatham Street, WC1A 1JB (7323 9223, www.wagamama.com). Holborn or Tottenham Court Road tube. **Open** noon-11pm Mon-Sat; noon-10pm Sun. **£. Noodle bar. Map** p117 D4 ㉚

Since starting life in the basement here in 1992, this chain of shared-table restaurants has become a global phenomenon, with branches as far as Cyprus and Boston. The British Wagamamas all serve the same menu: rice plate meals and Japanese noodles, cooked teppanyaki-style on a flat griddle or simmered in big bowls of spicy soup, and served in double-quick time.

Shopping

Ask

248 Tottenham Court Road, W1T 7QZ (7637 0353, www.askdirect.co.uk). Tottenham Court Road tube. **Open** 10am-7pm Mon-Wed, Fri, Sat; 10am-8pm Thur; noon-6pm Sun. **Map** p116 C4 ㉛

Some shops on Tottenham Court Road – London's main street for consumer electronics – feel gloomy and claustrophobic, and hit you with the hard sell. Ask has four capacious, well-organised floors that give you space to browse stock that spans digital cameras, MP3 players, radios, laptops as well as hi-fis and TVs with all the relevant accessories. Prices are competitive.

Lamb's Conduit Street

Holborn or Russell Square tube. **Map** p117 E3 ㉜

Tucked away among residential back streets, Lamb's Conduit Street is the perfect size for a browse, whether you fancy checking out quality tailoring at Oliver Spencer (no.62), cult menswear and cute women's knitwear from Folk (no.49), cutting-edge design at Darkroom (no.52) or even a recumbent bicycle at Bikefix (no.48). Head off the main drag to refuel at the Lamb (p121) or the Espresso Room (p121), pop into the ethical new People's Supermarket (nos.72-78), then go to Rugby Street for homeware at Ben Pentreath (no.17) or jewellery at French's Dairy (no.13).

London Review Bookshop

14 Bury Place, WC1A 2JL (7269 9030, www.lrbshop.co.uk). Holborn tube. **Open** 10am-6.30pm Mon-Sat; noon-6pm Sun. **Map** p117 D4 ㉝

An inspiring bookshop, from the stimulating presentation to the quality of the selection. Politics, current affairs and history are well represented on the ground floor, while downstairs, audio books lead on to exciting poetry and philosophy sections. Lovely café too.

Skoob

Unit 66, Brunswick Centre, WC1N 1AE (7278 8760, www.skoob.com). Russell Square tube. **Open** 10.30am-8pm Mon-Sat; 10.30am-6pm Sun. **Map** p117 D3 ㉞

A back-to-basics concrete basement that showcases 50,000 titles covering virtually every subject, from philosophy and biography to politics and the occult. You probably won't find quite what you were looking for here – but you're almost certain to come away happily clutching something else.

Nightlife

Bloomsbury Bowling Lanes

Basement, Tavistock Hotel, Bedford Way, WC1H 9EU (7183 1979, www.bloomsburybowling.com). Russell Square tube. **Map** p117 D3 ㉟

A hip destination for local students and those wanting a late drink away from Soho, the Lanes also puts on live bands and DJs on Monday, Friday and Saturday, sometimes with a 1950s theme. If you get bored of bands and bowling, hole up in a karaoke booth.

100 Club p118

Soho Square p129

King's Cross

North-east of Bloomsbury, the once-insalubrious area of King's Cross is undergoing massive redevelopment around the grand **St Pancras International** station and well-established 'new' **British Library**. The badlands to the north are being transformed (to the tune of £500m) into mixed-use nucleus King's Cross Central, with **Kings Place** one sign of good things to come.

Sights & museums

St Pancras International
(Pancras Road, 7843 7688, www.stpancras.com; see also p215) welcomes the high-speed Eurostar train from Paris with William Barlow's gorgeous Victorian glass-and-iron train shed. For all the public art, high-end boutiques and eateries, the real attractions are the beautiful original trainshed roof and the recently reopened neo-Gothic hotel that fronts the station (**St Pancras Renaissance**, see box p198).

British Library
96 Euston Road, NW1 2DB (7412 7332, www.bl.uk). Euston or King's Cross tube/rail. **Open** 9.30am-6pm Mon, Wed-Fri; 9.30am-8pm Tue; 9.30am-5pm Sat; 11am-5pm Sun. **Admission** free; donations appreciated. **Map** p117 D1 ㊱
'One of the ugliest buildings in the world,' opined a Parliamentary committee on the opening of the new British Library in 1997. Don't judge a book by its cover: the interior is a model of cool, spacious functionality, its focal point the King's Library, a six-storey glass-walled tower housing George III's collection in the central atrium. One of the greatest libraries in the world, the BL holds more than 150 million items. In the John Ritblat Gallery, the library's main treasures are displayed: the Magna Carta, original manuscripts from Chaucer and Beatles lyrics. Some great events too.

London Canal Museum
12-13 New Wharf Road, N1 9RT (7713 0836, www.canalmuseum.org.uk). King's Cross tube/rail. **Open** 10am-4.30pm Tue-Sun; 10am-7.30pm 1st Thur of the mth. **Admission** £3; free-£2 reductions. No credit cards. **Map** p117 E1 ㊲
The museum is housed in a former 19th-century ice warehouse, used by Carlo Gatti for his ice-cream, and includes an interesting exhibit on the history of the ice trade. The part of the collection looking at the history of the waterways and those who worked on them is rather sparse by comparison.

Wellcome Collection
183 Euston Road, NW1 2BE (7611 2222, www.wellcomecollection.org). Euston Square tube or Euston tube/rail. **Open** 10am-6pm Tue, Wed, Fri, Sat; 10am-10pm Thur; 11am-6pm Sun. **Admission** free. **Map** p116 C2 ㊳
Founder Sir Henry Wellcome, a pioneering 19th-century pharmacist and entrepreneur, amassed a vast, grisly and idiosyncratic collection of implements and curios – ivory carvings of pregnant women, used guillotine blades, Napoleon's toothbrush – mostly relating to the medical trade. It's now displayed in this swanky little museum, along with works of modern art. The temporary exhibitions are always wonderfully interesting, choosing subjects such skin, dirt or drugs.

Eating & drinking

The **Peyton & Byrne** café on the ground floor of the Wellcome Collection (above) is a handy stop.

Brill
6-8 Caledonian Road, N1 9DT (7833 7797, www.thebrill.co.uk). Kings Cross tube/rail. **Open** noon-10.30pm daily. **£**. **British**. **Map** p117 E1 ㊴

This likeable spot serves robust British food at great prices. Downstairs there's a cellar bar; next door, posh sandwiches and burgers are dispensed from a gleaming takeaway counter. Lunch in the restaurant is similarly simple, with sarnies boosted by the likes of duck salad and bacon. At night, tasty dishes such as ox cheek on mash are served to a background of chilled beats.

Camino

3 Varnishers Yard, Regents Quarter, N1 9AF (7841 7331, www.camino.uk. com). King's Cross tube/rail. **Open** noon-3pm, 6.30-11pm Mon-Fri; noon-4pm, 7-11pm Sat, noon-4pm Sun. **£££**. **Spanish**. Map p117 E1 ④

A big, Spanish-themed bar-restaurant in the heart of the King's Cross construction zone, Camino is a shining beacon of things to come. In the bar you can order good tapas, but it's worth sitting down for a proper meal in the restaurant, where the cooking adheres to the central principle of traditional Spanish food: fine ingredients, simply cooked. Just opposite and run by the same people, the tiny Andalusian *bodega*-style Bar Pepito is dedicated to Spanish sherry (15 types are on offer).

Euston Tap

NEW *West Lodge, 190 Euston Rd, NW1 2EF (7387 2890, www.eustontap.com). Euston tube/rail.* **Open** noon-11pm Mon-Fri; noon-midnight Sat; 2pm-midnight Sun. **Beer bar**. Map p117 C2 ④

Set away from the main station, this fantastic new beer bar occupies an impressive Grade II-listed Portland stone lodge – a relic from the original station built in the 1830s. The decor is a little worn, but there's an incredible selection of beers, with 19 genuinely rare craft beers on draught, guest beers from microbreweries and more than a hundred bottled varieties.

St Pancras Grand

Upper Concourse, St Pancras International, Euston Road, NW1 2QP
(7870 9900, www.searcys.co.uk/st pancrasgrand). King's Cross tube/rail. **Open** 7am-11pm Mon-Sat, 8am-11pm Sun. **£££**. **Brasserie**. Map p117 D1 ④

The revival of British cuisine had hardly been evident at its gateways to the world. Now, London has a station restaurant to be proud of: St Pancras Grand evokes a grand European café with contemporary-brasserie style. The well-sourced food is served simply but with ambition, by first-rate, stripy-aproned staff. The 'longest in Europe' trackside Champagne Bar got all the attention when St Pancras reopened, but the Grand is a far better option.

Shopping

London 2012 Shop

NEW *Unit 2A, St Pancras International, Pancras Road, NW1 2QP (7837 8558, http://shop.london2012.com). King's Cross tube/rail.* **Open** 7.30am-9pm Mon-Sat; 9am-7pm Sun. Map p117 D1 ④

If you want to browse for Games merchandise in person rather than online, drop in at one of the dedicated shops. You'll find everything from collectable pin badges, mugs and die-cast models of cabs or double-decker buses to Stella McCartney-designed sportswear and Wenlock and Mandeville mascot toys. Official merchandise is also available from John Lewis (p104) and at various train stations and transport hubs.

Nightlife

Big Chill House

257-259 Pentonville Road, N1 9NL (7427 2540, www.bigchill.net). King's Cross tube/rail. **Open** noon-midnight Mon-Wed, Sun; noon-1am Thur; noon-3am Fri, Sat. Map p117 E1 ④

A festival, record label, bar and club, the Big Chill empire rolls on. A good thing too, if it keeps offering such fine things as this three-floor space. There's a great terrace, but the real reasons to attend are the chill vibe and ace DJs. It costs £5 to enter after 10pm Fri and Sat.

Hawksmoor Seven Dials p142

West End Final

Where to eat, after hours.

For all London's excitement when it comes to cutting-edge nightlife, this really isn't a good city if you're looking to eat late. So when the **St John Hotel** restaurant (p200) opened in spring 2011, it felt rather as though it had invented quality late-night dining in the West End. Not only is the food very good, but it is served until 1.45am.

In fact, those with deep pockets already had a couple of excellent options. There are few better ways to impress a hungry weekend date than a late stop-off at **Hakkasan** (p114), the sleek and stylish basement cocktail bar and modern Chinese restaurant. Last orders are taken until 11.30pm from Sunday through to Wednesday, but as late as 12.30am on Thursday, Friday and Saturday. And for sheer sense of occasion, the lovely art deco interior of the **Wolseley** (p87) is perfect, with food orders taken until 11.45pm (10.45pm on Sunday).

Cheaper options can be found near Chinatown. The utilitarian **Café TPT** (21 Wardour Street, W1D 6PN, 7734 7980) takes orders for Chinese roast meats and seafood until 12.30am, but for exceedingly late closing times (3.30am daily), head to the **New Mayflower** (68-70 Shaftesbury Avenue, W1D 6LY, 7734 9207). They usually push set meals at tourists, but there are plenty of perfectly adequate Cantonese dishes on the menu.

Scala

275 Pentonville Road, N1 9NL (7833 2022, www.scala-london.co.uk). King's Cross tube/rail. **Map** p117 E1 ⑮

One of London's best-loved gig venues, this multi-floored monolith is the frequent destination for one-off super-parties now that many of London's superclubs have bitten the dust. Built as a cinema shortly after World War I, it is surprisingly capacious and hosts a laudably broad range of indie, electronica, avant hip hop and folk. Its chilly air-conditioning is unrivalled anywhere else in the city – a definite boon should the summer get sultry.

Arts & leisure

Kings Place

90 York Way, N1 9AG (0844 264 0321, www.kingsplace.co.uk). King's Cross tube/rail. **Map** p117 D1 ⑯

Part of a complex of galleries and office space (also housing the offices of the *Guardian* and *Observer* newspapers), the main 400-seat auditorium here opened a few years back with a typically wide-ranging series of concerts. Although this is the permanent home of both the London Sinfonietta and the Orchestra of the Age of Enlightenment, there's also jazz, folk, leftfield rock and spoken word – sometimes in a second, smaller but equally acoustically sophisticated room.

Event highlights Kings Place Festival (8-11 Sept 2011).

Place

17 Duke's Road, WC1H 9PY (7121 1000, www.theplace.org.uk). Euston tube/rail. **Map** p116 C2 ⑰

For genuinely emerging dance, look to the Place. The Robin Howard Dance Theatre here is only small – it has 300 seats, raked to a stage 15m by 12m wide – but that makes it an electrifying space in which to watch work by the best new choreographers and dancers.

Event highlights 'Resolution! Dance Festival' (Jan-Feb 2012).

Soho

Forever unconventional, Soho remains London at its most game. Shoppers and visitors mingle with the musos, gays and boozers who have colonised the area since the late 1800s. If you want to drink or eat, you could hardly find a better part of London to do so. Have a wander among the skinny streets off **Old Compton Street**, Soho's main artery – and see if you can't still find yourself a bit of mischief.

Sights & museums

Leicester Square

Leicester Square tube. **Map** p130 C3 ❶
Leicester Square isn't unpleasant by day, but by night becomes a sinkhole of inebriates out on a big night 'up west'. It was very different in the 18th century: satirical painter William Hogarth had a studio here, as did artist Sir Joshua Reynolds; both are commemorated in the small central gardens, although it's the Charlie Chaplin statue that gets all the attention. For a long time only tkts (p139) and unlikely neighbours the Prince Charles Cinema (p138) and Notre Dame de France (no.5, 7437 9363, www.notredamechurch.co.uk), with its Jean Cocteau murals, were worthy of attention, but now the W (p201) and St John (p200) hotels have arrived, things might be looking up.

Photographers' Gallery

NEW *16-18 Ramillies Street, W1A 1AU (0845 262 1618, www.photonet.org.uk).* *Oxford Circus tube.* **Map** p130 A1 ❷
The new six-storey space of this excellent photographic gallery is due to open in autumn 2011, three years after the gallery moved from its former Covent Garden home. A café and shop will also be on the premises.

Ripley's Believe It or Not!

1 Piccadilly Circus, W1J 0DA (3238 0022, www.ripleyslondon.com).
Piccadilly Circus tube. **Open** *July, Aug* 9am-midnight daily. *Sept-June* 10am-midnight daily. **Admission** £25.95; free-£23.95 reductions; £81.95 family. **Map** p130 B3 ❸
Over five floors of the Trocadero, this 'odditorium' follows a formula more or less unchanged since Robert Ripley opened his first display in 1933: an assortment of 800 curiosities is displayed, ranging from a two-headed calf to the world's smallest road-safe car.

Soho Square

Tottenham Court Road tube. **Map** p130 C1 ❹
This tree-lined quadrangle was once King's Square – a weather-beaten Charles II stands at the centre, very at home by the mock Tudor gardeners' hut. On sunny days, the grass is covered with smoochy couples and the benches fill up with snacking workers.

Eating & drinking

Since the 1950s, Gerrard and Lisle Streets have been the centre of Chinatown, marked by oriental gates, stone lions and telephone boxes topped with pagodas. Old-style diners like Mr Kong (21 Lisle Street, 7437 7341) and Wong Kei (41-43 Wardour Street, 0871 332 8296) are still here, but we prefer the likes of **Barshu** (p132).

For quick, cheap eats, there's a branch of **Hummus Bros** (p121) on Wardour Street; for **late eats** in the area, see box left.

Academy

12 Old Compton Street, W1D 4TQ (7437 7820, www.lab-townhouse.com). *Leicester Square or Tottenham Court Road tube.* **Open** 4pm-midnight Mon-Sat; 4-10.30pm Sun. **Cocktail bar**. **Map** p130 C2 ❺
The two-floor space that used to be LAB is always packed with Sohoites eager to be fuelled by the shakings of London's freshest mixologists.

Soho &
Covent Garden

© Copyright Time Out Group 2011

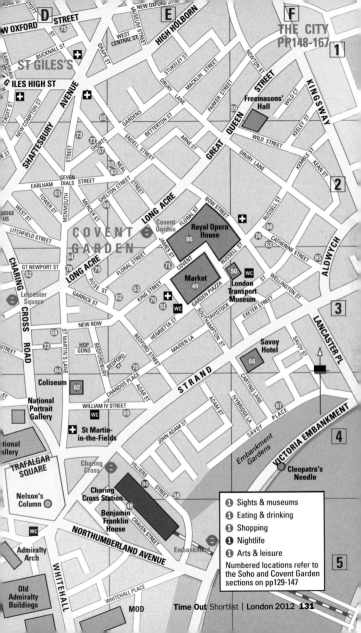

Map Labels

D · **E** · **F**

THE CITY
PR148-167

1

NEW OXFORD STREET

N OXFORD STREET

ST GILES'S

ILES HIGH ST

HIGH HOLBORN

75

MUSEUM STREET

WEST
CENTRAL ST

GRAPE ST

NEW OXFORD STREET

NEWTON ST

KINGSWAY

QUEEN STREET

GREAT

Freemasons'
Hall

59

WILD CT

WILD STREET

KEELEY ST

KEMBLE ST

KEAN ST

DRURY LANE

2

SHAFTESBURY AVENUE

BUCKNALL ST

NEW COMPTON ST

65

73

77

SHORTS

67

55

63

NEAL STREET

EARLHAM

SEVEN
DIALS

61

TOWER ST

MONMOUTH STREET

MERCER ST

60

SHELTON STREET

ENDELL STREET

GARDENS

BETTERTON ST

ARNE ST

STUKELEY ST

DRURY LANE

MACKLIN STREET

PARKER STREET

BOW STREET

ALDWYCH

88

RUSSELL ST

74

63

CATHERINE STREET

85

WEST ST

LITCHFIELD STREET

GT NEWPORT ST

52

54

Leicester
Square

LONG ACRE

LONG ACRE

FLORAL STREET

Covent
Garden

COVENT
GARDEN

Royal Opera
House

86

JAMES ST

71

COVENT

Market
49

Garden Piazza

50

WC

London
Transport
Museum

WELLINGTON ST

EXETER STREET

RUSSELL ST

CHARING CROSS ROAD

79

FLORAL STREET

ROSE ST

62

53

KING STREET

76

51

WC

SOUTHAMPTON ST

TAVISTOCK ST

GARRICK ST

NEW ROW

HENRIETTA ST

MAIDEN LA

STRAND

Savoy
Hotel

66

LANCASTER PL

68

72

ST MARTIN'S LANE

HOP
GDNS

BEDFORDBURY

BEDFORD STREET

70

CHANDOS PLACE

AGAR ST

84

Coliseum

82

WILLIAM IV STREET

WC

69

National
Portrait
Gallery

St Martin-
in-the-Fields

JOHN ADAM ST

ADAM ST

WYBRIDGE LA

CARTING LANE

SAVOY

SAVOY PLACE

Embankment
Gardens

VICTORIA EMBANKMENT

3

4

tional
allery

TRAFALGAR
SQUARE

Nelson's
Column

Charing
Cross

Charing
Cross Station

VILLIERS STREET

80

48

Benjamin
Franklin
House

58

Embankment

Cleopatra's
Needle

WC

Admiralty
Arch

Old
Admiralty
Buildings

WHITEHALL

NORTHUMBERLAND AVENUE

CRAVEN STREET

WHITEHALL PLACE

MOD

5

Legend

- **1** Sights & museums
- **1** Eating & drinking
- **1** Shopping
- **1** Nightlife
- **1** Arts & leisure

Numbered locations refer to
the Soho and Covent Garden
sections on pp129-147

Arbutus

63-64 Frith Street, W1D 3JW (7734 4545, www.arbutusrestaurant.co.uk). **Tottenham Court Road** tube. **Open** noon-2.30pm, 5-11pm Mon-Sat; noon-3pm, 5.30-10.30pm Sun. **£££. Modern European**. Map p130 C2 **6**

Providing very fine cooking at very fair prices isn't an easy trick, but this place makes it look easy. Although it's not cheap to eat à la carte, the set lunch and dinner are famously good value. It also pioneered offering 250ml carafes for sampling wine from the well-edited list.

Barshu

28 Frith Street, W1D 5LF (7287 6688, www.bar-shu.co.uk). Leicester Square or Tottenham Court Road tube. **Open** noon-11pm Mon-Thur, Sun; noon-11.30pm Fri, Sat. **££. Chinese.** Map p130 C2 **7**

Since opening five years ago, Barshu has done much to popularise Sichuan cuisine in London. The cooking continues to thrill and it is still an exceedingly charming venue, its decor modelled on that of an old Beijing teahouse. A dive into the large menu reveals a number of 'blood and guts' dishes: the likes of crunchy ribbons of jellyfish with a dark vinegar sauce and sesame oil.

Bocca di Lupo

12 Archer Street, W1D 7BB (7734 2223, www.boccadilupo.com). Piccadilly Circus tube. **Open** 12.30-3pm, 5.30-11pm Mon-Sat; noon-4pm Sun. **£££. Italian**. Map p130 B3 **8**

Take an outstanding gastronomic tour of most of Italy's 20 regions with the starter-sized portions of Bocca di Lupo's 'degustation' menu – or larger portions for those who prefer a more traditional Italian meal – served up in an atmosphere of understated luxury at surprisingly reasonable prices.

Busaba Eathai

106-110 Wardour Street, W1F 0TR (7255 8686, www.busaba.com). Oxford Circus or Tottenham Court Road tube.

Open noon-11pm Mon-Thur; noon-11.30pm Fri, Sat; noon-10pm Sun. **£.** **Thai**. Map p130 B2 **9**

You usually have to queue at the most central of five branches of this excellent Thai fast-food canteen. It combines shared tables and bench seats with a touch of oriental mystique (dark wood, incense) and food that is as good as at many top-price restaurants. Excellent.

Cha Cha Moon

15-21 Ganton Street, W1F 9BN (7297 9800). Oxford Circus tube. **Open** 11.30am-11pm Mon-Thur; 11.30am-11.30pm Fri, Sat; noon-10.30pm Sun. **£. Noodle bar**. Map p130 A2 **10**

Like Wagamama (p122) before it, Alan Yau's Cha Cha Moon offers fast food of mixed Asian inspiration at low prices, served on long cafeteria-style tables. The main focus is excellent noodle dishes (around £5) from Hong Kong, Shanghai and elsewhere in China.

Dehesa

25 Ganton Street, W1F 9BP (7494 4170). Oxford Circus tube. **Open** noon-11pm Mon-Sat; noon-5pm Sun. **££. Spanish-Italian tapas**. Map p130 A2 **11**

After running a no-reservations policy for a bit, this informal yet sophisticated spot now takes bookings. Dehesea (black-footed Ibérico pig) appears in nutty-flavoured ham and other charcuterie, but local sourcing comes to the fore in tapas such as confit Old Spot pork belly with cannellini beans.

Experimental Cocktail Club

NEW *13A Gerrard Street, W1D 5PS (7434 3559, www.chinatownecc.com). Leicester Square* tube. **Open** 6pm-3am Mon-Sat; 5-11pm Sun. **Cocktail bar**. Map p130 C3 **12**

Quite fancy, a little French and fairly flipping phenomenal, the ECC is a stylish speakeasy spread over two floors of a townhouse. The main bar, occupying the first floor, is classic, slightly colonial and cosy. Equally impressive is the intimate upstairs bar, complete with a small piano. The drinks, meanwhile, are extremely decent and the food is French and simple – boards of bread, cheese and charcuterie.

Fernandez & Wells

73 Beak Street, W1F 9SR (7287 8124, www.fernandezandwells.com). Oxford Circus or Piccadilly Circus tube. **Open** 7.30am-6pm Mon-Fri; 9am-6pm Sat; 9am-5pm Sun. **£**. **Café**. **Map** p130 B2 ⑬
If only there were more coffee bars like this in central London: one of their cheese toasties on sourdough bread or pastries make a fine breakfast. At lunch, seats are at a premium but worth the wait. The same people run a Spanish deli around the corner in Lexington Street; their St Anne's Court branch (no.16A) is nearby.

French House

49 Dean Street, W1D 5BG (7437 2799, www.frenchhousesoho.com). Leicester Square or Piccadilly Circus tube. **Open** noon-11pm Mon-Sat; noon-10.30pm Sun. **Pub**. **Map** p130 C2 ⑭
Titanic post-war drinkers, the Bacons and the Behans, frequented this small but significant boozer, while the venue's French heritage enticed De Gaulle to run his Resistance operation from the upstairs – now the tiny but hip restaurant Polpetto, from the people behind Polpo (p134). Little has changed: beer is served in half pints and bottles of Breton cider are plonked on the famed back alcove table.

Hix & Mark's Bar

66-70 Brewer Street, W1F 9UP (7292 3518, www.hixsoho.co.uk). Piccadilly Circus tube. **Open** *Restaurant* noon-3pm, 5-11.30pm Mon-Sat; noon-3pm, 5-10.30pm Sun. *Bar* noon-midnight daily. **£££**. **British/cocktail bar**. **Map** p130 B3 ⑮
Hix is altogether slicker than its Clerkenwell predecessor Hix Oyster & Chop House. In the dimly lit basement,

the superb Mark's Bar is a homage to New York – albeit with a bar billiards table – from the tin ceiling tiles to the cocktails (try a lip-pursing Forbidden Sour). The ground-floor dining room is more modern and pared down, apart from crazy mobiles by Damien Hirst and Sarah Lucas. Prices are centre-of-town high, but the food is delightful: perhaps hanger steak with watercress, horseradish and beets, fish fingers with chips and mushy peas, or Blythburgh pork chop with wild fennel and Mendip snails. The top-notch puddings range from traditional to decidedly unusual (sea buckthorn berry posset).

Imli

167-169 Wardour Street, W1F 8WR (7287 4243, www.imli.co.uk). Tottenham Court Road tube. **Open** noon-11pm Mon-Wed; noon-11.30pm Thur-Sat; noon-10pm Sun. **£**. **Indian tapas**. **Map** p130 B2 ⑯
Indian tapas is the hook here, but Imli is no passing fad. Cut-price relative of Mayfair's classy Tamarind (20 Queen Street, 7629 3561), this restaurant has plenty of culinary zip. Three dishes amount to a filling two-course meal.

Koya

NEW *49 Frith Street, W1D 4SG (7434 4463, www.koya.co.uk). Tottenham Court Road tube.* **Open** noon-3pm, 5.30-10.30pm Mon-Sat. **£**. **Japanese**. **Map** p130 C2 ⑰
This spartan, canteen-like venue specialises in Japanese udon noodles. These thick white wheat noodles are served three ways: in big bowls of hot broth, cold with a dip or (cold) pouring sauce, or cold with a bowl of hot broth for dunking. The menu also offers a small selection of rice-based dishes with miso soup.

Maison Bertaux

28 Greek St, W1D 5DQ (7437 6007). Leicester Square tube. **Open** 8.30am-11pm Mon-Sat; 8.30am-7.30pm Sun. **£**. No credit cards. **Café**. **Map** p130 C2 ⑱

Oozing arty, bohemian charm, this café dates back to 1871 when Soho was London's little piece of the Continent. Battered bentwood tables and chairs add to the feeling of being in a pâtisserie in rural France. The provisions (cream cakes, greasy pastries, pots of tea) really aren't the point.

Milk & Honey

61 Poland Street, W1F 7NU (7292 9949, www.mlkhny.com). Oxford Circus tube. **Open** (for non-members) 6-11pm Mon-Sat. **Cocktail bar**. Map p130 B2 ⑲

You could walk past the inconspicuous door of this semi-mythical, dimly lit speakeasy every day and never know it was here. It's members-only most of the time, but mere mortals can pre-book a table until 11pm. What the place lacks in atmosphere in the early evening, it more than makes up for with outstanding cocktails.

Nordic Bakery

14 Golden Square, W1F 9JG (3230 1077, www.nordicbakery.com). Oxford Circus or Piccadilly Circus tube. **Open** 8am-8pm Mon-Fri; 9am-7pm Sat; 11am-6pm Sun. **£. Café.** Map p130 B3 ⑳

A haven of über-stylish Scandinavian cool warmed up with baskets, tea towels, denim aprons and a nature-inspired wall rug. Their fresh-out-of-the-oven cinnamon buns – thick, fluffy and oozing spicy sweetness – are the real deal.

Polpo

41 Beak Street, W1F 9SB (7734 4479, www.polpo.co.uk). Piccadilly Circus tube. **Open** noon-3pm, 5.30-11pm Mon-Sat; noon-4pm Sun. **££. Italian/wine bar.** Map p130 A2 ㉑

In an 18th-century townhouse that was once home to Canaletto, this is a charming *bacaro* (Venetian-style wine bar). The room has a fashionably distressed look, the wines (served in rustic jugs of 250ml or 500ml) are selected from four good importers, and the food is a procession of small dishes, all of them packed with flavour. Some choices are classic Venetian (such as the cicheti bar snack); others are more adventurous.

Princi

135 Wardour Street, W1F 0UF (7478 8888, www.princi.co.uk). Leicester Square or Tottenham Court Road tube. **Open** 7am-midnight Mon-Sat; 9am-11pm Sun. **£. Bakery-café.** Map p130 B1 ㉒

Alan Yau teamed up with an Italian bakery for this busy venture. At the vast, L-shaped granite counter, choose from a broad range of savoury dishes and numerous cakes, tiramisus and pastries. The big slices of pizza have a springy base, the margherita pungent with fresh thyme; caprese salad comes with creamy balls of buffalo mozzarella and big slices of beef tomato.

St John Hotel

NEW *1 Leicester Street, off Leicester Square, WC2H 7BL (7251 0848, www.stjohnhotellondon.com). Leicester Square or Piccadilly Circus tube.* **Open** 7-10.45am, noon-2.45pm, 7.30pm-1.45am daily. **£££. British.** Map p130 C3 ㉓

St John's menus – at the original in Clerkenwell (p156), the Spitalfields branch and now here, in a spartan hotel (p200) – are masterpieces of brevity, with offal featuring heavily. A starter of 'pig's head, rabbit and radishes' might be followed by 'bacon and snails', both will be packed with earthy flavour. The resolutely British desserts are another St John strength.

Spice Market

NEW *W London, 10 Wardour Street, W1D 6QF (7758 1088, www.spicemarketlondon.com). Leicester Square tube.* **Open** 7-11am, noon-11pm Mon-Wed; 7-11am, noon-11.30pm Thur, Fri; 8-11.30am, noon-11.30pm Sat; 8-11.30am, noon-11pm Sun. **£££. South-east Asian.** Map p130 C3 ㉔

Of Jean-Georges Vongerichten's 29 restaurants across the world, this new outpost in the swanky W (p201) is his

LONDON BY AREA

only operation in London. His tables in New York are considered the hottest in town, and this operation is near-identical to its Meatpacking District cousin. The menu is a selective jaunt across Asia, picking up and playing with dishes along the way. Everything is good but expensive; the service is slick.

Spuntino

NEW *61 Rupert Street, W1D 7PW (www.spuntino.co.uk). Piccadilly Circus tube.* **Open** 11am-midnight Mon-Sat; noon-11pm Sun. **££. North American.** **Map** p130 B3 ㉕

This terrific new place is a homage to fashionably faux-bohemian New York diners. There's a discreet speakeasy-style entrance, with tattooed bar staff mixing drinks and pushing bar snacks or bigger dishes across the steel-topped bar to customers. You can eat 'sliders' (trendy, starter-sized burgers) or loosely Italian options such as the Mac & Cheese. Other creations are far more tongue-in-cheek: for example, an all-American peanut butter and jelly sandwich. Be warned: it's a small place and already very popular.

Yauatcha

15-17 Broadwick Street, W1F 0DL (7494 8888). Piccadilly Circus or Tottenham Court Road tube. **Open** noon-11.45pm Mon-Sat; noon-10.30pm Sun. **£££. Dim sum/tearoom.** **Map** p130 B2 ㉖

This groundbreaking dim sum destination is a sultry lounge-like basement den, with fish tanks and starry ceiling lights, where young professionals, families of Chinese and suited business people enjoy their succession of freshly prepared – and highly impressive – perennial favourites.

Shopping

There's a terrific West End branch of **Anthropologie** (158 Regent Street, W1B 5SW, 7529 9800, www. anthropologie.co.uk; see also p100).

Albam

23 Beak Street, W1F 9RS (3157 7000, www.albamclothing.com). Oxford Circus tube. **Open** noon-7pm Mon-Sat; noon-5pm Sun. **Map** p130 A3 ㉗

With its refined yet rather manly aesthetic, this menswear label dresses well-heeled gents, fashion editors and regular guys who like no-nonsense style. The focus is on high-quality, classic design with a subtle retro edge.

Berwick Street

Piccadilly Circus or Tottenham Court Road tube. **Map** p130 B2 ㉘

The buzzy street market (9am-6pm Mon-Sat), in an area better known for its lurid, neon-lit trades, is one of London's oldest. Dating back to 1778, it's still great for seasonal produce and cheap fabric. The indie record shops that used to be clustered here have taken a pasting over the last few years, but Revival Records (no.30) is full of vinyl beans, and Chris Kerr (no.52), son of legendary 1960s tailor Eddie, is still here crafting brilliant bespoke suits.

Carnaby Street

Oxford Street tube. **Map** p130 A2 ㉙

As famous as the King's Road back when the Sixties Swung, Carnaby Street was until a few years ago more likely to sell you a postcard of the Queen snogging a punk rocker than a fishtail parka. But the noughties have been kind and Carnaby is cool again. Among classy chains (Lush, Muji), Kingly Court (7333 8118, www.carnaby.co.uk) is the real highlight, a three-tiered complex containing a funky mix of chains and independents.

Foyles

113-119 Charing Cross Road, WC2H 0EB (7437 5660, www.foyles.co.uk). Tottenham Court Road tube. **Open** 9.30am-9pm Mon-Sat; noon-6pm Sun. **Map** p130 C2 ㉚

Probably London's single most impressive independent bookshop, Foyles built its reputation on the sheer volume and breadth of its stock (there are 56 specialist subjects in this flagship store). Its five storeys accommodate other shops too: Ray's Jazz, London's least beardy jazz shop, has moved up to the 3rd floor, giving more room to the first-floor café, which hosts great low-key gigs and readings.

Liberty

Regent Street, W1B 5AH (7734 1234, www.liberty.co.uk). Oxford Circus tube. **Open** 10am-9pm Mon-Sat; noon-6pm Sun. **Map** p130 A2 ③

A creaky, 1920s, mock Tudor department store masterpiece, Liberty has upped its game over the last few years – a store-wide 'renaissance' (in their words) that introduced a raft of cool new contemporary labels and a series of inspired events. Shopping here is about more than just spending money; artful window displays, exciting new collections and luxe labels make it an experience to savour. Despite being fashion-forward, Liberty respects its dressmaking heritage with a good haberdashery department.

Machine-A

NEW *60 Berwick Street, W1F 8SU (7998 3385, www.machine-a.com). Oxford Circus tube.* **Open** 11am-7pm Mon-Sat. **Map** p130 B1 ②

The avant-garde boutique that used to be Digitaria was renamed and revamped by owner Stavros Karelis. Shopping here is slightly unnerving, but once you navigate past the often controversial window displays, you'll find some of the most conceptual – and challenging – design in the capital.

Nightlife

Borderline

Orange Yard, off Manette Street, W1D 4JB (0844 847 2465, www. meanfiddler.com). Tottenham Court Road tube. **Map** p130 C2 ③

A cramped, sweaty dive bar-slash-juke joint, the Borderline has long been a favoured stop-off for touring American bands of the country and blues type, but you'll also find a variety of indie acts and singer-songwriters down here.

The Box

NEW *11-12 Walkers Court, Brewer Street, W1F 0ED (7434 4374, http:// theboxsoho.com). Piccadilly Circus tube.* **Map** p130 B2 ③

The 'theatre of varieties' has certainly secured column inches for its sex shows and alternative cabaret. Even Prince Harry has popped in for a look. See box right.

Comedy Store

1A Oxendon Street, SW1Y 4EE (0844 847 1728, www.thecomedystore.co.uk). Leicester Square or Piccadilly Circus tube. **Map** p130 C3 ③

The Comedy Store made its name as the home of 'alternative comedy' in the early 1980s. The venue is purpose-built for serious punters, with a gladiatorial semicircle of seats, and still has some of the circuit's best bills.

Leicester Square Theatre

6 Leicester Place, WC2H 7BX (0844 873 3433, www.leicestersquaretheatre. com). Leicester Square tube. **Map** p130 C3 ③

The main auditorium programmes a good mix of big-name comedy (such as Michael McIntyre and Bill Bailey), cabaret (Miranda Sings, Impropera) and straight plays, but keep an eye on the goings-on in the little basement performance space, with its champagne bar. On Friday and Saturday, Just the Tonic delivers top stand-up.

Madame JoJo's

8-10 Brewer Street, W1F 0SE (7734 3040, www.madamejojos.com). Leicester Square or Piccadilly Circus tube. **Map** p130 B3 ③

This red and slightly shabby basement space is a beacon for those escaping West End post-work chain pubs. Treasured nights include variety (the

The New Naughty

Is Soho rediscovering its love of cabaret?

The Box

Despite local council campaigns to 'clean up Soho', the former centre of London's sex trade and heart of the gay community seems to be taking to new styles of naughtiness in a big way. Over the last year, not one but two new venues have emerged as part of a city-wide resurgence in cabaret, burlesque and all manner of theatrical edginess.

The headlines have all been about the **Box** (left), which now occupies the former site of the Raymond Revuebar, the infamous Soho theatre and strip club that closed in 2004. Its unmarked door gives no indication of what lies within but A-listers from Kate

Moss to Keira Knightley, Prince Harry to Beth Ditto, have been lining up to get in. So what's actually on stage? It could hardly be more different from showgirls in glittery thongs. Acts have included *Time Out* fave Mat Fraser, who alternates his latter-day freak show performance as Seal-O the Seal Boy with intense mash-ups of Rat Pack crooning and simulated incestuous sexual assault, and Chrisalys, a pig-snouted fire-eater who mousetraps his tongue and does things with butt-plugs.

In truth, we're more excited about the opening of new comedy and cabaret spaces at the **Soho Theatre** (p139) for the first season of artistic director Steve Marmion. Marmion is a devotee of cabaret, announcing at the launch that 'the social insight cabaret and comedy provide reaches people in a way that other forms can't'.

There are two new stages, Upstairs and Downstairs. Upstairs focuses on education and new talent, including cabaret training, while Downstairs has a bar and table seating for 150 people. The ambitions for this space have been rather open-ended ('think '20s Berlin meets '50s New York meets 21st-century Soho'), but the programme has included the wonderfully terrifying accordion-led cabaret tunes of the Tiger Lillies (their first London run since 2008), as well as Jonny Woo's long-running Gay Bingo (the first Sunday of every month). The line-ups are good; even better is the theatre-world attention the Soho is bringing to cabaret as a form.

LONDON BY AREA

London Burlesque Social Club, Kitsch Cabaret, Finger in the Pie Cabaret's talent-spotting showcases) and Keb Darge's long-running Deep Funk.

Pizza Express Jazz Club

10 Dean Street, W1D 3RW (0845 602 7017, www.pizzaexpress.com). Tottenham Court Road tube. **Map** p130 C1 ❸

The upstairs restaurant (7437 9595) is a straightforward jazz-free pizza joint, but downstairs the 120-capacity basement venue is one of the best modern mainstream jazz venues in Europe.

Ronnie Scott's

47 Frith Street, W1D 4HT (7439 0747, www.ronniescotts.co.uk). Leicester Square or Tottenham Court Road tube. **Map** p130 C2 ❸

Opened (albeit on a different site) by the British saxophonist Ronnie Scott in 1959, this jazz institution was completely refurbished five years ago. The capacity was expanded to 250, the food got better and the bookings became drearier. Happily, Ronnie's has got back on track, with jazz heavyweights once more dominating in place of the mainstream pop acts who held sway for a while. Lots of fun.

Arts & leisure

Curzon Soho

99 Shaftesbury Avenue, W1D 5DY (0871 703 3988, www.curzoncinemas. com). Leicester Square tube. **Map** p130 C2 ❹

All the cinemas in the Curzon group programme a superb range of shorts, rarities, double bills and mini-festivals, but the Curzon Soho is the best – not least because it has a good ground-floor café and decent basement bar.

London Palladium

NEW *Argyll Street, W1F 7TF (0844 579 1940, www.wizardofozthemusical. com). Oxford Circus tube.* **Map** p130 A2 ❹

The home of Andrew Lloyd Webber's stage remake of MGM's 1939 blockbuster, *The Wizard of Oz*. The staging is spectacular, but that isn't quite enough for fully satisfying theatre. Production subject to change.

Odeon Leicester Square

Leicester Square, WC2H 7LQ (0871 224 4007, www.odeon.co.uk). Leicester Square tube. **Map** p130 C3 ❹

This art deco masterpiece is London's archetypal red-carpet premieres site. Catch one of the occasional silent movie screenings with live organ music if you can; otherwise, it will be a comfy viewing of a pricey current blockbuster.

Prince Charles Cinema

7 Leicester Place, Leicester Square, WC2H 7BY (0870 811 2559, www. princecharlescinema.com). Leicester Square tube. **Map** p130 C3 ❹

The downstairs screen here offers the best value in town (£5.50-£10) for releases that have ended their first run elsewhere. Upstairs, a new screen shows current releases at higher prices – but at under a tenner, still competitive for the West End. The weekend singalong screenings are very popular.

Prince Edward Theatre

28 Old Compton Street, W1D 4HS (0844 482 5151, www.jerseyboys london.com). Leicester Square or Piccadilly Circus tube. **Map** p130 C2 ❹

The Prince Edward shows *Jersey Boys*, the story of Frankie Valli and the Four Seasons. The pace is lively, the sets gritty and the doo-wop standards ('Big Girls Don't Cry', 'Can't Take My Eyes Off You') superbly performed. Production subject to change.

Queen's Theatre

Shaftesbury Avenue, W1D 6BA (7907 7071, www.delfontmackintosh. co.uk). Leicester Square tube. **Map** p130 C3 ❹

The capital's longest running musical, *Les Misérables*, offers quasi-operatic power ballads and some bona fide classics in a gritty tale of revolution and poverty. Production subject to change.

Soho Theatre

21 Dean Street, W1D 3NE (7478 0100, www.sohotheatre.com). Tottenham Court Road tube. **Map** p130 C2 ㊺

Its cool blue neon lights, front-of-house café and occasional late-night shows attract a younger, hipper crowd than most theatres. The Soho brings on aspiring writers through regular workshops, has regular solo comedy shows and has recently got really stuck in to cabaret (see box p137).

tkts

Clocktower Building, Leicester Square, WC2H 7NA (www.officiallondon theatre.co.uk/tkts). Leicester Square tube. **Open** 10am-7pm Mon-Sat; 11am-4pm Sun. **Map** p130 C3 ㊼

Avoid getting ripped off by the touts and buy tickets here for West End blockbusters at much-reduced rates, either on the day or up to a week in advance. It's not uncommon to find the best seats sold at half price.

Covent Garden

Covent Garden is understandably popular with visitors. A traffic-free oasis in the heart of the city, replete with shops, cafés and bars – and the **London Transport Museum** – it centres on a restored 19th-century covered market. On the west side, the portico of **St Paul's Covent Garden** hosts jugglers and escapologists. If you're looking for great performances rather than street performances, the **Royal Opera House** is here too.

Sights & museums

Presiding over the eastern end of Oxford Street, landmark **Centre Point** tower now contains a public restaurant (**Paramount**, p143).

Benjamin Franklin House

36 Craven Street, WC2N 5NF (7925 1405, www.benjaminfranklinhouse. org). Charing Cross tube/rail. **Open** pre-booked tours only. *Box office* 10.30am-5pm Wed, Sun. **Admission** £7; free-£5 reductions. **Map** p131 E5 ㊽

The house where Franklin lived from 1757 to 1775 can be explored on well-run, pre-booked multimedia 'experiences'. Lasting an intense 45mins, they are led by an actress in character as Franklin's landlady. Less elaborate 20min tours (£3.50) are given by house interns on Mondays.

Covent Garden Piazza

Covent Garden tube. **Map** p131 E3 ㊾

Visitors flock to Covent Garden Market for its winning combination of shopping, outdoor restaurant and café seats, performances by street artists and, in the lower courtyard, classical music renditions. Most tourists favour the old covered market (7836 9136, www. coventgardenlondon.uk.com), which combines small and sometimes quirky shops, many of them rather twee, with a range of upmarket gift chain stores. The Apple Market, in the North Hall, has a either arts and crafts (Tue-Sun) or antiques (Mon) stalls set up.

London Transport Museum

Covent Garden Piazza, WC2E 7BB (7379 6344, www.ltmuseum.co.uk). Covent Garden tube. **Open** 10am-6pm Mon-Thur, Sat, Sun; 11am-6pm Fri. **Admission** £10; free-£8 reductions. **Map** p131 F3 ㊿

Tracing the city's transport history from the horse age, this fine museum has emerged from major redevelopment with a much more confident focus on social history and design, illustrated by a superb array of buses, trams and trains. And, appropriately, it's also now much easier to get around. The collections are in broadly chronological order, beginning with the Victorian gallery and a replica of Shillibeer's first horse-drawn bus service from 1829.

Lucy in Disguise

Lily Allen quits pop to open London's finest vintage store.

Having opened its doors at the beginning of London Fashion Week, **Lucy in Disguise** (p146) was the hands-down biggest celebrity store opening of 2011. Popstar Lily Allen and her half-sister Sarah Owen channeled their love of vintage fashion into a 3,000sq ft shop in Covent Garden. The surprising thing about it is that the shop is actually pretty brilliant.

The place feels like a sprawling bachelorette apartment, with rails of pretty party dresses and bell jars housing rare accessories, all lit by retro chandeliers and a pair of pink neon lips. High-quality vintage – from frou-frou 1950s prom dresses to pieces by Chanel, Ossie Clark and Biba – sits alongside Donna Ida denim and Lucy in Disguise-branded candles, T-shirts, screen prints and Samsung laptops. The glittering stock and slick retro interior genuinely delight.

Allen and Owen might not be designers, but they love fashion and the shop allows them to be 'as creative and as involved with clothes as we can be'. They trawled Parisian vintage markets, rootled in little secondhand shops in British seaside towns and travelled to America to source top pieces for the shop, as well as handpicking selections from dealers around the world. 'I had to stop taking Lily out with me on buying appointments,' admits Owen. 'People saw her coming a mile off and, assuming she had loads of money, would try to charge us silly prices.' For this reason, Owen has assumed the role of managing director and Allen is creative director, sourcing items anonymously on the internet.

A retro hair and make-up salon (with cocktail list) set to pop up in the store's huge basement is a clever touch, as is the lending service: more expensive pieces can be hired out for three-day periods, at a tenth of the retail price. No chance for HABs (husbands and boyfriends) to get bored either, as there is a dedicated lounge area complete with a PlayStation Move and vintage men's mags.

Event highlights Depot guided tours (last Fri & Sat of the mth).

St Paul's Covent Garden

Bedford Street, WC2E 9ED (7836 5221, www.actorschurch.org). Covent Garden or Leicester Square tube. **Open** 8.30am-5pm Mon-Fri; 9am-1pm Sun. **Admission** free; donations appreciated. **Map** p131 E3 🖲

Known as the Actors' Church, this magnificently spare building was designed by Inigo Jones for the Earl of Bedford in 1631. Thespians commemorated on its walls range from those lost in obscurity to those destined for immortality. Surely there's no more romantic tribute in London than Vivien Leigh's plaque, simply inscribed with words from Shakespeare's *Antony & Cleopatra*: 'Now boast thee, death, in thy possession lies a lass unparallel'd.'

Eating & drinking

There's a busy **Masala Zone** (48 Floral Street, 7379 0101, www.masalazone.com; see also p169) near the Opera House and market.

Abeno Too

17-18 Great Newport Street, WC2H 7JE (7379 1160, www.abeno.co.uk). Leicester Square tube. **Open** noon-11pm Mon-Sat; noon-10.30pm Sun. **££. Japanese. Map** p131 D3 🖲

Okonomiyaki (hearty pancakes with nuggets of vegetables, seafood, pork and other titbits added to a disc of noodles) are cooked to order on hot-plates set into Abeno's tables and counter.

Clos Maggiore

🆕 *33 King Street, WC2E 8JD (7379 9696, www.closmaggiore.com). Covent Garden or Leicester Square tube.* **Open** noon-2.30pm, 5-11pm Mon-Sat; noon-2.30pm, 5-10pm Sun. **££. French. Map** p131 E3 🖲

Just off Covent Garden's bustling piazza, Clos Maggiore transports you to a picturesque corner of Provence. An elegant boxwood-lined dining room leads to an intimate indoor courtyard filled with fake blossoms and fairy lights. A Provençal-inspired menu highlights the provenance of produce, and those carefully sourced ingredients shine through in all of the dishes. Look out for the exceptionally good value set menu at lunchtime.

Dishoom

🆕 *12 Upper St Martin's Lane, WC2H 9FB (7420 9320, www.dishoom.com). Covent Garden or Leicester Square tube.* **Open** 8am-11pm Mon-Fri; 10am-11pm Sat; 10am-10pm Sun. **££. Pan-Indian. Map** p131 D3 🖲

Dishoom has got the look of a Mumbai 'Irani' café (the cheap, cosmopolitan eateries set up by Persian immigrants in the early 1900s) spot on. Solid oak panels, antique mirrors and ceiling fans say 'retro grandeur', and there's a fascinating display of old magazine covers, adverts and fading photos of Indian families. Parts of the menu are familiar street snacks (a terrific pau bhaji), but chocolate fondant, classy cocktails and intriguing lassi flavours move things upmarket.

Food for Thought

31 Neal Street, WC2H 9PR (7836 9072). Covent Garden tube. **Open** noon-8.30pm Mon-Sat; noon-5pm Sun. **£.** No credit cards. **Vegetarian café. Map** p131 E2 🖲

The menu of this much-loved veggie café changes daily, though you can expect three or four main courses, and a selection of salads and desserts. The laid-back premises are down a steep stairway that, during lunch, usually fills with a patient queue. The ground floor offers the same food to take away.

Gelupo

🆕 *7 Archer Street, W1D 7AU (7287 5555, www.gelupo.com). Piccadilly Circus tube.* **Open** 11am-11pm Mon-Wed, Sun; 11am-1am Thur-Sat. **£. Ice-cream. Map** p130 B3 🖲

London's already got great ice-cream places, but this is a real contender. Not actually Italian-run, it's run by people who do Italian food better than many Italians: Jacob Kenedy is a young British chef who cut his teeth at Moro, then opened his own place, Bocca di Lupo (p132). Flavours change daily, but might include chestnut, watermelon, sour cherry or espresso.

Giaconda Dining Room

9 Denmark Street, WC2H 8LS (7240 3334, www.giacondadining.com). Tottenham Court Road tube. **Open** noon-2.15pm, 6-9.15pm Mon-Fri. **££.** **Modern European.** Map p131 D1 ⑤⑦
A thoroughly likeable restaurant, despite being a little cramped. The food is what most people want to eat most of the time: the owners describe it as French-ish with a bit of Spain and Italy, meaning big-flavoured grills, fish and intriguing assemblages (chicken liver, chorizo, trotters and tripe, for instance).

Gordon's

47 Villiers Street, WC2N 6NE (7930 1408, www.gordonswinebar.com). Embankment tube or Charing Cross tube/rail. **Open** 11am-11pm Mon-Sat; noon-10pm Sun. **Wine bar.** Map p131 E4 ⑤⑧
Gordon's has been serving drinks since 1890, and it looks like it – the place is a specialist in yellowing, candle-lit alcoves. The wine list doesn't bear expert scrutiny and the food is buffet-style, but atmosphere is everything, and this is a great, bustling place.

Great Queen Street

32 Great Queen Street, WC2B 5AA (7242 0622). Covent Garden or Holborn tube. **Open** noon-2.30pm, 6-10.30pm Mon-Sat; noon-3pm Sun. **££.** **British.** Map p131 F1 ⑤⑨
The pub-style room here thrums with bonhomie. Ranging from snacks to shared mains, the menu is designed to tempt and satisfy rather than educate or impress. Booking is essential, and

the robust food is worth it. At the Sunday lunch session, diners sit and are served together. The Dive bar downstairs serves snacks and drinks.

Hawksmoor Seven Dials

NEW *11 Langley Street, WC2H 9JJ (7856 2154, www.thehawksmoor.co.uk). Covent Garden tube.* **Open** noon-3pm, 5-10.30pm Mon-Thur; noon-3pm, 5-11pm Fri, Sat; noon-4.30pm Sun. **£££.** **Grill.** Map p131 E2 ⑥⓪
Hawksmoor stands out as the benchmark to beat for best all-round bar and grill experience. The first Hawksmoor, which earned a reputation for great cocktails and great steaks, opened in 2006. This second branch is more of the same – only better. The site's a real beauty, evocative of old New York with its speakeasy feel and old brickwork. The cocktails are masterfully concocted and the steaks are sublime.

Kopapa

NEW *32-34 Monmouth Street, WC2H 9HA (7240 6076, www.kopapa.co.uk). Leicester Square tube.* **Open** 8am-10.45pm Mon-Thur; 8am-11.15pm Fri; 10am-11.15pm Sat; 10am-9.45pm Sun. **££.** **Global.** Map p131 D2 ⑥①
Kopapa serves breakfast, small dishes, great wines and great coffee, in a come-as-you-are café setting. Many of its bare tables are shared; around half are bookable, the rest are not. The lights are low, the seats close together. The coffees, smoothies and wines by the glass are all first rate, but it's fabulous tapas-style fusion food that really makes Kopapa stand out.

Lamb & Flag

33 Rose Street, WC2E 9EB (7497 9504). Covent Garden tube. **Open** 11am-11pm Mon-Thur; 11am-11.30pm Fri, Sat; noon-10.30pm Sun. **Pub.** Map p131 E3 ⑥②
A pub for over 300 years and a fixture on Rose Street for longer, the unabashedly traditional Lamb & Flag is always a squeeze, but no one minds.

The afternoon-only bar upstairs is 'ye olde' to a fault, and sweetly localised by pictures of passed-on regulars.

Opera Tavern

NEW *23 Catherine Street, WC2B 5JS (7836 3680, www.operatavern.co.uk). Covent Garden tube.* **Open** noon-3pm, 5-12.30am Mon-Fri; noon-12.30am Sat; noon-5pm Sun. **££. Spanish-Italian tapas.** Map p131 F2 **63**

Low-lit, bang on-trend and immediately appealing, this is a restaurant of real character, once a rarity in this part of town. The grand old pub premises date from 1879, but received a major refit. It's equally accomplished as a bar and restaurant, with a menu that craftily meshes Italianate small plates and Spanish tapas.

Paramount

NEW *32nd floor, Centre Point, 101-103 New Oxford Street, WC1A 1DD (7420 2900, www.paramount.uk.net). Tottenham Court Road tube.* **Open** 8-10am, noon-3pm, 6-11pm Mon-Fri; 10am-3pm, 6-11pm Sat. **£££. Modern European.** Map p130 C1 **64**

With its lofty location at the top of the landmark Centre Point building, it's not surprising that the handsome Tom Dixon-designed interior of this smart restaurant is upstaged by the superb view. Still, Colin Layfield's menu holds its own, with carefully constructed dishes that appeal to the eye and tongue. The attached bar is open only to members or diners.

Rock & Sole Plaice

47 Endell Street, WC2H 9AJ (7836 3785, www.rockandsoleplaice.com). Covent Garden tube. **Open** 11.30am-10.30pm Mon-Sat; noon-9.30pm Sun. **££. Fish & chips.** Map p131 D1 **65**

A chippie since 1874, this busy establishment has walls covered in theatre posters. The ground-floor tables are often all taken (check whether there's space in the basement), and the outside seats are never empty in summer.

Savoy Grill

NEW *100 Strand, WC2R 0EW (7592 1600, www.gordonramsay.com/the savoygrill). Charing Cross tube/rail or Embankment tube.* **Open** noon-2.30pm, 5.30-10.30pm daily. **£££. British.** Map p131 F3 **66**

The glamour of the refurbished Savoy hotel (p201) demanded much of Gordon Ramsay's Savoy Grill, and he's largely delivered. The room is suitably low-lit, with the right balance of intimacy and openness. The menu is full of grills and seafood, but with more imaginative British dishes that show the kitchen's talent: a starter of potted salt beef was slow-cooked and tender, while mutton pie was a deliciously clever play on shepherd's pie. It's expensive but not overpriced. Book well ahead.

Scoop

40 Shorts Gardens, WC2H 9AB (7240 7086, www.scoopgelato.com). Covent Garden tube. **Open** 11am-9pm daily. **£. Ice-cream.** Map p131 D2 **67**

Frequent queues are a testament to the quality of the ice-cream, even dairy-free health versions, at this Italian artisan's shop. Flavours include a very superior Piedmont hazelnut type, which can be eaten in at a few tables or taken away.

J Sheekey

28-34 St Martin's Court, WC2N 4AL (7240 2565, www.j-sheekey.co.uk). Leicester Square tube. **Open** noon-3pm, 5.30pm-midnight Mon-Sat; noon-3.30pm, 6-11pm Sun. **£££. Fish & seafood.** Map p131 D3 **68**

Sheekey's Oyster Bar opened in 2009, yet another enticement to visit this fine restaurant. Unlike many of London's period pieces (which this certainly is: it was chartered in the mid 19th century), Sheekey's buzzes with fashionable folk. Even if you opt for the main restaurant, your party of four may be crammed on to a table for two, but the accomplished menu will take your mind off it, stretching from modern European to comforting faves (fish pie, salmon fish cakes).

Terroirs

5 William IV Street, WC2N 4DW (7036 0660, www.terroirswinebar. com). Charing Cross tube/rail. **Open** 11am-10pm Mon-Fri; 11am-4pm Sat. **£££. Wine bar. Map** p131 E4 ⑥⑨

Now extending over two floors, Terroirs is a superb and very popular wine bar that specialises in the new generation of organic and biodynamic, sulphur-, sugar- or acid-free wines. The list is only slightly shorter than the Bible and the food is terrific: a selection of French bar snacks, charcuterie and seafood. A new Columbia Road Market (p175) branch, Brawn, is as popular.

Wahaca

66 Chandos Place, WC2N 4HG (7240 1883, www.wahaca.co.uk). Covent Garden or Leicester Square tube. **Open** noon-11pm Mon-Sat; noon-10.30pm Sun. **£. Mexican. Map** p131 E3 ⑦⓪

Wahaca has a look as cheery as its staff, created from lamps made out of tomatillo cans dotted with bottle tops, wooden crates packed with fruit, and tubs of chilli plants. The menu is really designed for sharing, tapas style, but you can choose one of the large plato fuertes (enchiladas, burritos or grilled dishes) if you want your own plate.

Shopping

Apple Store

NEW *1-7 The Piazza, WC2E 8HA (7447 1400, www.apple.com). Covent Garden tube.* **Open** 9am-9pm Mon-Sat, noon-6pm Sun. **Map** p131 E3 ⑦①

A cathedral to geekery, this is the world's biggest Apple Store, with separate rooms – set out over three storeys – devoted to each product line. The exposed brickwork, big old oak tables and stone floors make it an inviting place, and it's also the world's first Apple Store with a Start Up Room where staff will help set up your new iPad, iPhone, iPod or Mac, or transfer files from your old computer to your new one – all for free.

Cecil Court

www.cecilcourt.co.uk. Leicester Square tube. **Map** p131 D3 ⑦②

Bookended by Charing Cross Road and St Martin's Lane, picturesque Cecil Court is known for its antiquarian book, map and print dealers. Notable residents include children's specialist Marchpane (no.16), the Italian Bookshop (no.5), Watkins (nos.19 & 21), for occult and New Age titles, and 40-year veteran David Drummond at Pleasures of Past Times (no.11), who specialises in theatre and magic.

Coco de Mer

23 Monmouth Street, WC2H 9DD (7836 8882, www.coco-de-mer.co.uk). Covent Garden tube. **Open** 11am-7pm Mon-Wed, Fri, Sat; 11am-8pm Thur; noon-6pm Sun. **Map** p131 D2 ⑦③

London's most glamorous erotic emporium sells a variety of tasteful books, toys and lingerie, from glass dildos that double as objets d'art to crotchless culottes and corsets.

Hope & Greenwood

1 Russell Street, WC2B 5JD (7240 3314, www.hopeandgreenwood.co.uk). Covent Garden tube. **Open** 11am-7.30pm Mon-Wed; 11am-8pm Thur, Fri; 10.30am-7.30pm Sat; 11.30am-5.30pm Sun. **Map** p131 F2 ⑦④

This adorable 1950s-style, letterbox-red cornershop is the perfect place to find the sherbets, chews and chocolates that were once the focus of a proper British childhood. Even the staff look the part: beautifully turned out in a pinny, ready to pop your sweets in a striped paper bag with a smile.

James Smith & Sons

53 New Oxford Street, WC1A 1BL (7836 4731, www.james-smith.co.uk). Holborn or Tottenham Court Road tube. **Open** 9.30am-5.15pm Mon-Fri; 10am-5.15pm Sat. **Map** p131 D1 ⑦⑤

For more than 175 years, this charming shop, Victorian fittings still intact, has held its own in the niche market of

Lady's Day

Josie Rourke takes over at the Donmar Warehouse theatre.

Over nearly a decade, artistic director Michael Grandage has made Covent Garden's **Donmar Theatre** (p147) the most talked-about stage in London, putting on hugely successful West End seasons and attracting a string of hot Hollywood stars to the tiny stage. So who is it that's taking over from him on 1 January 2012?

Josie Rourke – warm, intelligent, business-like and refreshingly Northern (she was born in Lancashire) – is artistic director of west London's shoestring powerhouse Bush Theatre (www.bushtheatre.co.uk). There she has staged some of the capital's best and most political new writing, defeated proposed 40% cuts to the theatre's Arts Council subsidy, and – just before leaving – will oversee the theatre's relocation into the former Shepherd's Bush Library, 'a fantastic arts and crafts building', she says. In a city where almost every theatre is controlled by a middle-aged man, she's a sight for sore eyes.

When we talked to her, before the appointment, she was certainly up for a challenge. 'To want to have a career in theatre is such a radical act of imagination if that's not what your parents do: it's only led by a combination of education, the right kind of public funding and example.' She also mentioned how, when first at the Donmar, it 'was wonderful to hear those people talk about what it is to have a theatre – not just the building, but the ideal you're in pursuit of.'

Rourke started in London as an assistant director at the Donmar, where she assisted Grandage, Nick Hytner (now in charge at the National Theatre, p76) and Oscar-winner Sam Mendes. During five years as a freelance, she directed plays at the Young Vic (p77), Old Vic (p77) and for the Royal Shakespeare Company, and was well reviewed more recently for her revival of Scottish tenement classic *Men Should Weep*, her debut at the National.

Given that Rourke's latest enterprise – the hottest ticket of spring 2011, a version of *Much Ado About Nothing* starring David Tennant and Catherine Tate – is only due to close at Wyndham's in September 2011, she leaves herself little time to prepare for filling her predecessor's boat-sized shoes. But then, as Grandage is happy to point out, Rourke is an 'inspired appointment'.

LONDON BY AREA

umbrellas and walking sticks. Forget throwaway brollies that break at the first sign of bad weather and invest in a hickory-crooked City umbrella.

Lucy in Disguise

NEW *10 King Street, WC2E 8HN (7240 6590, www.lucyindisguise london.com). Covent Garden or Leicester Square tube.* **Open** 11am-7pm Mon-Wed; noon-6pm Thur-Sat; 11am-8pm Sun. **Map** p131 E3 76

Former pop star Lily Allen's fine new vintage store. See box p140.

Neal's Yard Dairy

17 Shorts Gardens, WC2H 9UP (7240 5700, www.nealsyarddairy.co.uk). Covent Garden tube. **Open** 11am-7pm Mon-Thur; 10am-7pm Fri, Sat. **Map** p131 D2 77

Neal's Yard buys from small farms and creameries and matures the cheeses in its own cellars until they're ready to sell. Names such as Stinking Bishop and Lincolnshire Poacher are as evocative as the aromas in the shop.

St Martin's Courtyard

NEW *Between St Martin's Lane & Long Acre (www.stmartinscourtyard.co.uk). Covent Garden tube.* **Map** p131 D3 78

The two dozen shops in this courtyard development include Corgis, Banana Republic, and Sienna and Savannah Miller's boutique Twenty8Twelve. There are also good-quality Italian, British and Mexican restaurants.

Stanfords

12-14 Long Acre, WC2E 9LP (7836 1321, www.stanfords.co.uk). Covent Garden or Leicester Square tube. **Open** 9am-7.30pm Mon, Wed, Fri; 9.30am-7.30pm Tue; 9am-8pm Thur; 10am-8pm Sat; noon-6pm Sun. **Map** p131 D3 79

Three floors of travel guides, literature, maps, language guides, atlases and magazines. The basement houses the full range of British Ordnance Survey maps, and you can plan your next move over Fairtrade coffee in the café.

Nightlife

Heaven

Underneath the Arches, Villiers Street, WC2N 6NG (7930 2020, www.heaven-london.com). Embankment tube or Charing Cross tube/rail. **Map** p131 E4 80

London's most famous gay club is a bit like *Les Misérables* – it's camp, full of history and tourists love it. Popcorn on Mondays has long been a good bet, but it's really all about G-A-Y on Thursdays, Fridays and Saturdays. For as long as anyone can remember, divas with an album to flog (Madonna, Kylie, Girls Aloud) have turned up to play here at the weekend.

12 Bar Club

Denmark Street, WC2H 8NL (7240 2622, www.12barclub.com). Tottenham Court Road tube. **Open** 7pm-3am Mon-Sat; 6pm-12.30am Sun. No credit cards. **Map** p131 D1 81

This cherished hole-in-the-wall – if smoking were still allowed, this is the kind of place that would be full of it – books a grab-bag of stuff. The size (capacity 100, a stage that barely accommodates a trio) dictates a predominance of singer-songwriters.

Arts & leisure

Coliseum

St Martin's Lane, WC2N 4ES (0871 911 0200, www.eno.org). Leicester Square tube or Charing Cross tube/rail. **Map** p131 D4 82

Built as a music hall in 1904, the home of the English National Opera (ENO) is in sparkling condition following a renovation in 2004. The ENO itself is in solid shape under the youthful stewardship of music director Edward Gardner, with occasional duds offset by surprising sell-outs (among them a hugely flamboyant version of Ligeti's *Grand Macabre*). All works are in English, and prices are generally cheaper than at the Royal Opera House.

Donmar Warehouse

41 Earlham Street, WC2H 9LX (0844 871 1624, www.donmarwarehouse. com). Covent Garden or Leicester Square tube. **Map** p131 E2 🟣

Having kept the Donmar on a fresh, intelligent path for a decade, artistic director Michael Grandage will hand over to Josie Rourke (see box p145). The theatre's combination of intimacy (the space seats only 250 people) and artistic integrity has given it an enviable track record of attracting A-list film stars to perform: Nicole Kidman, Gwyneth Paltrow and Jude Law are only some of the theatre's alumni.

Duke of York's Theatre

St Martin's Lane, WC2N 4BG (0871 297 5454, www.dukeofyorkstheatre. co.uk). Leicester Square tube. **Map** p131 D3 🟣

Ghost Stories is London's scariest show. You're in a lecture theatre, with the jovially obnoxious Professor of the Paranormal debunking ghost stories. You know you're being lulled into a false sense of security: the subsequent jump-out-of-your-seat shocks are effective, but the real darkness is saved for the end. Production subject to change.

Novello Theatre

🆕 *Aldwych, WC2B 4LD (7907 7071, www.delfontmackintosh.co.uk). Covent Garden or Holborn tube.* **Map** p131 F3 🟣

Cameron Mackintosh's latest wheeze, *Betty Blue Eyes* starts out reasonably faithful to the sly, wry Yorkshire-isms of the Alan Bennett screenplay from which it is adapted but ends up somewhere altogether more fabulous. The musical numbers and choreography are hilariously kitsch, but an animatronic pig voiced by Kylie steals the show. Production subject to change.

Royal Opera House

Bow Street, WC2E 9DD (7304 4000, www.roh.org). Covent Garden tube. **Map** p131 E2 🟣

The Royal Opera House was founded in 1732 on the profits of his production of John Gay's *Beggar's Opera*; the current building, built roughly 150 years ago but extensively remodelled, is the third on the site. Organised tours explore the massive eight-floor building, taking in the main auditorium, the costume workshops and sometimes a ballet rehearsal. The glass-roofed Floral Hall, the Crush Bar and the Amphitheatre Café Bar (with its terrace over the market) are open to the general public. Critics argue the programming can be a little spotty, especially given the famously elevated ticket prices at the top end. Never mind: there are still fine productions, many of them under the baton of Antonio Pappano. This is also home to the Royal Ballet.

Event highlights *Rigoletto* (30 Mar-21 Apr 2012); *Otello* (12-24 July 2012).

Savoy Theatre

The Strand, WC2R 0ET (0844 847 2345, www.ambassadortickets.com). Charing Cross tube/rail. **Map** p131 F4 🟣

A pepped-up, candy-coloured hymn to sisterhood – in which Malibu Barbie Elle Woods takes on the overprivileged preppies at Harvard and wins. Laurence O'Keefe and Nell Benjamin's music and lyrics give the movie an irresistible makeover: highlights are supersmart rhyming dialogues that actually propel the plot, rhythmic, catchy tunelets, and a flawless British cast. Production subject to change.

Theatre Royal Drury Lane

🆕 *Catherine Street, WC2B 5JF (7907 7071, www.shrekthemusical. co.uk). Covent Garden tube.* **Map** p131 F2 🟣

DreamWorks' *Shrek*, a scatologically jolly green giant of a stage show and Broadway hit, has now taken off in the West End. *Shrek*'s farts-and-all humour and carnivalesque spirit have survive in David Lindsay-Abaire's book. Production subject to change.

LONDON BY AREA

St Paul's (p159) from One New Change (p164)

The City

Holborn to Clerkenwell

The City of London collides with the West End in Holborn and Clerkenwell. Bewigged barristers inhabit the picturesque **Inns of Court**, while City boys pull on trainers to head from their loft apartments to the latest restaurant in one of London's foodiest areas – or to superclub **Fabric**.

Sights & museums

Courtauld Gallery

Strand, WC2R 1LA (7848 2526, www. courtauld.ac.uk/gallery). Temple tube. **Open** 10am-6pm daily. **Admission** £5; free-£4 reductions. Free 10am-2pm Mon. **Map** p150 A4 ❶

In the north wing of Somerset House (p152), the Courtauld's select collection of paintings has several works of world importance. There are outstanding works from earlier periods (don't miss Lucas Cranach's fine *Adam & Eve*), but the strongest suit is Impressionist and post-Impressionist paintings, such as Manet's astonishing *A Bar at the Folies-Bergère* and numerous works by Cézanne. Hidden downstairs, the sweet little gallery café is often overlooked.

Dr Johnson's House

17 Gough Square, EC4A 3DE (7353 3745, www.drjohnsonshouse.org). Chancery Lane tube or Blackfriars tube/rail. **Open** *May-Sept* 11am-5.30pm Mon-Sat. *Oct-Apr* 11am-5pm Mon-Sat. **Admission** £4.50; free-£3.50 reductions; £10 family. No credit cards. **Map** p150 B4 ❷

Famed as the author of one of the first – surely the most significant and beyond doubt the wittiest – dictionary of the English language, Dr Samuel Johnson (1709-84) also wrote poems, a novel and one of the earliest travelogues. You can tour the stately Georgian townhouse where Johnson came up with his inspired definitions – 'to make dictionaries is dull work,' was his definition of the word 'dull'.

Fleet Street

Chancery Lane or Temple tube.
Map p150 B4 ❸
The first printing press on this legendary street of newspapers was installed behind St Bride's Church (below) in 1500 by William Caxton's assistant, Wynkyn de Worde, but it wasn't until 1702 that London's first daily newspaper, the *Daily Courant*, rolled off the presses. By the end of World War II, half a dozen newspaper offices were churning out scoops between the Strand and Farringdon Road, but they gradually all moved away once Rupert Murdoch had won his bitter war with the print unions in the 1980s; the last of the news agencies, Reuters, followed in 2005. Fine buildings that remain from the roaring days of the industry include Reuters (no.85), the Daily Telegraph (no.135) and the jet-black Daily Express (nos.121-128).

Hunterian Museum

Royal College of Surgeons, 35-43 Lincoln's Inn Fields, WC2A 3PE (7869 6560, www.rcseng.ac.uk/museums). Holborn tube. **Open** 10am-5pm Tue-Sat. **Admission** free. No credit cards. **Map** p150 A4 ❹
John Hunter (1728-93) was a pioneering surgeon and anatomist, and physician to King George III. His huge collection of medical specimens can be viewed in this two-floor museum. The grisly exhibits include various bodily mutations, Winston Churchill's dentures and the brain of 19th-century mathematician Charles Babbage.

Museum & Library of the Order of St John

St John's Gate, St John's Lane, EC1M 4DA (7324 4005, www.museumstjohn. org.uk). Farringdon tube/rail. **Open** 10am-5pm Mon-Sat. *Tours* 11am, 2.30pm Tue, Fri, Sat. **Admission** free;

suggested donation £5, £4 reductions.
Map p150 C2 ❺
This museum celebrates the Order of St John. Now known for its ambulance service, the order's roots lie in the Christian medical practices developed during the Crusades of the 11th to 13th centuries. Artefacts related to the Order of Hospitaller Knights, from Jerusalem, Malta and the Ottoman Empire, are displayed: there's a separate collection relating to the evolution of the modern ambulance service. The museum reopened in 2010 after major refurbishment reorganised the galleries in the Tudor gatehouse and, across St John's Square, opened the Priory Church, its gorgeous garden and its 12th-century crypt to the public.

St Bartholomew-the-Great

West Smithfield, EC1A 9DS (7606 5171, www.greatstbarts.com). Barbican tube or Farringdon tube/rail. **Open** 8.30am-5pm Mon-Fri (until 4pm Nov-Feb); 10.30am-4pm Sat; 8.30am-8pm Sun. **Admission** £4; £3.50 reductions; £10 family. **Map** p150 C3 ❻
This atmospheric medieval church was chopped about during Henry VIII's reign: the interior is now firmly Elizabethan, although it also contains donated works of contemporary art and an ancient font. You may recognise the main hall from such movies as *Shakespeare in Love* and *Four Weddings & a Funeral*.

St Bride's Church

Fleet Street, EC4Y 8AU (7427 0133, www.stbrides.com). Temple tube or Blackfriars tube/rail. **Open** 8am-6pm Mon-Fri; 11am-3pm Sat; 10am-6.30pm Sun. Times vary Mon-Sat, so phone ahead. **Admission** free. No credit cards. **Map** p150 B4 ❼
St Bride's, 'the journalists' church', contains a shrine to hacks killed in action. The interior was rebuilt after Blitz bombing. Down in the crypt, a quietly excellent museum displays fragments of the churches that have existed on

The City

- **1** Sights & museums
- **1** Eating & drinking
- **1** Shopping
- **1** Nightlife
- **1** Arts & leisure

THE
WEST END
pp101-147

CLERKENWELL

Charles
Dickens
Museum

Mount
Pleasant
Sorting
Office

Museum of the
Order of St John

St Barts
Medical
College

Charterhouse

Gray's
Inn
Gardens

Smithfield
Market

St Bartholomew
the Great

HIGH HOLBORN

HOLBORN

Sir John
Soane's
Museum

Lincoln's
Inn

WEST SMITHFIELD

St Bartholomew's
Hospital

Postman's
Park

Lincoln's Inn Fields

Hunterian
Museum

Old
Bailey

Royal Courts
of Justice

Dr Johnson's
House

St Dunstan

Stationers'
Hall

Cutlers'
Hall

St Paul's
Cathedral

Prince
Henry's
Room

FLEET STREET

St Bride's

LUDGATE HILL

ST PAUL'S CHYD

St Clement
Danes

Temple
Church

City
Thames
link station

Apothecaries'
Hall

St Andrews
by the Wardrobe

City
Information
Centre

College
of Arn

King's College
Institute

Courtauld
Institute

Somerset
House

Middle
Temple

Inner
Temple

Blackfriars
(reopens Late
2011)

QUEEN

VICTORIA EMBANKMENT

Blackfriars
Millennium
Pier

UPPER
WHITE LION HILL

THAME

Cleopatra's
Needle

River Thames

0   300 m

0   300 yds

© Copyright Time Out Group 2011

Oxo Tower
Wharf

THE SOUTH BANK
pp62-77

Savoy
Pier

eopatra's
Needle

National
Film
Theatre

Gabriel's
Wharf

London
Studios

Bankside
Gallery

Tate
Modern

Shakespeare's
Globe

Queen Elizabeth
Hall & Purcell
Room

National
Theatre

SOUTHWARK ST

Festival
Pier

Hayward
Gallery

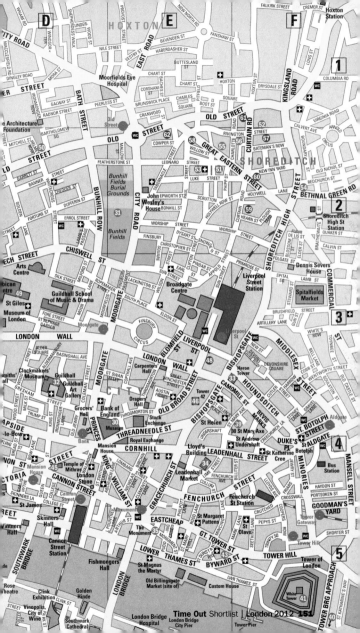

this site since the sixth century and tells the story of the newspapers on Fleet Street. According to local legend, the spire was the inspiration for the classic tiered wedding cake.

Sir John Soane's Museum

13 Lincoln's Inn Fields, WC2A 3BP (7405 2107, www.soane.org). Holborn tube. **Open** 10am-5pm Tue-Sat; 10am-5pm, 6-9pm 1st Tue of mth. *Tours* 11am Sat. **Admission** free; donations appreciated. *Tours* free-£5. **Map** p150 A3 **8**

Architect Sir John Soane (1753-1837) was an obsessive collector of art, furniture and architectural ornamentation, partly for enjoyment and partly for research. He turned his house into an amazing museum to which 'amateurs and students' should have access. Much of the museum's appeal derives from the domestic setting, but the real wow is the Monument Court. At its lowest level is a 3,000-year-old sarcophagus of alabaster so fine that it's almost translucent, as well as the cell of Soane's fictional monk Don Giovanni. The first phase of a long-term programme of renovation and expansion is due for completion in May 2012 (see box right).

Event highlights Monthly candlelit tours – always book in advance.

Somerset House & the Embankment Galleries

Strand, WC2R 1LA (7845 4600, www.somersethouse.org.uk). Temple tube or Charing Cross tube/rail. **Open** 10am-6pm daily. **Admission** free. *Embankment Galleries* prices vary; see website for details. **Map** p150 A5 **9**

Architect Sir William Chambers spent the last 20 years of his life from 1775 working on this neo-classical edifice overlooking the Thames. Effectively the first purpose-built office block in the world, it was built to accommodate learned societies such as the Royal Academy, and also the Inland Revenue. The Inland Revenue is still here, but the rest of the building is open to the public. It houses the wonderful Courtauld (p148) and has a beautiful courtyard with choreographed fountains, a terraced café and restaurant. It also hosts temporary exhibitions.

Temple Church & Inner Temple

Fleet Street, EC4Y 7BB (7353 8559, www.templechurch.com). Temple tube. **Open** 2-4pm Tue-Fri; phone or check website for details. **Admission** free. No credit cards. **Map** p150 B4 **10**

The quadrangles of Middle Temple (7427 4800, www.middletemple.org.uk) and Inner Temple (7797 8250, www.innertemple.org.uk) have been lodgings for training lawyers since medieval times, with Temple Church – the private chapel of the mystical Knights Templar, its structure inspired by Jerusalem's Church of the Holy Sepulchre – serving both. Its rounded apse contains the worn gravestones of several Crusader knights. Tours of Inner Temple can be arranged (minimum five people, £10 each; 7797 8241).

Event highlights Organ recitals in Temple Church (Wed lunchtimes).

Eating & drinking

Bistrot Bruno Loubet

Zetter, St John's Square, 86-88 Clerkenwell Road, EC1M 5RJ (7324 4455, www.thezetter.com). Farringdon tube/rail. **Open** 7.30-10.30am, noon-2.30pm, 6-10.30pm Mon-Fri, 7.30am-3pm, 6-10.30pm Sat; 7.30am-3pm, 6-10pm Sun. **£££**. **Modern European**. **Map** p150 C2 **11**

The menu at this bistro is thoughtfully constructed to satisfy novelty seekers, but won't scare off the conservative palate – you might find slow-cooked hare on the menu, but also the likes of confit lamb shoulder with white beans pepped up with North African preserved lemon and harissa. Playful French desserts are another strength. The staff are smiley and very efficient, and there's a buzz of happy diners.

Moving in Next Door

A major expansion for the Soane's 200th anniversary.

A favourite of many locals, the little **Sir John Soane's Museum** (left) has changed status over the years from a treasured secret to something approaching a must-visit. These days you can expect queues at the front door of this eccentric house of curiosities (more than 93,000 people visit each year) and the monthly candlelit tours are always booked up in a trice.

In May 2012, the 200th anniversary of the building of the house will be marked by the completion of the first phase of an ambitious £7m restoration. A staff lavatory will once again be the Tivoli Recess – the city's first gallery of contemporary sculpture, with a stained-glass window and skylights with plaster sunbursts. Further stained glass will illuminate the Shakespeare Recess, with William's likeness from his Stratford-upon-Avon tomb set there. Less exciting, but arguably at least as important, is the use to which the next-door building (no.12) is now being put. The old entrance to the house – a narrow corridor where all those visitors had to sign in, buy their guides and postcards, and leave coats, bags and umbrellas with the volunteers – was far too cramped for the purpose. After the restoration is complete, you will leave your clutter at no.12, before strolling into the main house untrammelled and ready to be enthralled.

Once you've toured the house's treasures, seen the ingenious fold-out walls of paintings and admired the clever lighting effects and archaeological oddments, you exit through no.12, past a new shop and an Exhibition Room that gives details on Soane and the objects you've just seen. (Soane wasn't much given to labelling, and the museum is obliged – by the 1833 Act of Parliament that set up the museum – to follow his lead.)

Over the years up to 2014, the entire second floor of Soane's house will open to the public – for the first time since his death in 1837. Working from watercolour paintings done in around 1825, the museum will recreate his bedroom (pictured), Model Room (containing 80 fine architectural models), the Oratory (a memorial to his dead wife, using what was already antiquarian stained glass) and the mirrored bookshelves of the Book Passage. Most typical of all will be one small feature of the the Ante Room: once restored, this space full of sculptures and plastercasts will also have a hole in the floor, through which Soane's modern-day guests will be able to peer into a Catacomb full of funerary urns from ancient Rome.

Clerkenwell Kitchen

27-31 Clerkenwell Close, EC1R 0AT
(7101 9959, www.theclerkenwellkitchen.
co.uk). Angel tube or Farringdon
tube/rail. Open 8am-5pm Mon-Wed,
Fri; 8am-5pm, 6.30-11pm Thur. **££**.
Eco-restaurant. Map p150 B2 ⑫
Tucked into an office development for
creatives, Clerkenwell Kitchen has a
ready supply of enthusiasts who pop
in for coffees, sandwiches, lunch meet-
ings and quiet moments with the
Wi-Fi. High-quality, fair-priced meals
made with seasonal produce are served
from noon – restaurant-calibre food
served in a stylishly informal café setting, to be enjoyed with a glass of wine
or Meantime beer.

Le Comptoir Gascon

61-63 Charterhouse Street, EC1M 6HJ
(7608 0851, www.comptoirgascon.com).
Farringdon tube/rail. Open noon-2pm,
7-10pm Tue, Wed; noon-2pm, 7-10.30pm
Thur, Fri; 10.30am-2.30pm, 7-10pm Sat.
££. **French**. Map p150 C3 ⑬
Comptoir is the modern rustic cousin
(dainty velour chairs, exposed pipes,
open brickwork, pottery dishes) of
the more serious-minded Club Gascon
(57 West Smithfield, 7796 0600, www.
clubgascon.com), but exudes as much
class and confidence as its forebear in
the presentation of delectable regional
specialities of Gascony. The posh café
vibe is enhanced by capable and amiable French staff.

Eagle

159 Farringdon Road, EC1R 3AL
(7837 1353). Farringdon tube/rail.
Open noon-11pm Mon-Sat; noon-5pm
Sun. **££**. **Gastropub**. Map p150 B2 ⑭
Widely credited with being the first
gastropub (it opened in 1991), this is
still recognisably a pub that serves
quality food: noisy, often crowded,
with no-frills service and dominated by
an open range where T-shirted cooks
toss earthy grills in theatrical bursts of
flame. The Med-influenced menu stays
true to 'big flavours'.

Jerusalem Tavern

55 Britton Street, EC1M 5UQ (7490
4281, www.stpetersbrewery.co.uk).
Farringdon tube/rail. Open 11am-11pm
Mon-Fri. **Pub**. Map p150 C3 ⑮
Tilting, creaking and uneven, the tatty
Jerusalem serves sought-after ales
from Suffolk's St Peter's brewery. A
rag-tag and loyal crowd muses over the
Evening Standard crossword and, in
winter, a cosy fireplace encourages the
desire for warm sustenance. Haddock
and salmon fish cakes fit the bill nicely.

Look Mum No Hands

NEW *49 Old Street, EC1V 9HX (7253*
1025, www.lookmumnohands.com).
Barbican tube or Old Street tube/rail.
Open 7.30am-10pm Mon-Fri; 9am-
10pm Sat; 10am-10pm Sun. **£**. **Cafe**.
Map p151 D2 ⑯
Look Mum is a cyle-friendly café-bar
with 'secure' cycle parking in a courtyard (bring your own lock anyway), a
one-person workshop and plenty of
space to hang out, snack, use the Wi-Fi,
and – in the evenings – drink bottled
beer or well-priced wine. Live afternoon
screenings of cycle races take place in
the big main room. The food's simple –
platters of cured meats (£12) or veggie
platters (£10), Greek salads, baked tarts,
morning pastries and cakes.

Modern Pantry

47-48 St John's Square, EC1V 4JJ
(7250 0833, www.themodernpantry.
co.uk). Farringdon tube/rail. Open
Café 8am-11pm Mon-Fri; 9am-11pm
Sat; 10am-10pm Sun. *Restaurant* noon-
3pm, 6-10.30pm Tue-Fri; 6-11pm Sat.
££. **International**. Map p150 C2 ⑰
A culinary three-parter in a pair of
Georgian townhouses that feels savvy
and still of the moment a few years
after opening. Both pantry (takeaway)
and café are at street level; upstairs are
adjoining, informal dining rooms.
Service is spot on and the menu brilliantly fuses all kinds of ingredients.
Weekend brunch is always special –
but usually busy.

Morito

NEW *32 Exmouth Market EC1R 4QL (7278 7007). Farringdon tube/rail or bus 19, 38, 341.* **Open** 5-11pm Mon; 12.30-3.30pm, 4.30-11pm Tue-Sat. **££**. **Tapas**. Map p150 B2 ⑱

While the busy, unassailably popular Moro (34-36 Exmouth Market, EC1R 4QE, 7833 8336, www.moro.co.uk) is all smart clothes and clattering expanse, Morito – Sam and Sam Clark's new tapas venture next door – is tiny, pared-back and intimate. Wine is served by the tumbler, carafe or bottle, while draught beers come in third-of-a-pint 'chatos'. From stools at the bright orange Formica bar, you can watch chefs cook at an open grill. As with Moro, the menu reaches far beyond Spain – the trademark cuisine is 'Moorish' (Spanish, but with heavy North African influences). It's all understated, but right on the money.

Prufrock Coffee

NEW *23-25 Leather Lane, EC1N 7TE (07852 243470 mobile, www.prufrock coffee.com). Chancery Lane tube or Farringdon tube/rail.* **Open** 8am-5pm Mon-Fri; 10am-4pm Sat. **£**. **Cafe**. Map p150 B3 ⑲

Even with London's recent growth of boutique coffee shops and professional baristas, Prufrock is a special place. It feels like an airy art gallery crossed with a laboratory: the high windows display an antique coffee machine, music is of the classical sort and the large counter in the middle holds an impressive array of hardware – an espresso machine, grinders, siphons with halogen beam heaters, Japanese pour-over filters, even a Trifecta. The man behind it, Gwilym Davies, was crowned World Barista Champion in 2009; his staff are every bit as good.

St John

26 St John Street, EC1M 4AY (7251 0848, www.stjohnrestaurant.com). Barbican tube or Farringdon tube/rail. **Open** noon-3pm, 6-11pm Mon-Fri; 6-11pm Sat; 1-3pm Sun. **£££**. **British**. Map p150 C2 ⑳

Leading light of the modern British cooking revival, St John is an austere-looking place, opened in 1995 in the shell of a smokehouse by chef-patron Fergus Henderson. Its menu hasn't changed: the focus is on unusual seasonal British ingredients, simply cooked and presented. Less expensive is the short menu at the boisterous no-reservations bar. The new St John Hotel (p200) is in Soho.

Seven Stars

53 Carey Street, WC2A 2JB (7242 8521). Chancery Lane or Holborn tube. **Open** 11am-11pm Mon-Fri; noon-11pm Sat; noon-10.30pm Sun. **££**. **Gastropub**. Map p150 A4 ㉑

If you can squeeze into the small interior, you'll get a slice of low-rent, bohemian London: Roxy Beaujolais's pub is a fantastic social hub for local characters, from eccentric lawyers to burlesque babes. One of the few City pubs where your large burgundy will be well priced for top quality.

Three Kings of Clerkenwell

7 Clerkenwell Close, EC1R 0DY (7253 0483). Farringdon tube/rail. **Open** noon-11pm Mon-Fri; 7-11pm Sat. No credit cards. **Pub**. Map p150 B2 ㉒

Rhino heads, Egyptian felines and Dennis Bergkamp provide the decorative backdrop against which a discerning boho regulars glug real ale, cider or lager, and tap the well-worn tables to the Cramps and other gems from a superb jukebox.

Vinoteca

7 St John Street, EC1M 4AA (7253 8786, www.vinoteca.co.uk). Farringdon tube/rail. **Open** noon-11pm Mon-Sat. **Wine bar**. Map p150 C3 ㉓

Inspired by the Italian *enoteca* (a blend of off-licence and wine bar, with bar snacks thrown in), Vinoteca is in fact more of a gastropub in spirit. But even if you want no more to eat than a plate of bread and olive oil, come here for the impressive 200-bottle wine list, of which a range of 19 labels are available by the glass.

Ye Old Mitre

1 Ely Court, at the side of 8 Hatton Gardens, EC1N 6SJ (7405 4751). Chancery Lane tube or Farringdon tube/rail. **Open** 11am-11pm Mon-Fri. **Pub. Map** p150 B3 ㉔

The secluded location requires you to slink down an alleyway just off Hatton Garden, where you'll be transported to a parallel pub universe where the clientele are friendly and the staff (in pristine black and white uniforms) briskly efficient. Open only during the week, it's a pint-sized pub that's earned its top-notch reputation.

Zetter Townhouse

NEW *49-50 St John's Square, EC1V 4JJ (7324 4545, www.thezettertownhouse.com). Farringdon tube/rail.* **Open** 6.30pm-midnight Mon-Wed, Sun; 6.30pm-1am Thur-Sat. **Map** p150 C2 ㉕

Spread across the ground floor of the Zetter hotel's new sister site (p203), this cosy cocktail lounge is a collaboration with the founders of 69 Colebrooke Row (p171). Colebrooke's head barman Tony Conigliaro is an expert alcohol alchemist renowned for creating leftfield liquids and libations in his laboratory. Here the drinks list is unique, experimental yet refreshingly uncomplicated, with 13 house cocktails are priced at £8.50. Switched-on staff are delighted to talk you through your tipple. You can turn up unannounced, but book ahead to be sure of a seat.

Shopping

A terrific collection of shops are scattered along **Exmouth Market**, the short pedestrianised street that's home to **Morito** (left). They include little CD shop-cum-café Brill (no.27), jewellery at ec

one (no.41) and terrific books at Clerkenwell Tales (no.30).

Kate Kanzier

NEW *67-69 Leather Lane, EC1N 7TJ (7242 7232, www.katekanzier.com). Chancery Lane tube or Farringdon tube/rail.* **Open** 8.30am-6.30pm Mon-Fri; 11am-4pm Sat. **Map** p150 B2 ㉖

Adored for great-value directional footwear for women, Kate Kanzier is the place to visit for brogues (£30), ballerinas (£20), sandles and leather boots in a huge range of colours. Sexy high-heeled pumps in patent, suede, leather and animal prints are marked out by vintage designs. Handbags and clutches are also stocked.

Out of Town

NEW *30C Great Sutton Street, EC1V 0UD (7549 2168, www.outoftown london.com). Farringdon tube/rail.* **Open** 8.30am-7pm Mon-Fri; 9.30am-4pm Sat. **Map** p150 C2 ㉗

Nestling on shelves and rails here are classic men's brands (Levi's, Bass Weejuns loafers, North Sea knitwear), vintage clothes and a regularly updated mix of mid 20th-century prints, maps, US military clothing, fine furnishings, crockery and curios. Everything in the shop is for sale – even the chairs and tables at which customers sit to enjoy Out of Town's delicious family-made cakes and pastries.

Nightlife

Fabric

77A Charterhouse Street, EC1M 3HN (7336 8898, www.fabriclondon.com). Farringdon tube/rail. **Open** 10pm-6am Fri; 11pm-8am Sat; 11pm-6am Sun. **Map** p150 C3 ㉘

Fabric is the club most party people come to see in London: the main room has the stomach-wobbling Bodysonic dancefloor, the second is a rave-style warehouse, the third is where the cool stuff happens. Fridays belong to the bass: highlights include DJ Hype, who

LODNON BY AREA

takes over all three rooms once a month for his drum 'n' bass and dubstep night Playaz. Saturdays rock to techy, minimal, deep house sounds. Recent years have also seen Fabric On + On dance marathons. Stellar DJs – and big queues – are a given.

Volupté

7-9 Norwich Street, EC4A 1EJ (7831 1622, www.volupte-lounge. com). Chancery Lane tube. **Open** noon-4pm, 5pm-1am Tue-Fri; noon-3am Sat. **Map** p150 B3 ㉙
Expect to suffer extreme wallpaper envy as you enter the ground-floor bar, then descend to the club proper. Punters enjoy some of the best cabaret talent in town from tables set beneath absinthe-inspired vines. Nights include Harlem Swing Club, taking the time machine to the 1920s.

The City

Fewer than 10,000 souls live within the Square Mile (1.21 square miles, in fact), but every working day the population increases tenfold, as bankers, brokers, lawyers and traders storm into their towering office blocks. The City still holds to boundaries set by the 2nd-century walls of Roman Londinium (a few sections of which remain), although it then had six times more residents than now. The streets are full of historic gems, but the real crowd-pullers are **St Paul's** and the **Tower of London**.

Sights & museums

The art gallery at **Barbican** (£8-£10, free-£6 reductions; p164) has good exhibitions of art, design and architecture, while the free Curve space shows excellent commissions. Of the three classic skyscrapers in the City – **Lloyd's** (right), the Gherkin (**30 St Mary Axe**, p161) and Tower 42 (the

NatWest Tower) – only the latter's bar, **Vertigo 42** (p162), is open to the public. However, **Heron Tower** (right), now the City's tallest building, is due to open a rooftop bar. See also box p160.

Bank of England Museum

Entrance on Bartholomew Lane, EC2R 8AH (7601 5545, www.bankofengland. co.uk/museum). Bank tube/DLR. **Open** 10am-5pm Mon-Fri. **Admission** free. **Map** p151 E4 ㉚
Housed in the bank's former Stock Offices, this engaging museum explores the history of the national bank. As well as a rare opportunity to lift a 13kg gold bar (albeit one encased in a secure box you poke your hand into), you can learn about Kenneth Grahame: *The Wind in the Willows* author was a long-term employee here.

Bunhill Fields

Old Street tube/rail. **Admission** free. **Map** p151 E2 ㉛
The importance of this nonconformist burial ground was recognised in 2011, when it was protected from development by a Grade I listing. It's a moving little place, hemmed in by office walls and crammed with memorials to dead dissenters, such as John Bunyan, Daniel Defoe and William Blake. Opposite, the former home and chapel of John Wesley are now a museum of Methodism (49 City Road, 7253 2262, www.wesleyschapel.org.uk).

Guildhall Art Gallery & Clockmakers' Museum

Guildhall Yard, EC2P 2EJ (7332 3700, www.guildhall-art-gallery.org.uk). St Paul's tube or Bank tube/DLR. **Open** 10am-4.30pm Mon-Sat; noon-4pm Sun. **Admission** free. **Map** p151 D4 ㉜
The City of London's gallery (free to enter since spring 2011) contains dull portraits of royalty and some former mayors, and plenty of wonderful surprises, including a brilliant Constable, high-camp Pre-Raphaelite works and

various absorbing paintings of historic London. A sub-basement has the scant remains of a 6,000-seat Roman amphitheatre, built around AD 70. Across the big courtyard, the single-room Clockmakers' Museum (www.clockmakers.org, closed Sun, free admission) is a symphony of ticking, chiming clocks and watches.

Heron Tower

NEW *110 Bishopsgate, EC2M 4AY (www.herontower.com). Liverpool Street tube/rail.* **Map** p151 E3 ③

The 755ft-tall Heron Tower (radio mast included) was due to open in autumn 2011 – having become the City's tallest building back in 2009. (The tallest buildings in London, however, are One Canada Water, p178, and the Shard, p70.) On top of all the so-called office 'villages', a bit under 600ft up in the distinctive stepped roof, a Restaurant & Sky Bar will open to the public.

Lloyd's of London

1 Lime Street, EC3M 7HA (www.lloyds.com). Monument tube. **Map** p151 E4 ③

Lord Rogers' high-tech building has all its mechanical services (ducts, stair-wells, lift shafts) on the outside, a design that still looks modern after 25 years. The original Lloyd's Register, decorated with bas-reliefs of sea monsters and nautical scenes, is on nearby Fenchurch Street. No public access.

Monument

Monument Street, EC3R 8AH (7626 2717, www.themonument.info). Monument tube. **Open** 9.30am-5pm daily. **Admission** £3; free-£2 reductions. No credit cards. **Map** p151 E5 ③

The world's tallest free-standing stone column was designed by Sir Christopher Wren and his (often over-looked) associate Robert Hooke as a memorial to the Great Fire of London. It measures 202ft from the ground to the tip of the golden flame on the orb at its top, exactly the distance east to

Farriner's bakery in Pudding Lane, where the fire is supposed to have begun on 2 September 1666. Reopened after a glorious £4.5m refurbishment, the Monument can now be climbed up a spiral interior staircase for fine views.

Museum of London

150 London Wall, EC2Y 5HN (7001 9844, www.museumoflondon.org.uk). Barbican or St Paul's tube. **Open** 10am-6pm daily. **Admission** free; suggested donation £3. **Map** p151 D3 ③

This expansive museum (set in the middle of a roundabout) tells the whole history of London – with help from east London's Museum of London Docklands (p178). Themes include 'London Before London' – flint axes, fossils, grave goods – and 'Roman London', which has a reconstructed dining room complete with mosaic floor. Also on the ground floor, sound effects and audio-visual displays illustrate the medieval city, along with cases of shoes and armour, and there's a moving exhibit on the Black Death. Rush downstairs for outstanding new galleries on modern London. Among many fine exhibits are an unexploded Blitz bomb, an Alexander McQueen dress and a genuine 18th-century debtors' prison cell.

Postman's Park

St Paul's tube. **Map** p151 C3 ③

This peaceful, fern-filled park contains the Watts Memorial to Heroic Sacrifice: a wall of Victorian ceramic plaques, each of which commemorates a fatal act of bravery by an ordinary person.

St Paul's Cathedral

Ludgate Hill, EC4M 8AD (7236 4128, www.stpauls.co.uk). St Paul's tube. **Open** 8.30am-4pm Mon-Sat. *Galleries, crypt & ambulatory* 9.30am-4.15pm Mon-Sat. **Admission** £12.50; free-£11.50 reductions; £29.50 family. *Tours* £3; £1-£2.50 reductions. **Map** p150 C4 ③

Booze, Chews and Views

London's newest skyscrapers are welcoming in the public.

Heron Tower

We love the Gherkin (**30 St Mary Axe**, right) and the **Lloyd's** building (p159), but we can't help thinking they missed a trick. Each year, locals scour the brochure for the **Open-City London** architecture festival (p44) to see which iconic skyscrapers will be open to the public. Last year, admission to the **BT Tower** (p114) was organised by ballot, such was the demand for entry. For many of the city's most distinctive modern buildings, there's no way in unless you're lucky enough to work there.

For the new breed of London skyscrapers, this isn't going to be a problem. Perhaps taking note of **Vertigo 42** (p162), the champagne bar high in the City skyscraper you'd most like to be looking out of rather than at, a new breed of behemoth is courting the public.

The City's new tallest building, **Heron Tower** (p159), leads the charge in the financial centre. It should be opening a Restaurant and Sky Lounge as this guide hits the shelves, where you can drink or dine in a venue even promising exterior terraces – 570 feet up.

Across the river, Renzo Piano's **Shard of Glass** (p70) is also offering public access when it opens in 2012. It not only has restaurants (Floors 31-33) and a Shangri-La hotel (Floors 34-52), but a public Observatory – above even the hotel, on Floors 68-72.

Until these new stars open, **Galvin at Windows** (p108) offers excellent views of the west of town, but architecture fans will be more interested in **Paramount** (p143), the fine restaurant atop the landmark Centre Point tower.

Height isn't everything: two other City locations have great views but from a relatively low vantage. **One New Change** (p164) should have opened its Roof Terrace Café by the time you read this, giving eye-level views of the statues on St Paul's dome, but the SkyLounge at **Mint Tower of London** hotel (p203) is already a hit – we're told the overspill of bankers and lawyers has been having to wait in a second, ground-level bar. On our recent Sunday night visit, however, it was easy enough to get a 12th-floor window seat with a grand Thames vista. And there's an outside terrace for balmy weather.

LODNON BY AREA

A £40m restoration has left the main façade of St Paul's looking as brilliant as it must have when the first Mass was celebrated here in 1710. The vast open spaces of the interior contain memorials to national heroes such as Wellington and Lawrence of Arabia, as well as superb mosaics and gilt added by the Victorians. The Whispering Gallery, inside the dome, is reached by 259 steps from the main hall (the acoustics are so good a whisper can be clearly heard across the dome). Stairs continue up to first the Stone Gallery (119 steps), with its high external balustrades, then outside to the Golden Gallery (152 steps), with its giddying views. Head down to the crypt (where a new 270° projector, the Oculus, runs a film on the cathedral's history) to see Nelson's grand tomb and the small tombstone of Sir Christopher Wren himself, inscribed: 'Reader, if you seek a monument, look around you.'

30 St Mary Axe

www.30stmaryaxe.com. Liverpool Street tube/rail. **Map** p151 F4 ③⑨
Completed only in 2004, Lord Foster's distinctively curved skyscraper has already become a cherished icon of modern London, its 'Erotic Gherkin' nickname plainly apt. Unfortunately, there's no public access.

Tower Bridge Exhibition

Tower Bridge, SE1 2UP (7403 3761, www.towerbridge.org.uk). Tower Hill tube or Tower Gateway DLR. **Open** *Apr-Sept* 10am-6.30pm daily. *Oct-Mar* 9.30am-6pm daily. **Admission** £7; free-£5 reductions; £11 family. **Map** p151 F5 ④⓪
Opened in 1894, this is the 'London Bridge' that wasn't sold to America. Originally powered by steam, the drawbridge is now opened by electric rams when big ships need to venture this far upstream (check when the bridge is next due to be raised on the website). An entertaining exhibition on the history of the bridge is displayed in the old steamrooms and on the west walkway, which provides a crow's-nest view along the Thames.

Tower of London

Tower Hill, EC3N 4AB (0844 482 7777, www.hrp.org.uk). Tower Hill tube or Tower Gateway DLR. **Open** *Mar-Oct* 10am-5.30pm Mon, Sun; 9am-5.30pm Tue-Sat. *Nov-Feb* 10am-4.30pm Mon, Sun; 9am-4.30pm Tue-Sat. **Admission** £17; free-£14.50 reductions; £47 family. **Map** p151 F5 ④①
Despite exhausting crowds and long climbs up narrow stairways, this is one of Britain's finest historical sites. Who wouldn't be fascinated by a close-up look at the crown of Queen Victoria or the armour (and mighty codpiece) of Henry VIII? The buildings of the Tower span 900 years of history and the bastions and battlements house a series of interactive displays on the lives of monarchs – and excruciatingly painful deaths of traitors. The highlight has to be the Crown Jewels, viewed from a slow-moving travelator (get there early to minimise queuing), but the other big draw is the Royal Armoury in the White Tower: four floors of swords, armour, pole-axes, halberds and other gruesome tools for chopping people up. Executions of noble prisoners were carried out on the green in front of the Tower – the site is marked by a glass pillow sculpture.

Tickets are sold in the kiosk just west of the palace and visitors enter through the Middle Tower, but there's a free audio-visual display in the Welcome Centre outside the walls. There's plenty enough to do to fill a day, but skip to the highlights using the audio tour (which takes an hour), or by joining the highly entertaining free tours led by the Yeoman Warders (Beefeaters), who also care for the Tower's ravens.
Event highlights Regular historical costumed re-enactments; 'Royal Beasts – the story of the Royal Menagerie' (until 31 Dec 2011).

LODNON BY AREA

Eating & drinking

Cinnamon Club (p84) has a sibling in the City: Cinnamon Kitchen (9 Devonshire Square, EC2M 4YL, 7626 5000, www.cinnamonkitchen.co.uk); for a cheap lunch, the Cheapside branch of **Hummus Bros** (p121) is well located for St Paul's Cathedral (but closed at weekends). For drinks and eats with a view, see box p160.

Black Friar

174 Queen Victoria Street, EC4V 4EG (7236 5474). Mansion House tube or Blackfriars tube/rail. **Open** 10am-11pm Mon-Sat; noon-10.30pm Sun. **Pub**. Map p150 C4 ⓶

This wedge-shaped pub at the north end of Blackfriars Bridge offers a handful of real ales, wine by the glass, standard lagers and decent pub nosh, but it's the extraordinary Arts & Crafts interior, resplendent with carvings of monks and odd mottos, that makes the place worth a visit.

Bodean's

16 Byward Street, EC3R 5BA (7488 3883, www.bodeansbbq.com). Tower Hill tube. **Open** noon-3pm, 6-10pm Mon-Fri; 6-10pm Sat. **££. American**. Map p151 E5 ⓷

Across Bodean's five branches – also in Soho, Westbourne Grove, Fulham and Clapham – the shtick remains unchanged: generous portions of Kansas City barbecued meat, served in an informal upstairs or smarter downstairs where US sport is on TV.

Restaurant at St Paul's

St Paul's Cathedral, St Paul's Churchyard, EC4M 8AD (7248 2469, www.restaurantatstpauls.co.uk). St Paul's tube. **Open** noon-4.30pm daily. **£££. British**. Map p150 C4 ⓸

This is a handsome, light-filled space in the cathedral crypt, with sensuous and textural decor – great for a restaurant, surprising in a place of worship.

The food is excellent – along the lines of asparagus and poached duck egg, prettily pink barnsley chop, portobello mushroom wellington and a gooseberry cobbler for pudding – and well-priced at £21.50 for two courses, £25.95 for three. There's also a cafe; both are closed in the evening.

Sweetings

39 Queen Victoria Street, EC4N 4SA (7248 3062). Mansion House tube. **Open** 11.30am-3pm Mon-Fri. **£££. Fish & seafood**. Map p151 D4 ⓹

In these days of makeovers and global menus, Sweetings is that rare thing – a traditional British restaurant that clings to its traditions as if the Empire depended on it. It opens only for lunch, takes no bookings, and is full soon after noon, so order a silver pewter mug of Guinness and enjoy the wait.

Vertigo 42

Tower 42, 25 Old Broad Street, EC2N 1HQ (7877 7842, www.vertigo42.co.uk). Bank tube/DLR or Liverpool Street tube/rail. **Open** noon-3pm, 5-11pm Mon-Fri; 5-11pm Sat. **££££. Champagne bar**. Map p151 E4 ⓺

Short of introducing iris-recognition scanning, the process of going for a drink in Tower 42 (book in advance, then get X-rayed and metal-detected on arrival) could scarcely be more MI5. But it's worth it: the 42nd floor location delivers stupendous views. There are nibbles and the champagne list offers five labels by the flute (pricey at £13.50, plus 12.5% service).

Shopping

The City's strategy for improving the area's shopping, spearheaded by new mall **One New Change** (p164), hasn't yet come to much – but check out **Daunt Books** (61 Cheapside, EC2V 6AX, 7248 1117, www.dauntbooks.co.uk), a short walk east of the mall; the first Daunt is on Marylebone High Street (p104).

Barbican Centre p164

One New Change

NEW *1 New Change, EC4M 9AF (www.onenewchange.com). St Paul's tube.* **Map** p150 C4 🜛

Designed by Pritzker Prize-winning French starchitect Jean Nouvel, this dark, low-slung 'groundscraper' mall isn't an immediately lovable building – and even the shops (Reiss, Topshop, Swarovski) and eateries (Eat, Nando's, a Searcys champagne bar) feel a little predictable. But take the glass elevators up to the top floor and you'll be rewarded with superb views on a level with the dome of St Paul's. A terrace restaurant and bar should also now be open up there.

Nightlife

Bathhouse

7-8 Bishopsgate Churchyard, EC2M 3TJ (7920 9207, www.thebathhouse venue.com). Liverpool Street tube/rail. **Open** noon-midnight Mon-Wed; noon-1am Thur; noon-5am Fri; 8pm-4am Sat. **Admission** free-£7. **Map** p151 E3 🜛

This Victorian Turkish bathhouse is now a party space. All marble and gilt mirrors, it seems almost too appropriate for retro, burlesque and glam nights, such as Golden Birdcage or the Tassel Club's Dinner Party.

Arts & leisure

Barbican Centre

Silk Street, EC2Y 8DS (7638 4141, 7638 8891 box office, www.barbican. org.uk). Barbican tube or Moorgate tube/rail. **Map** p151 D3 🜛

The Barbican is a prime example of 1970s brutalism, softened by square ponds of friendly resident ducks. The complex has a concert hall, theatre, cinema and art galleries, a labyrinthine array of spaces that isn't at all easy to navigate. Programming, however, is first class. At the core of the classical music roster, performing 90 concerts a year, is the brilliant London Symphony Orchestra (LSO), supplemented by top

rock, jazz and world-music gigs. The annual BITE season cherry-picks exciting theatre and dance from around the globe, and the cinema shows a mixture of mainstream, art-house and international films.

Event highlights Junya Ishigami: 'Architecture as Air' (until 16 Oct 2011); BITE12 (mid Jan-Apr 2012); Gergiev's Stravinsky Festival (11-15 May 2012).

LSO St Luke's

161 Old Street, EC1V 9NG (7490 3939, 7638 8891 box office, www.lso. co.uk/lsostlukes). Old Street tube/rail. **Map** p151 D2 🜛

The London Symphony Orchestra's conversion of this Hawksmoor church into a 370-seat concert hall cost £20m, but the classical concerts and sheer variety of pop/rock gigs prove it was worth every penny.

Shoreditch

Just north-east of the City proper, the pleasure zones of Shoreditch soak up bankers' loose change. The area's edginess and artiness have begun to follow cheaper rents north and east into Dalston and Hackney (pp172-178), but in and around the triangle made by Shoreditch High Street, Great Eastern Street and Old Street the many bars and clubs remain lively – on a Friday or a Saturday night, often unpleasantly so. It's still a scruffy bit of town, though, notwithstanding the fashion kids traipsing around.

Eating & drinking

Book Club

100-106 Leonard Street, EC2A 4RH (7684 8618, www.wearetbc.com). Old Street tube/rail. **Open** 8am-midnight Mon-Thur; 10am-2am Fri, Sat; 10am-midnight Sun. **Admission** free-£5. **Bar/café**. **Map** p151 E2 🜛

The lovely-looking, open and airy Book Club fuses lively creative events with late-night drinking seven nights of the week. Locally themed cocktails include the Shoreditch Twat (a mix of tequila, Jagermeister, vermouth, vanilla sugar and egg), and food is served all day. There's also free Wi-Fi, a pool table, ping pong and lots of comfy seats. The programme might include Scroobius Pip's We.Are.Lizards or perhaps a Thinking & Drinking lecture.

Calllooh Callay

65 Rivington Street, EC2A 3AY (7739 4781). Shoreditch High Street rail or Old Street tube/rail. **Open** 5-11pm Mon, Thur, Sun; 5.30pm-1am Fri; 6pm-1am Sat. **Bar. Map** p151 F1 ⓢ

All warm and whimsical, the neo-Victorian decor here is as eclectic as Jabberwocky, the Lewis Carroll nonsense poem from which the bar gets its name. The quirkiest touch is the hoodwinking oak Narnia wardrobe, through which you'll find a lounge, mirrored bar and loos tiled in old cassettes. The 'Mad Hatter Tiki Punchbowl' is served up in a gramophone speaker trumpet.

Eyre Brothers

70 Leonard Street, EC2A 4QX (7613 5346, www.eyrebrothers.co.uk). Old Street tube/rail. **Open** noon-2.45pm, 6.30-10.45pm Mon-Fri; 7-11pm Sat. **££. International. Map** p151 E2 ⓢ

News has got around: Eyre Brothers does everything exceptionally well, thus it can be hard to book a table. Brothers David and Robert clearly spend as much time crafting the changing menu as they must have fashioning the clean-lined decor – all chic leather furniture, designer lamps and divided dining areas. Authentic Portuguese dishes reflect their upbringing in Mozambique, while Spanish and French flavours add range and luxury to the offerings.

Pizza East

⬛NEW⬛ *56 Shoreditch High Street, E1 6JJ (7729 1888, www.pizzaeast.com). Shoreditch High Street rail.* **Open**

noon-11pm Mon-Wed, Sun; noon-midnight Thur; noon-1am Fri, Sat. **£. Pizza. Map** p151 F2 ⓢ

Pizza East is in a big space that used to be a club and still looks like one floor of an old factory. There's more than pizza on the Italian-American menu (calamari with caper aioli, polenta with deep-fried chicken livers), but the pizzas are well-made and adventurous (witness clam pizza, a New England speciality). Being in Shoreditch and vast, this place is noisy – even without the DJs on Thur-Sat evenings – but the food is good and the welcome friendly.

Shopping

Just south of Shoreditch is one of the city's best shopping areas. We've listed key boutiques around **Old Spitalfields Market** and **Brick Lane** on pp175-177.

A Child of the Jago

10 Great Eastern Street, EC2A 3NT (7377 8694, www.achildofthejago.com). Shoreditch High Street rail. **Open** 11am-7pm Mon-Sat; noon-5pm Sun. **Map** p151 E2 ⓢ

Joe Corre (Vivienne Westwood's son) and fashion designer Simon 'Barnzley' Armitage's eclectic shop is about as far from 'high street' as it gets, with its deft and very Shoreditch combination of modern and vintage clothes. You'll find the likes of Barnzley's cashmere hooded tops (they're handmade in Scotland) and Westwood's World's End collection.

Three Threads

47-49 Charlotte Road, EC2A 3QT (7749 0503, www.thethreethreads.com). Old Street tube/rail. **Open** 11am-7pm Mon-Sat; noon-5pm Sun. **Map** p151 F2 ⓢ

Free beer, a jukebox well stocked with dad rock and conveniently placed bar stools around the till… the Three Threads tempts even the most shopphobic male. Exclusive, cult labels such as Japan's Tenderloin, Fjall

Three Threads p165

Raven, Danish label Won Hundred and New York's Built by Wendy are here, but the vibe is more like a pal's house. It also stocks great womenswear from Carhartt and YMC, and Mimi bags.

Nightlife

In addition to the table tennis table, **Book Club** (p164) offers a terrific range of unusual night-time events, from music to spoken word.

Comedy Café

66-68 Rivington Street, EC2A 3AY (7739 5706, www.comedycafe.co.uk). Old Street tube/rail or Shoreditch High Street rail. **Map** p151 F2 ⑰
Comedy Café is a purpose-built club, with a fun atmosphere and food is an integral part of the experience.

East Village

89 Great Eastern Street, EC2A 3HX (7739 5173, www.eastvillageclub.com). Old Street tube/rail. **Open** 5pm-midnight Tue, Wed; 5pm-1am Thur; 5pm-1am Fri; 9pm-4am Sat; 2-11pm Sun. **Map** p151 E2 ㊳
Stuart Patterson, one of the Faith crew who have been behind all-day house-music parties across London for more than a decade, created this two-floor, 'real house' bar-club in 2008 – and it's still punching above its weight. The top-notch DJs should suit any sophisticated clubber; you can expect the likes of Chicago house don Derrick Carter and London's own Mr C. It also hosts Rootikal, House Not House and our very own bimonthly Nite Sessions.

Horse & Groom

28 Curtain Road, EC2A 3NZ (7503 9421, www.thehorseandgroom.net). Old Street tube/rail. **Open** 6pm-1am Tue-Thur, Sun; 6pm-2am Fri, Sat. **Map** p151 F2 ㊴
This two-floor, self-proclaimed 'disco pub' hosts nights ranging from house and electro to contemporary classical and pub quizzes.

Old Blue Last

38 Great Eastern Street, EC2A 3ES (7739 7033, www.theoldbluelast.com). Old Street tube/rail or Shoreditch High Street rail. **Open** noon-midnight Mon-Wed; noon-12.30am Thur, Sun; noon-1.30am Fri, Sat. **Map** p151 F2 ㊿
Klaxons, Arctic Monkeys and Lily Allen have all played secret shows to the high-fashion rock 'n' rollers in the sauna-like upper room at this shabby two-floor Victorian boozer. The Old Blue Last's programme was recently revamped, and regular club nights might include the pop-punk favourite What's My Age Again, Skill Wizard, Bounty and electro night Dollop.

Plastic People

147-149 Curtain Road, EC2A 3QE (7739 6471, www.plasticpeople.co.uk). Old Street tube/rail or Shoreditch High Street rail. **Open** 10pm-2am Thur; 10pm-4am Fri, Sat; 7-11pm Sun. **Map** p151 F1 ㊱
The long-established, long-popular Plastic People subscribed to the old-school line that all you need for a party is a dark basement and a kicking sound system – then to everybody's surprise closed for a refurb. The programming remains true to form: from deep techno to house, with all-girl DJ line-ups and many a star arriving to play a secret gig on the exemplary sound system.

XOYO

NEW *32-37 Cowper Street, EC2A 4AP (7729 5959, www.xoyo.co.uk). Old Street tube/rail.* **Map** p151 E2 ㊲
XOYO stands out from its competitors because of its size (its 900-person capacity is big for the area), but also because it functions as a club, a gig hub and an exhibition space, with a stark white gallery-like room upstairs and a dance basement below (offset by an unusually high ceiling). One of the founders, Cymon Eckel, describes it as 'essentially… a disco loft-club', but it has a pleasingly open attitude to all tribes of clubber.

Camden Lock

Neighbourhood London

LONDON BY AREA

Like many modern cities, London is really two different kinds of metropolis: the centre, for work, play and lucky tourists, and the periphery, where rent is cheaper and most locals live. Restaurants and bars are often more vital in these neighbourhoods – and cool scenes are more apt to develop.

To the north are **Camden** and **Islington** (p171). In the east, **Spitalfields to Dalston** (p172) is the city's hippest zone, but do also visit **Docklands** (p178) and, of course, the **Olympic Park** (p179). Head south of the Thames for spectacular **Greenwich** (p181) and lively **Brixton & Vauxhall** (p184), or shop in **Notting Hill** (p186) to the west of town.

London is a huge city, which means some sights are a day trip in themselves. We've included these in their own chapter: **Worth the Trip** is on pp188-190.

Camden

The key north London destination is rapidly gentrifying Camden. Famous for its **market** and close to **London Zoo**, it's one of London's liveliest nightlife areas. West of Camden, snooty **St John's Wood** is the spiritual home of cricket.

Sights & museums

Jewish Museum

Raymond Burton House, 129-131 Albert Street, NW1 7NB (www.jewish museum.org.uk). Camden Town tube. **Open** 10am-5pm Mon-Thur, Sun; 10am-2pm Fri. **Admission** £7.50; free-£6.50 reductions; £18 family. This expanded museum reopened in 2010, and it's a brilliant exploration of Jewish life since 1066. Access is free to the downstairs café, beside an ancient ritual bath, and shop. You must pay to go upstairs, but there you can wield the iron in a tailor's sweatshop, sniff chicken soup and pose for a wedding photo. There's a powerful Holocaust section, focused on a single survivor, Leon Greenman. Opposite, a beautiful room of religious artefacts, including a 17th-century synagogue ark and centrepiece chandelier of Hanukkah lamps, introduces Jewish ritual.

Lord's & MCC Museum

St John's Wood Road, NW8 8QN (7616 8595, www.lords.org). St John's Wood tube. **Tours** phone or see website for details. **Admission** £14; free-£8 reductions; £37 family.

The opposite side of Regent's Park from Camden, Lord's is more than just a famous cricket ground – as the headquarters of the Marylebone Cricket Club (MCC), it is official guardian of the rules of cricket. As well as staging test matches and internationals, the ground is home to the Middlesex County Cricket Club (MCCC) and will host the Archery for the London 2012 Games. Visitors can take an organised tour round the futuristic, pod-like NatWest Media Centre and august, portrait-bedecked Long Room.

ZSL London Zoo

Regent's Park, NW1 4RY (7722 3333, www.zsl.org/london-zoo). Baker Street or Camden Town tube then 274, C2 bus. **Open** 10am-6pm daily. **Admission** £17.60-£20.50; free-£19 reductions.

London Zoo has been open in one form or another since 1826. Spread over 36 acres and containing more than 600 species, it cares for many of the endangered variety – as well as your nippers at the children's zoo. The emphasis throughout is on upbeat education. Exhibits are always entertaining – we especially like the recreation of a kitchen overrun with cockroaches – but sometimes the zoo sensibly just lets the animals be the stars: witness the much expanded Penguin Beach, which opened in spring 2011.

Eating & drinking

Proud (p170) is great for rock 'n' roll boozing, while the original **Haché** (24 Inverness Street, 7485 9100, www.hacheburgers.com; see also p99) provides sustenance.

Chin Chin Laboratorists

NEW *49-50 Camden Lock Place, NW1 8AF (www.chinchinlabs.com). Camden Town tube.* **Open** 11am-6pm Wed, Thur, Sun; 11am-7pm Fri, Sat. **No credit cards.** **£.** **Ice-cream.**

The 'laboratorists' are husband-and-wife duo Ahrash Akbari-Kalhur and Nyisha Weber. In their ice-cream parlour, which looks like a mad scientist's lab, they use liquid nitrogen to make ice-cream on demand. The ice-cream, frozen so fast no coarse ice-crystals can form, is wonderfully smooth. The practical application of science has never been cooler, tastier or more fun.

Market

43 Parkway, NW1 7PN (7267 9700, www.marketrestaurant.co.uk). Camden Town tube. **Open** noon-2.30pm, 6-10.30pm Mon-Sat; 1-3.30pm Sun. **££.** **British.**

Camden's other Market is a utilitarian but excellent British restaurant. Stripped-back hardly covers it: brick walls are ragged and raw; zinc-topped tables are scuffed; old-fashioned wooden chairs look like they were once used in a classroom. Food is similarly pared down, reliant on the flavours of high-quality seasonal produce.

Masala Zone

25 Parkway, NW1 7PG (7267 4422, www.masalazone.com). Camden Town tube. **Open** 12.30-3pm, 5.30-11pm Mon-Fri; 12.30-11pm Sat; 12.30-10.30pm Sun. **££.** **Indian.**

This branch of the Masala Zone chain is popular with hip youngsters who come for the buzzy vibe, reasonable prices and decent pan-Indian food: earthy curries, thalis and zesty street snacks. The eye-catching decor is themed round colourful 1930s-style posters and retro artefacts.

Shopping

Alfie's Antique Market
13-25 Church Street, NW8 8DT (7723 6066, www.alfiesantiques.com). Edgware Road tube or Marylebone tube/rail. **Open** 10am-6pm Tue-Sat. No credit cards.

To the south-east of Regent's Park, Church Street is probably London's most important area for antiques shops, with a cluster centred on estimable Alfie's. The market itself has more than 100 dealers in vintage furniture and fashion, art, books and maps.

Camden Market
Camden Lock *Camden Lock Place, off Chalk Farm Road, NW1 8AF (www. camdenlockmarket.com).* **Open** 10am-6pm daily (reduced stalls Mon-Fri).
Camden Lock Village *east of Chalk Farm Road , NW1 (www.camdenlock. net).* **Open** 10am-8.30pm daily.
Camden Market *Camden High Street, at Buck Street, NW1 (www. camdenmarkets.org).* **Open** 9.30am-5.30pm daily.
Stables Market *off Chalk Farm Road, opposite Hartland Road, NW1 8AH (7485 5511, www.stablesmarket. com).* **Open** 10.30am-6pm Mon-Fri (reduced stalls); 10am-6pm Sat, Sun.
All *Camden Town or Chalk Farm tube.*

Amid T-shirts, corsets and chintz, between endless tourists who want a snap beside a genuine British punk, there are treats here. Our advice? Go later in the afternoon during the week, when it's quieter. Camden Market itself sells garish neon sunglasses and slogan T-shirts. Almost next door is the listed Electric Ballroom, which sells vinyl on weekends. Inverness Street Market opposite sells similar garb to the Camden Market, as well as a diminishing supply of fruit and veg. North, you'll find crafts, clothes, trinkets and small curiosities with a Japanese pop culture influence at Camden Lock and Camden Lock Village, the latter having opened after major fire damage to the market in spring 2009. North again is the Stables Market, with its Horse Hospital section, selling vintage clothing, snacks and classic furniture.

Nightlife

Koko
1A Camden High Street, NW1 7JE (0870 432 5527, 0844 847 2258 box office, www.koko.uk.com). Mornington Crescent tube.

Avoid standing beneath the sound-muffling overhang downstairs and you may find that this one-time music hall is one of London's finest venues. The 1,500-capacity hall stages weekend club nights and gigs by indie rockers, from cultish to those on the up.

Lock Tavern
35 Chalk Farm Road, NW1 8AJ (7482 7163, www.lock-tavern.co.uk). Chalk Farm tube.

A tough place to get into at weekends, with queues of artfully distressed rock urchins and one of Camden's most arbitrary door policies. It teems with aesthetic niceties inside (cosy black couches and warm wood panels downstairs; open-air terrace on the first floor), but it's the unpredictable after-party vibe that packs in the punters.

Proud Camden
Horse Hospital, Stables Market, Chalk Farm Road, NW1 8AH (7482 3867, www.proudcamden.com). Chalk Farm tube.

North London guitar slingers do rock-star debauchery at this former Horse Hospital, whether draping themselves – cocktail in hand – over the luxurious textiles in the stable-style booths, sinking into deck chairs on the terrace, or spinning round in the main band room to trendonista alt-sounds. Proud2 (p184) is a more elaborate night out.

Roundhouse

Chalk Farm Road, NW1 8EH (7424 9991 information, 0844 482 8008 box office, www.roundhouse.org.uk). Chalk Farm tube.
A one-time railway turntable shed, the Roundhouse was used for experimental theatre and hippie happenings in the 1960s before becoming a rock venue in the '70s. The venue reopened a few years ago, and now mixes arty rock gigs with dance, quality theatre and multimedia events. Sightlines can be poor, but acoustics are good.

Islington

Camden's north London neighbour Islington combines bars, boutiques and small arts venues.

Eating & drinking

For great weekend vibes, get down at the **Old Queen's Head** (below).

Ottolenghi

287 Upper Street, N1 2TZ (7288 1454, www.ottolenghi.co.uk). Angel tube or Highbury & Islington tube/rail. **Open** 8am-10pm Mon-Wed; 8am-10.30pm Thur-Sat; 9am-7pm Sun. **££. Bakery-café.**
This is more than an inviting bakery. Behind the pastries piled in the window is a slightly prim deli counter with lush salads, available day and evening, eat-in or take away. As a daytime café, it's brilliant, but people also flock here for fine fusion food at dinner.

69 Colebrooke Row

NEW *69 Colebrooke Row, N1 8AA (07540 528593 mobile, www.69 colebrookerow.com). Angel tube.*
With just a handful of tables plus a few stools at the bar, 69 may be smaller than your front room, but the understated, intimate space proves a fine environment in which to enjoy pristine cocktails (liquorice whisky sours, perhaps), mixed with quiet ceremony by

elegantly bow-tied mixologist Tony Conigliaro. Impeccably attired staff, handwritten bills and tall glasses of water poured from a cocktail shaker mark out this lovely enterprise.

Shopping

Just off Upper Street near Angel tube, **Camden Passage** (7359 0190, www.camdenpassage antiques.com) retains some of the quirky antiques dealers who first brought shoppers here, as well as wonderful boutiques.

Diverse

294 Upper Street, N1 2TU (7359 8877, www.diverseclothing.com). Angel tube. **Open** 10.30am-6.30pm Mon-Wed, Fri, Sat; 10.30am-7.30pm Thur; 11.30am-5.30pm Sun.
This stalwart boutique does a fine job of keeping N1's style queens in fashion-forward mode. Despite the cool clobber, chic layout and striking window displays, this is the sort of place where you can rock up in jeans and scuzzy Converse and not feel uncomfortable.

Smug

13 Camden Passage, N1 8EA (7354 0253, www.ifeelsmug.com). Angel tube. **Open** 11am-6pm Wed, Fri, Sat; noon-7pm Thur; noon-5pm Sun.
Graphic designer Lizzie Evans has decked out this cute lifestyle boutique with all her favourite things: rainbow kitchen accessories, Lisa Stickley wash bags, vintage-inspired soft toys and 1950s and '60s furniture.

Nightlife

Old Queen's Head

44 Essex Road, N1 8LN (7354 9993, www.theoldqueenshead.com). Angel tube. **Open** noon-midnight Mon-Wed, Sun; noon-1am Thur; noon-2am Fri, Sat.
Another place with long weekend queues – no wonder, when DJs such as Freestylers, Eno and Mr Thing are on

the roster. There are two floors and out-side seating, and during the week you can lounge on the sofas. Weekends are for dancing, minor celeb-spotting and chatting up the bar staff.

Arts & leisure

Almeida

Almeida Street, N1 1TA (7359 4404, www.almeida.co.uk). Angel tube.
A well-groomed 325-seat venue with a funky bar attached, the Almeida turns out thoughtfully crafted theatre directed by such star directors as Thea Sharrock and Rupert Goold.

Arsenal Football Club

Emirates Stadium, Ashburton Grove, Highbury, N7 7AF (0844 277 3625, www.arsenal.com). Arsenal tube.
Before fading, Arsenal finally mounted a serious challenge for the 2010/11 Premiership, some validation of the club's insistence on attractive passing football and bringing through exciting young players. The team's new sta-dium – north of Islington – is one of the country's best, and has a club museum.

Sadler's Wells

Rosebery Avenue, EC1R 4TN (0844 412 4300, www.sadlerswells.com). Angel tube.
Purpose-built on the site of the original 17th-century theatre, this dazzling complex is home to an impressive line-up of local and international contempo-rary dance. Perhaps the key London venue for dance.

Screen on the Green

83 Upper Street, N1 0NP (0870 066 4777, www.everymancinema.com). Angel tube.
Boutique cinema chain Everyman now owns three former Screen cinemas, of which this is the best – refurbished a few years back, it lost seats to make space for the more comfortable kind, gained an auditorium bar and stage for live events, but kept its retro neon sign.

On the doorstep of the City, **Spitalfields** is known for its covered market, around which spread restaurants and bars. To the east, **Brick Lane** may be world-famous for its curries, but it is increasingly home to hip bars and boutiques. Slightly north, **Hoxton** begins where the City overspill into Shoreditch (p164) comes to an end: it's a good bet for late drinking and clubbing. Eastwards, **Bethnal Green** has the Museum of Childhood; to the north, unheralded **Dalston** has stealthily become a fine cluster of out-there music and arts venues, with the London Overground line (p216) having made them all more accessible.

Sights & museums

Geffrye Museum

136 Kingsland Road, E2 8EA (7739 8543, www.geffrye-museum.org.uk). Hoxton rail. **Open** 10am-5pm Tue-Sat; noon-5pm Sun. **Admission** free; donations appreciated.
In a set of 18th-century almshouses, the Geffrye offers a vivid physical history of the English interior. Displaying orig-inal furniture, paintings, textiles and decorative arts, the museum recreates a sequence of typical middle-class liv-ing rooms from 1600 to the present – a fascinating take on domestic history. **Event highlights** Kei Ito's installation 'Sitting the Light Fantastic' (from 16 Sept 2011).

V&A Museum of Childhood

Cambridge Heath Road, E2 9PA (8983 5235, www.museumofchildhood.org.uk). Bethnal Green tube/rail or Cambridge Heath rail. **Open** 10am-5.45pm daily. **Admission** free; donations appreciated.
Home to one of the world's finest col-lections of kids' toys, dolls' houses, games and costumes, the Museum of

Albion p174

Childhood shines brighter than ever after extensive refurbishment, which has given it an impressive entrance. Part of the Victoria & Albert (p93), the museum has been amassing child-related objects since 1872, with Barbie Dolls complementing Victorian praxinoscopes. There are plenty of interactive exhibits and a decent café too.
Event highlights 'Magic Worlds' (8 Oct 2011-4 Mar 2012).

Whitechapel Gallery

77-82 Whitechapel High Street, E1 7QX (7522 7888, www.whitechapel gallery.org). Aldgate East tube. **Open** 11am-6pm Tue, Wed, Fri-Sun; 11am-9pm Thur. **Admission** free.

This East End stalwart has enjoyed a major redesign that saw the Grade II-listed building expand into the equally historic former library right next door – cleverly, the architects left the two buildings stylistically distinct rather than smoothing out their differences. The gallery gave itself an archive centre, restaurant and café, and tripled its exhibition space, improving a reputation as an art pioneer that was built on shows of Picasso (in 1939, his *Guernica* was shown here), Pollock and Kahlo. A permanent Rachel Whiteread piece is planned for the London 2012 Festival.

Eating & drinking

Beside Old Spitalfields Market, **St John Bread & Wine** (7251 0848, www.stjohnbreadandwine.com) is the fine offshoot of St John (p156).

Albion

2-4 Boundary Street, E2 7DD (7729 1051, www.albioncaff.co.uk). Old Street tube/rail or Shoreditch High Street rail. **Open** 8am-midnight daily. **£**. **Café**.

Boundary Project is a terrific operation in otherwise dishevelled Shoreditch. Albion is the ground-floor 'caff' (their description), food shop and bakery; Boundary is the smarter French restaurant in the basement, while a rooftop bar-grill and hotel rooms top off the enterprise (p202). Everything from Albion's Brit nostalgia menu tastes delicious, from a little appetiser of perfect crackling to a proper Irish stew.

Brick Lane Beigel Bake

159 Brick Lane, E1 6SB (7729 0616). Liverpool Street tube/rail, Shoreditch High Street rail or bus 8. **Open** 24hrs daily. **£**. No credit cards.
Bagel bakery.

This little East End institution produces perfect bagels both plain and filled (cream cheese, brilliant salt beef), superb bread and moreish cakes. Even at 3am, fresh baked goods are being pulled from the ovens; no wonder the queue trails out the door when local bars and clubs begin to close.

Dreambagsjaguarshoes

34-36 Kingsland Road, E2 8DA (7729 5830, www.dreambagsjaguarshoes. com). Hoxton rail. **Open** noon-1am daily. **Bar**.

Still as trendy as the day it first opened, this bar offers a fast-track education in what makes Shoreditch cool. Grungey but glam scruffs lounge in decor that changes, regularly and completely – artists are commissioned at intervals to give the place a makeover. The background music is self-consciously edgy and good pizzas roll in from next door.

Poppies

NEW *6-8 Hanbury Street, E1 6QR (7247 0892, www.poppiesfishandchips. co.uk). Liverpool Street tube/rail or Aldgate East tube.* **Open** 11am-11pm daily. **££**. **Fish & chips**.

A worthy replacement for the East End caff that preceded it, Poppies serves perfectly fried fish from Billingsgate Market (cod, haddock, rock, scampi, halibut) with hand-cut chips, home-made tartare sauce and mushy peas. You can sit in – service is by sharply dressed, authentically amiable Italian chaps. The location between Brick Lane and Spitalfields (p176) is handy.

Song Que

134 Kingsland Road, E2 8DY (7613 3222). Hoxton rail or Old Street tube/ rail then bus 243. **Open** noon-3pm, 5.30-11pm Mon-Sat; 12.30pm-11pm Sun. **£. Vietnamese**.

North-east London holds its monopoly on the best Vietnamese restaurants in the city, with Song Que the benchmark. It's a canteen-like operation to which diners of all types are attracted – be prepared to share tables at busy times. Beef pho and barbecued quail with citrus dipping sauce are superb.

Tayyabs

83 Fieldgate Street, E1 1JU (7247 9543, www.tayyabs.co.uk). Aldgate East or Whitechapel tube. **Open** noon-11.30pm daily. **£. Pakistani**.

A bit of a walk south-east of Brick Lane, Tayyabs is the East End equivalent of the caffs favoured by truckers in South Asia. It has been around since the 1970s, and although the interior has been extended, it's a challenge to bag a table. Cooking is big, bold and sassy. When it's just too busy, try Needoo Grill, round the corner (87 New Road).

Viajante

NEW *Patriot Square, E2 9NF (7871 0461, www.viajante.co.uk). Bethnal Green tube/rail or Cambridge Heath rail.* **Open** noon-2pm, 7-9.30pm daily. **££££. Modern European**.

In nowhere-land north of Bethnal Green station, fêted young chef Nuno Mendes has opened his own restaurant in a posh new hotel (p205). A stint at El Bulli informs his cooking: the six-, nine- or 12-course tasting menus (£60-£85, with matched wines for extra £30-£60) are firmly in the 'experimental' camp. Expect culinary fireworks. Inventive tapas are served at the bar and there's a more affordable three-course lunch.

Shopping

On Sundays, the whole area from **Old Spitalfields Market** (p176) east to Brick Lane is hectic with shoppers. Watch out for the new **Box Park** (www.boxpark.co.uk) at Shoreditch High Street station – a 'shopping mall' in 40 recycled shipping containers.

Broadway Market

www.broadwaymarket.co.uk. London Fields rail or bus 236, 394.

Broadway Market has huge fashion kudos, but it's high-quality produce (this is primarily a specialist food market), well-edited vintage clothing and independent boutiques (Artwords, Black Truffle) that make it really worth a visit. The market wasn't always like this: after years of decline, in 2004 the local traders' and residents' association set about transforming their ailing fruit and veg market. Now, it's one of the city's most successful local markets.

Columbia Road Market

Columbia Road, E2. Hoxton rail or bus 26, 48, 55. **Open** 8am-2pm Sun.

On Sunday mornings, this unassuming East End street is transformed into a swathe of fabulous plant life and the air is fragrant with blooms. But it's not just about flora: alongside the market is a growing number of shops selling everything from pottery and Mexican glassware to cupcakes and perfume. Get there early for the pick of the crop, or around 2pm for the bargains; refuel at Jones Dairy (23 Ezra Street).

LN-CC

NEW *18-24 Shacklewell Lane, E8 2EZ (3174 0726, www.ln-cc.com). Dalston Kingsland rail.* **Open** by appointment.

The various rooms in this 5,000sq ft basement have been transformed by in-demand set designer Gary Card to play host to myriad designer labels: for men, New Power Studio, Rick Owens, Maison Martin Margiela and archive Raf Simons; for women, archive Yohji Yamamoto, Comme des Garçons and Issey Miyake. There are also rare books and even an events space.

Old Spitalfields Market

Commercial Street, between Lamb Street & Brushfield Street, E1 6AA (7247 8556, www.spitalfieldsoldmarket. com). Liverpool Street tube/rail or Shoreditch High Street rail. **Open** 9.30am-5pm Thur, Fri, Sun. *Antiques* 8.30am-4.30pm Thur. *Food* 10am-5pm Fri-Sun. *Fashion* 9.30am-5pm Fri. *Records & books* 10am-4pm 1st & 3rd Fri of the mth. No credit cards.

Since the 2003 renovation and total overhaul of the much-loved Spitalfields Market, it's a leaner, cleaner affair, bulked out with slightly soulless boutiques. A pitch here is expensive, so expect gastro-nibbles, wittily sloganed baby T-shirts and leather bags. If you want to avoid the crowds and make more idiosyncratic finds, forget the busy Sunday market and come on a Thursday for heaps of vintage fashion.

Dray Walk

Liverpool Street tube/rail or Shoreditch High Street rail.
The great brick buildings of the Old Truman Brewery, about halfway up Brick Lane, are home to a formidable array of funky retailers: Junky Styling (no.12) for innovative reworkings of second-hand clothes; Folk (no.11) for cutting-edge brands such as Sessun and Hillside; Traffic People (no.10) for classic polos and girly flower-print designs; Number 6 (no.6) for hip new casual attire; and, of course, Rough Trade East (below). Open only one day a week, the buzzy Sunday (Up)Market (7770 6100, www.sundayupmarket. co.uk) collects 140 stalls selling edgy fashion from fresh young designers, vintage gear and well-priced jewellery. It's more relaxed, cheaper and hipper than Old Spitalfields Market (above).

123 Boutique

NEW *123 Bethnal Green Road, E2 7DG (www.123bethnalgreenroad.co.uk). Shoreditch High Street rail.* **Open** noon-7pm Tue, Wed, Fri, Sat; noon-8pm Thur; 11am-6pm Sun.

Ross Barry and his sister Michelle Goggi are part of a textile dynasty – an east London family business called LMB, with a history of recycling clothing and wholesaling vintage. Searching for a small site to open their first store, they discovered something more exciting – 123 Bethnal Green Road, a huge Grade II-listed building looming high over Brick Lane. After a two-year renovation project, they opened their vintage and sustainable fashion store to wide acclaim. Look out for pieces by Noki designer JJ Hudson and accessories by Judy Blame.

Redchurch Street

NEW *Shoreditch High Street rail.*
A shabby Shoreditch cut-through, Redchurch is suddenly a strong contender for the London's best shopping street. Vintage homeware specialist Caravan (no.3), Aussie botanical beauty shop Aesop (no.5A), classic menswear brand Sunspel (no.7) gather at one end. Further up are darkly lit menswear store Hostem (nos.41-43), decadent interiors at Maison Trois Garçons (no.45), vintage-style up-dos and manicures at hair salon the Painted Lady (no.65) and even a grungy thrift shop, Sick (no.105), that specialises in 1990s, er, vintage. Two key arrivals are concept store Aubin & Wills (nos.64-66), where you can buy men's, women's and homeware lines, or catch a film in the small cinema, and expansive new premises for long-term favourite Labour & Wait (no.85), selling its aesthetically pleasing mops, enamel bread bins and stylish ladles.

Rough Trade East

Dray Walk, Old Truman Brewery, 91 Brick Lane, E1 6QL (7392 7788, www. roughtrade.com). Liverpool Street tube/ rail. **Open** 8am-9pm Mon-Thur; 8am-8pm Fri, Sat; 11am-7pm Sun.

Since opening on Dray Walk (above) in 2007, the indie music store has never looked more upbeat. This 5,000sq ft record store, café and gig space offers a dizzying range of vinyl and CDs, spanning punk, indie, dub, soul, electronica and more. With 16 listening posts and a stage for live sets, this is close to musical nirvana.

Vintage Emporium

NEW *14 Bacon Street, E1 6LF (7739 0799, www.thevintageemporiumcafe. com). Shoreditch High Street rail.*
Open 10am-7pm daily.
We love this relaxed vintage store and café (complete with bright yellow 1960s coffee machine, open until 10pm daily). Partners Jess Collins and Oli Stanion opened the emporium on a shoestring on a Brick Lane back alley, selling clothes from the Victorian era through to the 1950s. Oh, and it hosts naked life-drawing classes – a sight to behold as you sip your herbal tea.

Nightlife

Bethnal Green Working Men's Club

42-44 Pollard Row, E2 6NB (7739 7170, www.workersplaytime.net). Bethnal Green tube/rail.
The sticky red carpet and broken lampshades perfectly suit the programme of quirky lounge, retro rock 'n' roll and fancy-dress burlesque parties from spandex-lovin' dance husband-and-wife duos and the like. The mood is friendly, the playlist upbeat and the air always full of artful, playful mischief.

Café Oto

18-22 Ashwin Street, E8 3DL (7923 1231, www.cafeoto.co.uk). Dalston Junction or Dalston Kingsland rail.
No credit cards.
This 150-capacity Dalston café and music venue can't easily be categorised, though it offers the tidy definition: 'creative new music that exists outside of the mainstream'. That means Japanese noise rockers, electronica pioneers, improvising noiseniks and artists from the strange ends of the rock, folk and classical spectrums.

The High Life

The cross-Thames cable car.

First there were Boris bikes (see box p181). Now London's media-savvy mayor has announced a cross-river cable car project that will provide a direct link between two major London 2012 venues – the North Greenwich Arena (p207) south of the Thames and, on Royal Victoria Dock on the north side, ExCeL (p207).

Each of 34 suspended gondolas will carry up to ten people at a time, travelling 50 metres above the murky depths on a five-minute crossing that is promised to offer a 'truly sublime, bird's-eye view of our wonderful city'.

The height of the crossing means it won't interfere with shipping and it should be much cheaper and quicker to build than a bridge or tunnel. That said, projected costs have soared from an original estimate of £25m, and fundraising is sufficiently difficult that the project may not be complete for the 2012 Games.

The Mace consortium – previous projects include the London Eye (p67) and the Shard (p70) – will build and run the cable car, and Boris is so confident his flying gondolas will be a success he's said to be considering a second route linking the North Greenwich Arena to Canary Wharf. No fare structure has been finalised, but Transport for London plans to integrate the service into the Oyster system and forecasts £2.50 singles for Oyster pay-as-you-go (p216) or £3.50 for cash.

Dalston Superstore

*117 Kingland High Street, E8 2PB
(7254 2273). Dalston Kingsland rail.*
Open noon-2am Mon-Fri; 11am-2am
Sat, Sun.
The opening of this gay arts-space-
cum-bar cemented Dalston's status as
the final frontier of east London's gay
scene. It's a confidently cool, New
York-style dive bar split between two
floors, clad in cement, brick and steel
vents, but enlivened with fluoro
flashes, graffiti and art installations.
During the day there's café grub and
Wi-Fi; at night, expect queues for the
impressive and eclectic guest DJs.

Nest

NEW *36 Stoke Newington Road, N16
7XJ (7354 9993, www.ilovethenest.com).
Dalston Kingsland rail.*
Cult venue Bardens Boudoir – a 350-
capacity basement under a disused furniture store in the heart of Turkish
Dalston – reopened as a brighter and
chirpier version last year, controlled by
pub-club pros from the Old Queen's
Head (p171) and Paradise (p187). It programmes out-there line-ups nightly for
the hipsters that love them.

Vortex Jazz Club

*Dalston Culture House, 11 Gillet Street,
N16 8JN (7254 4097, www.vortexjazz.
co.uk). Dalston Kingsland rail.*
The Vortex is on the first floor of a
handsome new-build, with a restaurant
on the ground floor. The space can feel
a bit sterile, but the programming is
superb, packed with left-field talent
from Britain, Europe and the US.
London's most exciting jazz venue.

Docklands

The flagship for finance-led urban
redevelopment under the last Tory
government in an area that had
been thriving docks, Docklands
was for many years a chunk of
barely populated tower blocks
awaiting economic revival.

Nowadays, the northern end of the
Thames peninsula known as the
Isle of Dogs is all shiny megabanks.
West of the Isle of Dogs, among
further decommissioned docks,
ExCeL conference centre (p207)
will host many London 2012 events.

Sights & museums

Museum of London Docklands

*No.1 Warehouse, West India Quay,
Hertsmere Road, E14 4AL (7001
9844, www.museumindocklands.org.
uk). Canary Wharf tube or West India
Quay DLR.* **Open** 10am-6pm daily.
Admission free.
Housed in a 19th-century warehouse
(itself a Grade I-listed building), this
huge sibling of the Museum of London
(p159) provides an excellent introduction to the complex history of London's
docks and the river. Displays over
three storeys take you from the arrival
of the Romans all the way to the docks'
1980s closure and the area's redevelopment. A new exhibition sheds light on
London's shameful involvement in the
transatlantic slave trade.

One Canada Square

Canary Wharf tube/DLR.
Cesar Pelli's dramatic office block was
the country's tallest habitable building
from 1991 to 2010, when it was finally
overtaken by the Shard (p70). It
remains a blank-faced icon of financial
overconfidence, its pyramid roof
instantly recognisable across London.

Thames Barrier Park

*North Woolwich Road, E16 2HP
(www.thamesbarrierpark.org.uk).
Pontoon Dock DLR.*
Crisply beautiful, this was London's
first new park in half a century when
it opened in 2001. It has a lush sunken
garden of waggly hedges and offers
perhaps the best views from land of
the shiny metal fins of the massive
Thames Barrier. A white footbridge,

high above Royal Victoria Dock, brings you here from the ExCeL centre (p207).

Trinity Buoy Wharf

64 Orchard Place, E14 0JW (7515 7153, www.trinitybuoywharf.com). East India DLR. **Open** *Long Player* 11am-5pm Sat, Sun.

In the 1860s, London's only lighthouse was built here to train lighthouse keepers and trial new light technology. The former repairs yard – which has great views of the O2 Arena (p184) on the far bank – now hosts regular art events, and the lighthouse is a permanent home for the meditative sounds of the *Long Player* art installation. There's also a 1940s diner car (7987 4334, www.fatboysdiner.co.uk, 10am-5pm Tue-Sun) and café (8am-3pm Mon-Fri).

Eating & drinking

Yi-Ban

London Regatta Centre, Dockside Road, E16 2QT (7473 6699, www.yi-ban.co.uk). Royal Albert DLR. **Open** noon-11pm Mon-Sat; 11am-10.30pm Sun. **££**. **Chinese**.

Very handy for ExCeL (p207), Yi-Ban has a fun view across Royal Albert Dock to London City Airport (p214). The long room takes cues from hotel dining areas, but the food doesn't have to follow sweet-and-sour pork clichés. Experiment instead with the daytime dim sum, west lake soup or Cantonese-style crispy roast pork belly. The staff are charming, serving the terrific food with style and efficiency.

Olympic Park

East London is where you'll find the six **Host Boroughs**. The **Olympic Park** (below) itself extends into four of them: Hackney, Newham, Tower Hamlets and Waltham Forest. Additional key venues are in Greenwich (pp181-184), while Barking & Dagenham became the final Host Borough in

spring 2011. We suggest a good route along some of the area's many waterways on pp58-60. For architectural highlights and key London 2012 events, see pp8-17; for basic orientation, see pp206-213.

Sights & museums

Olympic Park

Stratford tube/rail/DLR or Pudding Mill DLR (www.london2012.com).

An extraordinary transformation has been made to the mostly derelict, former industrial land between Stratford International station and the River Lea. In just a few years, a cluster of remarkable stadiums have sprung up – impressive in scale and design – as well as the red girders of Anish Kapoor's vast ArcelorMittal Orbit; for our favourites, see pp8-11. The View Tube (see box p182) offers the best vantage point on the site.

Three Mills

Three Mill Lane, E3 3DU (8980 4626, www.housemill.org.uk). Bromley-by-Bow tube. **Tours** May-Oct 1-4pm Sun. *Mar, Apr, Dec* 11am-4pm 1st Sun of mth. **Admission** £3; £1.50 reductions; free under-16s. **No credit cards.**

Just south of the Olympic Park, this pretty island on the River Lea takes its name from the three mills that ground flour and gunpowder here. The House Mill, built in 1776, is the oldest and largest tidal mill in Britain and it is occasionally opened to the public. Even when the House Mill is closed, the island provides pleasant walks that can feel surprisingly rural. Victorian sewer engineer Sir Joseph Bazalgette's extraordinary, Byzantine Abbey Mills Pumping Station can be seen nearby.

Eating & drinking

Container Cafe

View Tube, the Greenway, Marshgate Lane, E15 2PJ (07702 125081 mobile, www.theviewtube.co.uk). Pudding Mill

LONDON BY AREA

Lane DLR. **Open** 9am-4.30pm daily. **£**. **No credit cards. Café**.

Right opposite the Olympic Stadium, this is a perfect location from which to cast your eyes over the Olympic Park while drinking a carefully prepared coffee (see box p182). A pleasant riverbank walk to the north, next door to Forman's Restaurant (below), the Counter Cafe (Stour Space, 7 Roach Road, Fish Island, E3 2PA, 07834 275920 mobile, www.thecountercafe. co.uk) is run by the same cheerful bunch – and has a formidable view of the Stadium across the river.

Forman's Restaurant

Stour Road, Fish Island, E3 2PA (8525 2365, www.formans.co.uk/restaurant). Pudding Mill Lane DLR or Hackney Wick rail. **Open** *Restaurant* 7-11pm Thur, Fri; 9am-noon, 7-11pm Sat; noon-4pm Sun. *Gallery Bar* 5-9pm Thur, Fri; noon-5pm Sat, Sun. **££-£££**. **British**.
Come here to enjoy a truly local speciality in a truly amazing setting: London-cure smoked salmon, made in the East End in the same way since 1905, scoffed in plain view of the Olympic Park. The rather posh restaurant and cafe-bar serve buckwheat blinis with the salmon, as well as other seasonal produce such as smoked eel and Hampshire buffalo mozzarella.

Hackney Pearl

11 Prince Edward Road, E9 5LX (8510 3605, www.thehackneypearl. com). Hackney Wick rail. **Open** 10am-11pm Tue-Sun. **££**. **Café-bar**.
Hackney Pearl is a friendly neighbourhood hangout, with the owners having made something special out of not very much. Two shop units in a post-industrial enclave between Victoria Park and the Lea Navigation have been enlivened by furniture that seems salvaged from a groovy thrift shop – colourful rugs, Formica tables and old dressers – and a compact menu that lists simple but imaginative food, with an eastern European slant.

Shopping

Westfield Stratford City

NEW *http://uk.westfield.com/stratford city. Stratford tube/DLR/rail.*
Due to open as this guide hits the shelves, Westfield will steal its own crown, as the £1.45bn Stratford City overtakes its predecessor Westfield London as Europe's largest urban mall. Over three levels and 1.9m sq ft of space, the centre will contain 300 shops (including high-street staples John Lewis and Marks & Spencer) and 50 eateries (Wagamama and Nando's among them), as well as a 17-screen Vue multiplex, Britain's largest casino and three brand-new hotels. It will also be the key gateway into the Games: 70% of spectators are expected to pass through on the way from the station.

Arts & leisure

Just east of Stratford International station, **Theatre Square** has a little cluster of entertainment venues: a multiplex, the Stratford Circus arts venue (0844 357 2625, www.stratford-circus.com) and the Theatre Royal Stratford East.

Theatre Royal Stratford East

Gerry Raffles Square, E15 1BN (8534 0310, www.stratfordeast.com). Stratford tube/rail/DLR.
The Theatre Royal is a community theatre, with many shows written, directed and performed by black or Asian artists. Musicals are big here – *The Harder They Come* went on to West End success – but there's also a fine comedy night, the Christmas pantomime and some harder-hitting fare.

Greenwich

Greenwich is laden with centuries of royal and maritime heritage. The most easterly of London's UNESCO World Heritage Sites – and with the

LONDON BY AREA

Grandstand Seats

Look out over the Olympic Park from the View Tube.

If you wanted contemporary east London packed up in a box, this would be it – and what a brightly coloured box it is. Made out of recycled metal shipping containers and painted a vivid yellow-green, the **View Tube** (www.theviewtube.co.uk) is carefully placed on a ridge a short walk from Pudding Mill Lane DLR to provide the best possible vantage on the Olympic Park.

Almost in touching distance is the Populous-designed Olympic Stadium, on your right is Zaha Hadid's low-slung Aquatics Centre, and between them you can see the distant Velodrome and Basketball Arena. Handy boards show the layout of the park and explain how it was all built.

View Tube combines its ace setting with a commitment to the local community (upstairs, a 'Classroom with a View' welcomes school trips) and local producers (Beetroot & Culture veg, H Forman smoked salmon in the cream cheese bagels), which supply the excellent café.

Appropriately named, the **Container Café** is furnished with blue stools that echo the angular London 2012 logo, but all eyes are on the floor-to-ceiling windows looking out over the Park. Spare a glance, though, for the short blackboard list of hot eats (bacon baguette and homemade relish, pie, soup of the day) and drinks (coffee from Square Mile beans). Further temptations rest on the counter: chocolate brownies, appealingly overstuffed savoury croissants. It's usually busy, but also very relaxed and cheerful.

Since soon after opening, all East End life has been here. On sunny days cyclists troop in for cookies and walking families scoff toast and scrambled eggs. Mostly Antipodean baristas turn out top-quality flat whites and long blacks, while the visitors take in the view.

Getting here from the DLR stop is easy: follow the signs marking pedestrian and cycle access. But it's also fun to approach along the Greenway. For one possible route, see our Itinerary on pp58-60.

shimmering riverside colonnades of the Old Royal Naval College one of the most breathtaking – it merits a day's exploration by itself. Those visiting **Greenwich Park** for the London 2012 Equestrian events are certainly set for a good day out.

Sights & museums

Cutty Sark

NEW *King William Walk, SE10 9HT (www.cuttysark.org.uk). Cutty Sark DLR or Greenwich DLR/rail.*
The *Cutty Sark* is to reopen in spring 2012, fully patched up after surviving a serious fire in 2007. Built in Scotland in 1869, this tea clipper was the quickest in the business when it was launched in 1870, but steam soon overtook sail and it was retired in the 1950s to this dry dock. Despite the fire, the vessel will be 90 per cent original, with figurehead, masts, rigging and coach house intact, and is to be raised ten feet above the ground, so visitors for the first time will enter from beneath.

Discover Greenwich & Old Royal Naval College

2 Cutty Sark Gardens, SE10 9LW (8269 4799, www.oldroyalnavalcollege. org.uk). Cutty Sark DLR. **Open** 10am-5pm daily. **Admission** free.
Designed by Wren in 1694, with Hawksmoor and Vanbrugh helping to complete it, the Old Royal Naval College was originally a hospital for seamen, with pensioners living here from 1705 to 1869, when the complex became the Royal Naval College. The public are allowed into the impressive rococo chapel, where there are free organ recitals, and the Painted Hall, a tribute to William and Mary that took Sir James Thornhill 19 years to complete. In 2010, the Pepys Building (the block of the Naval College nearest the *Cutty Sark*, the pier and Cutty Sark DLR) reopened as the excellent Discover Greenwich. It's full of focused, informative exhibits on the

surrounding buildings, the life of the pensioners, Tudor royalty and so forth, delivered with a real sense of fun: while grown-ups read about scagliola (a fake stone building material), the kids can try on a knight's helmet. There's also a shop and tourist information (p221).

National Maritime Museum

Romney Road, SE10 9NF (8858 4422, 8312 6565 information, www.nmm.ac.uk). Cutty Sark DLR or Greenwich DLR/rail. **Open** 10am-5pm daily. **Admission** free; donations appreciated.
The world's largest maritime museum contains a huge store of creatively organised art, cartography, models and regalia, telling the stories of great sea expeditions back to medieval times, and displaying such artefacts as Nelson's uniform, complete with fatal bullet-hole. There are also fine interactives: the Bridge is a fun ship simulator, and you can also load cargo or try out being a ship's gunner.

In summer 2011, the opening of £35m Sammy Ofer Wing marks the start of a five-year transformation of the museum. It provides a new main entrance into Greenwich Park, towards the Royal Observatory, as well as a restaurant-cafe, archive and digital lounge (view the logbook of the man who killed Blackbeard) and a multimedia exhibit tracing Britain's seaborne life from the 16th century, with sound, video and a 30m wall of objects (among them Drake's sun jewel).

From the museum a colonnaded walkway leads to the Queen's House (8312 6565), designed by Inigo Jones and holding art by Hogarth and Gainsborough. At the top of the hill in the park, the Royal Observatory and Flamsteed House (8312 6565, www.rog. nmm.ac.uk; £10, free-£7.50 reductions) are also part of the museum – you can straddle the Prime Meridian Line or take in a star show in the Planetarium (£6.50, £4.50 reductions).

Eating & drinking

Old Brewery

Pepys Building, Old Royal Naval College, SE10 9LW (3327 1280, www. oldbrewerygreenwich.com). Cutty Sark DLR. **Open** 10am-10.30pm daily. **££**. **Modern British/microbrewery**.

The Meantime Brewing Company, creator of unusual artisan beers that have won international awards, runs the microbrewery, pub and café-diner in Discover Greenwich (p183), on the site of a 1717 brewery. Here you can enjoy authentic, historical brews – such as the London Porter – from a selection of around 50 beers on draught or bottled, listed by style, and a menu that runs from pickled herring with vinegary spring vegetables and mussels to neck of mutton with purple sprouting broccoli, new potatoes and anchovy sauce.

Nightlife

O2 Arena & IndigO2

Millennium Way, SE10 0BB (8463 2000 information, 0844 856 0202 box office, www.theo2.co.uk). North Greenwich tube.

Since its launch in 2007, this conversion of the Millennium Dome has been a huge success. The O2 Arena – a state-of-the-art, 23,000-capacity enormodome with good acoustics and sightlines – hosts the headline rock and pop acts. Its little brother, Indigo2, isn't actually that little (capacity 2,350) but is a good fit for big soul, funk and pop-jazz acts (Roy Ayers, Stacey Kent), old pop stars (Gary Numan, Ultravox) and all points between. Thames Clippers (p217) run half hourly back into town.

Proud2

NEW *O2 Arena, Peninsula Square, SE10 0DX (8463 3070, www.proud2. com). North Greenwich tube.*

The most ambitious of the growing network of Proud nightlife venues (including Proud Cabaret in the City and Proud Camden, p170), Proud2 has had a blinding kaleidoscopic paint job, laid on £2 shuttle buses to central London and created a Vegas-style night out. From plush seating – even the beds circling the new outside bar – to the multisensory carnival within, few London clubs have been this bold on this scale. See box right.

Brixton & Vauxhall

The key hub in south London, **Brixton** has been through its troubles (the 30th anniversary of the 1981 race riots brought recent progress in the area into sharp focus), but is now a vibrant area. Right on the river to the north of Brixton, anonymous **Vauxhall** – central, but pretty much off the radar on the wrong side of the river from Westminster (p78) – has some of the fiercest gay nightlife in the city: Fire (below) never seems to close, and RVT (right) is an iconic alt-cabaret venue. To the west in **Battersea**, the BAC (right) is a hotbed of exciting new theatre.

Eating & drinking

Franco Manca

4 Market Row, Electric Lane, SW9 8LD (7738 3021, www.francomanca.co.uk). Brixton tube/rail. **Open** noon-5pm Mon-Sat. **£**. **Pizza**.

Franco Manca is the sort of discreet place you might walk past while ogling the Afro-Caribbean goodies in the surrounding market. Don't. It uses well-sourced, quality ingredients (many organic), top-notch equipment and good sourdough bases, quickly baked at high temperatures in the Neopolitan manner to seal in the flavour and lock in the moisture of the crust.

Nightlife

Fire

South Lambeth Road, SW8 1UQ (www. fireclub.co.uk). Vauxhall tube/rail.

Craving clubs full of shirts-off muscle boys going at night-and-day techno? For a number of years the 'Vauxhall Village' has been destination of choice for hardcore gay clubbers, the sort who think nothing of starting on Friday and finding themselves still dancing on Monday, but key venues such as Fire now host dance nights for hedonists of any sexual persuasion. The Lightbox here is an all-round LED sensation.

Plan B

418 Brixton Road, SW9 7AY (7733 0926, www.plan-brixton.co.uk). Brixton tube/rail.
It may be small, but Plan B is very cool. Since reopening after a fire a few years back, packing a delicious Funktion 1 Soundsystem, the flow of top-notch hip hop and funk stars just hasn't stopped. Community, Plan B's Saturday night shindig, is an absolute beauty.

RVT

372 Kennington Lane, SE11 5HY (7820 1222, www.rvt.org.uk). Vauxhall tube/rail. **Open** 7pm-midnight Mon, Wed, Thur; 6pm-midnight Tue; 7pm-2am Fri; 9pm-2am Sat; 2pm-midnight Sun. **Admission** £5-£7.
If you're seeking a very London gay experience, the Royal Vauxhall Tavern is where to start. It operates a famously broad, anything-goes booking policy, but there are some fixtures: Saturday's alt-cabaret performance night Duckie (www.duckie.co.uk) might range from strip cabaret to rude puppets.

Arts & leisure

BAC

Lavender Hill, SW11 5TN (7223 2223, www.bac.org.uk). Clapham Common tube, Clapham Junction rail or bus 77, 77A, 345.
Housed in the old town hall, the forward-thinking Battersea Arts Centre hosts young theatre troupes – increasingly literally, with bedrooms installed to facilitate artist collaboration. Expect

Superclub Revival?

Proud2 and Pulse arrive.

Chandeliers hang over the dancefloor, while Daft Punk blares from the soundsystem and scantily clad women and men in suits strain to see a burlesque act slinking around on a podium. Gilded lions line every surface. Busty bar staff whose outfits Ann Summers would be proud of dish out shots. Room two is a children's playpen filled with UV polka dots, roller-skating hostesses and hula-hooping dancers. It's a bizarre setting – and it's even more bizarre to think that this new vision of gaudy glam was Fabric's concrete dream-club, Matter.

Such is the ever-evolving nature of London nightlife. Just when Ministry of Sound (p76) and Fabric (p157) looked like they were the only big nightclubs that could survive and everyone's attentions had turned to east London's raw and intimate basement clubs– spring 2011 saw two new nightclubs bring Ibiza-size hedonism to town.

At the O2 Arena, Matter is now **Proud2** (left), run on Fridays and Saturdays by the people who own **Proud Camden** (p170) and Proud Cabaret. Meanwhile, under Blackfriars Bridge in Southwark, London's largest state-of-the-art club space, **Pulse** (p76), opened with Erick Morillo's Voodoo Nights. Together, they have a capacity of nearly 7,000.

The era of the superclubs may be over, but the age of ambitious clubbing certainly isn't.

quirky, fun and physical theatre from the likes of cult companies Kneehigh and 1927. There are also exciting festivals that combine theatre and performance art, or showcase stand-up comedy and spoken word.

Notting Hill

Notting Hill Gate, Ladbroke Grove and Westbourne Park tube stations form a triangle that contains lovely squares, grand houses and fine gardens, along with shops, bars and restaurants that serve the kind of bohemian who can afford to live here. Off Portobello Road are the boutiques of Westbourne Grove and Ledbury Road.

Sights & museums

Museum of Brands, Packaging & Advertising

Colville Mews, Lonsdale Road, W11 2AR (7908 0880, www.museumof brands.com). Notting Hill Gate tube. **Open** 10am-6pm Tue-Sat; 11am-5pm Sun. **Admission** £6.50; free-£4 reductions.
Robert Opie began collecting the things others throw away when he was 16. Over the years the collection has grown to include milk bottles, vacuum cleaners and cereal packets. The emphasis is on British consumerism through the last century, though there are items as old as an ancient Egyptian doll.

Eating & drinking

Hereford Road

3 Hereford Road, W2 4AB (7727 1144, www.herefordroad.org). Bayswater tube. **Open** noon-3pm, 6-10.30pm Mon-Fri; noon-3.30pm, 6-10.30pm Sat; noon-4pm, 6-10pm Sun. **££. British**.
Hereford Road has real self-assurance, even though its only been around a few years. It's an easy place in which to relax, with a mixed crowd and a happy

buzz. Starters include the likes of (undyed) smoked haddock with white beans and leeks, while mains might feature mallard cooked with braised chicory and lentils.

Ledbury

127 Ledbury Road, W11 2AQ (7792 9090, www.theledbury.com). Westbourne Park tube. **Open** noon-2.30pm, 6.30-10.30pm Mon-Sat; noon-3pm, 7-10pm Sun. **£££. French**.
Notting Hillites flock to this elegant gastronomic masterpiece, where the food is as adventurous and accomplished as any, but less expensive than many. Flavours are delicate but intense, often powerfully earthy. A well-priced, top-quality wine list too.

Portobello Star

171 Portobello Road, W11 2DY (7229 8016). Ladbroke Grove tube. **Open** 11am-11pm Mon-Thur; 11am-12.30am Fri; 10am-12.30am Sat; 11am-11.30pm Sun. **Cocktail bar**.
Fronted by a couple of pavement tables, Portobello Star is just a long, thin room, but it's a handsome space, more appealing than it seems at first. The USPs are the likeable bartenders' convincing renditions of cocktails both traditional (a richly flavourful mint julep, a margarita modified by agave) and modern (Dick Bradsell's Bramble). You may have to shout to make yourself heard when the DJs crank it up – the music policy bounces from generic indie to more danceable tunes.

Shopping

The strip of boutiques along **Ledbury Road** is shopping catnip for yummy mummies – but Wolf & Badger (right) is our current favourite. Due west of Notting Hill is the 46-acre **Westfield London** shopping mall (Ariel Way, W12 7GF, 7333 8118, www.westfield.com/london), predecessor to the new Westfield Stratford City (p181) and packed with shops and restaurants.

Mary's Living & Giving Shop

NEW *177 Westbourne Grove, W11 2SB (7727 6166, www.savethechildren.org. uk). Notting Hill Gate tube.* **Open** 11am-7pm Mon-Sat; noon-5pm Sun.

Part of an ongoing project with Save the Children, TV star shopper Mary Portas has rebranded one of the organisation's west London sites to create an extraordinarily popular shop that's more boutique than bargain basement. It's had donations from labels Acne, Stella McCartney, Agent Provocateur and Paul Smith, plus celebs including Lauren Laverne. The vintage Chanel bag collection (from £699 each) is a cult favourite with the posh local shoppers.

Portobello Road Market

Portobello Road, Notting Hill, W10 (www.portobelloroad.co.uk). Ladbroke Grove or Notting Hill Gate tube. **Open** 8am-6.30pm Mon-Wed, Fri, Sat; 8am-1pm Thur. *Antiques* 4am-4pm Fri, Sat. No credit cards.

Portobello is always busy, but fun. Antiques start at the Notting Hill end, further down are food stalls, and emerging designer and vintage clothes congregate under the Westway and along the walkway to Ladbroke Grove on Fridays (usually marginally quieter) and Saturdays (invariably manic). Portobello also has fine shops, such as Honest Jon's record emporium (no.278), approaching 40 years in the business.

Wolf & Badger

NEW *Wolf & Badger, 46 Ledbury Road, W11 2AB (7229 5698, www. wolfandbadger.com). Notting Hill Gate tube.* **Open** 10am-6pm Mon-Sat; 11am-5pm Sun.

This new concept boutique has a somewhat rare philosophy – to bypass well-known luxury labels and showcase young designers instead. Retail space is rented out to fledgling labels, who gain business advice on how to grow their brand while being snapped up by style-savvy west Londoners. Owners

Samir Ceric and Zoë Knight have excellent style credentials – one is a gallery owner, the other designs accessories.

Nightlife

Notting Hill Arts Club

21 Notting Hill Gate, Notting Hill, W11 3JQ (7460 4459, www.nottinghillarts club.com). Notting Hill Gate tube.

Cool west London folk are grateful for this small basement club. It isn't much to look at, but somehow almost single-handedly keeps this side of town on the radar thanks to nights like Thursday's yOyO – for fans of crate-digging, from funk to 1980s boogie.

Paradise

19 Kilburn Lane, W10 4AE (8969 0098, www.theparadise.co.uk). Kensal Green tube or Kensal Rise rail. **Open** noon-midnight Mon-Wed; noon-1am Thur; noon-2am Fri, Sat; noon-11.30pm Sun.

A mile north of Notting Hill is perhaps London's finest exponent of the art of pub-clubbing. This is Paradise, a place that manages to be relaxed and cool, thanks to canny promotion work by DJ Tayo. Themed supper clubs, vintage burlesque shows and kicking rave-ups make it more than just a good local spot – it's a destination in its own right.

Arts & leisure

Lyric Hammersmith

Lyric Square, King Street, W6 0QL (0871 221 1722, www.lyric.co.uk). Hammersmith tube.

Hammersmith, south-west of Notting Hill, is hardly a glamorous bit of town, but the Lyric is a theatre people will cross the city for. Artistic director Sean Holmes has brought writers back to the Lyric, making space for neglected modern classics and new plays alongside the cutting-edge physical and devised work for which the theatre had become known. The roof terrace bar is a real attraction in good weather.

Hampstead Heath

Worth the Trip

North

Hampstead Heath

Hampstead tube or Hampstead Heath rail.

The trees and grassy hills of the heath make it a surprisingly wild patch of the metropolis. Aside from the pleasure of walking, sitting and even swimming in the ponds, there's Kenwood House/ Iveagh Bequest (Hampstead Lane, 8348 1286, www.english-heritage.org.uk), every inch the stately pile. Built in 1616, it was bought by brewing magnate Edward Guinness, who donated his brilliant art collection in 1927. Highlights include a Rembrandt self-portrait.

Lee Valley White Water Centre

NEW *Station Road, Waltham Cross, Herts EN9 1AB (0845 677 0606, www.gowhitewater.co.uk). Liverpool Street tube/rail to Waltham Cross rail (25min journey).*
See box p190.

North-west

Wembley Stadium

Stadium Way, Wembley, Middx HA9 0WS (0844 980 8001, www.wembley stadium.com). Wembley Park tube or Wembley Stadium rail.

Reopened in 2007, this 90,000-seater stadium is impressive, its steel arch an imposing feature on the skyline. It's a very appropriate venue for London 2012 – get a flavour of the heritage on one of the stadium guided tours.

South-west

Hampton Court Palace

East Molesey, Surrey KT8 9AU (0844 482 7777, www.hrp.org.uk). Hampton Court rail, or riverboat from Richmond or Westminster to Hampton Court Pier (Apr-Oct). **Open** *Palace Apr-Oct 10am-6pm daily; Nov-Mar 10am-4.30pm daily.* **Admission** *Palace, courtyard, cloister & maze £14; free-£11.50 reductions; £38 family.*

Maze £3.50; *free*-£2.50 *reductions.*
Gardens Apr-Oct £4.60; *free*-£4
reductions; *Nov-Mar free.*

A half-hour train ride from central London, this is a spectacular palace, once owned by Henry VIII. It was built in 1514 and for 200 years was a focal point of English history: Shakespeare gave his first performance to James I here in 1604; and, after the Civil War, Oliver Cromwell was so besotted by the building he moved in. Centuries later, the rosy walls of the palace still dazzle. Its vast size can be daunting, so take advantage of the costumed guided tours. The Tudor Kitchens are great fun, with their giant cauldrons and fake pies, and the exquisitely landscaped gardens contain fine topiary and the famous maze. One of the free events for London 2012, the Cycling Road Time Trial, starts and finishes here.

Royal Botanic Gardens (Kew Gardens)

*Kew, Richmond, Surrey TW9 3AB
(8332 5655, www.kew.org). Kew
Gardens tube/rail, Kew Bridge rail or
riverboat to Kew Pier.* **Open** *Apr-Aug*
9.30am-6.30pm Mon-Fri; 9.30am-7.30pm
Sat, Sun. *Sept, Oct* 9.30am-6pm daily.
Nov-Jan 9.30am-4.15pm daily. *Feb,
Mar* 9.30am-5.30pm daily. **Admission**
£13.50; *free*-£11.50 reductions.

The unparalleled collection of plants at Kew was begun by Queen Caroline, wife of George II, with exotic plants brought back by voyaging botanists (Charles Darwin among them). In 1759, 'Capability' Brown was employed by George III to improve on the work of his predecessors, setting the template for a garden that attracts thousands of visitors each year. Head straight for the 19th-century greenhouses, filled to the roof with tropical plants, and next door the Waterlily House's quiet and pretty indoor pond (closed in winter). Brown's Rhododendron Dell is at its best in spring, while the Xstrata Treetop Walkway, some 60ft above the ground, is terrific fun among autumn leaves.

Wimbledon Lawn Tennis Museum

*Museum Building, All England Lawn
Tennis Club, Church Road, SW19 5AE
(8946 6131, www.wimbledon.org/
museum). Southfields tube or bus 39,
493.* **Open** 10am-5pm daily; ticket
holders only during championships.
Admission £18; *free*-£15.75 reductions.

This museum on the history of tennis has a 200° screen that simulates playing on Centre Court and a re-creation of a 1980s men's dressing room, complete with 'ghost' of John McEnroe. The ticket price includes a behind-the-scenes tour: you can admire Centre Court's new retractable roof, which will permit extended evening play – as well as preventing rain delays – for both the annual Wimbledon tournament and the London 2012 Tennis competition.

WWT Wetland Centre

*Queen Elizabeth's Walk, Barnes,
SW13 9WT (8409 4400, www.wwt.
org.uk/london). Hammersmith tube
then 33, 72, 209 or 283 bus.* **Open**
Summer 9.30am-6pm daily. *Winter*
9.30am-5pm daily. *Tours* 11am, 2pm
daily. *Feeding tours* 3pm daily.
Admission £9.95; *free*-£7.40
reductions; £27.75 family.

Reclaimed from industrial reservoirs a decade ago, the 43-acre wetland reserve is four miles from central London, but feels a world away. Quiet ponds, rushes, rustling reeds and wildflower gardens all teem with bird life – some 150 species – as well as the now very rare water vole. Naturalists ponder its 27,000 trees and 300,000 aquatic plants and swoon over 300 varieties of butterfly, 20 types of dragonfly and four species of bat (now sleeping in a stylish new house designed by Turner Prize-winning artist Jeremy Deller). You can explore water-recycling initiatives in the RBC Rain Garden or check out the new interactive Pond Safari and Down the Plughole exhibits. Traditionalists needn't be scared – plain old pairs of binoculars can be hired.

Ride the White Water

The first London 2012 venue has opened to the public.

Think of a challenging white water rafting or kayaking course and Zambia's Zambezi or the Whataroa in New Zealand might spring to mind. But London's Lee Valley Park? We spoke about it to GB Slalom kayaker and 2012 hopeful Huw Swetnam, who helped to develop the **Lee Valley White Water Centre** (p188) and trains here every day. 'The centre's the best [artificial] white water facility in Britain and one of the best in the world,' he told us. 'It imitates some of the best natural white water rivers, such as the Etive in Scotland, the Grandtully course on the Tay, and the Tryweryn in Wales.' Swetnam explained that the course is special because you can change the features to make it harder or easier to negotiate.

Even better, the site of the London 2012 Canoe Slalom contests is the only new venue open to the public in the run-up to the Games. It offers exhilarating half-day sessions of rafting for £49. Booking ahead is essential – and you'll have to be quick: the

centre closes for the Games at the end of September.

The centre, which cost £35m to build, looks impressive. As well as the two water courses (the public get to use the 300m Standard Competition Course, with the 160m Legacy Loop reserved for training), there's a roomy wood-decked viewing terrace that traps sunlight all day. Finishing touches to the site will include landscaping and the addition of 12,000 temporary grandstand seats.

The course for the Games is 300m from start to finish and has a 5.5m drop. Five powerful machines pump up to 15,000 litres of water per second, so there's plenty of white froth. The rapids are equivalent to a grade three or four river, but because the course isn't as long as a river, public rafting sessions involve four or five runs that take about an hour and a half. And there's no hauling the boat up a steep bank – one of the best bits is the giant conveyer that takes you and your canoe or raft to the starting pool.

Essentials

Hoxton Hotel p202

Hotels

Given general gloom about the British economy, London's hotel sector is extremely buoyant, with numerous openings looking to supply beds for visitors to the capital for the London 2012 Olympic & Paralympic Games and, before that, the Queen's Diamond Jubilee in June. For some succinct advice about booking your room for the Games, see **Essentials: The 2012 Games** (p211).

The luxury end of the market has been especially busy. Two very different new hotels are up and running on central Leicester Square (**St John Hotel**, p200; **W London**, p201), the **Savoy** (p201) is back in business after years of diligent restoration, and the **St Pancras Renaissance** (see box p198) has finally reopened after its own painstaking process of refurbishment. Further exciting openings as we go to press include

the Dorchester's luxury offering **45 Park Lane** (p199).

Mid-range business hotels are also booming: a superb new addition is the **Mint Tower of London** (p203) and the fabulous Townhouse extension to the **Zetter** (p203) is looking lovely. Meanwhile, an opening to watch out for in this price bracket is **Ecclestone Square** (p194).

The sheer amount of activity is pushing hoteliers into surprising new parts of town – the **Town Hall Hotel** (p205) is a great example, opening in historically unfashionable Bethnal Green – and has driven up quality, especially at the top of the market. The 195-room Shangri-La, opening in the **Shard** (p70) in early 2012, is likely to intensify competition at the superluxe end of the market.

Pressure is also beginning to build on prices: the stylish budget category, in which the **Hoxton** has had few credible competitors (see box p204), may get a shake up: the 'Tiny' rooms (their own, and justified, description) at the superb **Dean Street** (p197) start from £90, while rates at its equally good new sister **Shoreditch Rooms** (p203) start at £75.

One trend we've enjoyed in the last couple of years has been what you might term 'B&B deluxe'. **40 Winks** (p204) is only the artiest addition to a field that already includes **Rough Luxe** (p200) and the **Fox & Anchor** (p202).

Still, you can't expect bargains in London: there is good value to be found, but to get a room that's genuinely cheap you'll either have to book months in advance, drop your standards or get online and trust to last-minute deals.

Money matters

When visitors moan about London prices (you know you do), their case is strongest when it comes to hotels. The average room rate has been dipping somewhat, but the signs are that it will rise steeply in advance of the London 2012 Games before stabilising. In any case, we reckon any decent double averaging under £120 a night is good value: hence, **£** in the listings below represents a rack rate of around £100 and below. Hotels do offer special deals, though, notably at weekends; check their websites or ask when you book, and also look at discount websites such as www.lastminute.com, www.london-discount-hotel.com or www.alpharooms.com.

The South Bank

Bermondsey Square Hotel
Bermondsey Square, Tower Bridge Road, SE1 3UN (0870 111 2525,

---

SHORTLIST

Best new
- Mint Tower of London (p203)
- St John Hotel (p200)
- St Pancras Renaissance (see box p198)
- Shoreditch Rooms (p203)
- W Leicester Square (p201)

All-round winners
- Claridge's (p197)
- Covent Garden Hotel (p197)
- Dean Street Townhouse & Dining Room (p197)

Best for old London
- Connaught (p197)
- Fox & Anchor (p202)
- Hazlitt's (p199)

Affordable style
- Hoxton Hotel (p202)
- Lux Pod (p196)
- Shoreditch Rooms (p203)

Best eating & sleeping
- Albion at the Boundary (p202)
- Bistrot Bruno Loubet at the Zetter (p203)
- St John Hotel (p200)
- Viajante at the Town Hall Hotel (p205)

Best hotel bars
- Connaught (p197)
- Zetter Townhouse (p203)

Best bargains
- Designer rooms at the Hoxton Hotel (see box p204)
- 'Tiny' rooms at Dean Street Townhouse (p197)
- Weekend stays at the Fox & Anchor (p202)
- Weekend suites at Mint Westminster (p194)

Best hostels
- Clink78 (p197)
- YHA Central (p201)

ESSENTIALS

www.bespokehotels.com). Borough tube or London Bridge tube/rail. **££**.

This is a deliberately kitsch new-build on a newly developed square. Suites are named after the heroines of psychedelic rock classics (Lucy, Lily and so on), there are classic discs on the walls, and you can kick your heels from the suspended Bubble Chair at reception. But, although occupants of the Lucy suite get a multi-person jacuzzi (with a great terrace view), and anyone can get sex toys from reception, the real draw isn't the gimmicks – it's well-designed rooms for competitive prices. The Brit food restaurant-bar is a bit hit-or-miss, but the hotel's pretty and the cheerful staff are helpful.

Park Plaza County Hall

1 Addington Street, SE1 7RY (7021 1800, www.parkplaza.com). Lambeth North tube or Waterloo tube/rail. **££**.
From the tube the approach is rather grimy, but this enthusiastically – if somewhat haphazardly – run hotel is well located just behind County Hall. Each room has its own kitchenette (microwave, sink), room sizes aren't bad (floor-to-ceiling windows help them feel bigger) and there's a handsomely vertiginous atrium, into which you peer down on the restaurant from infrequent glass lifts. The huge new Park Plaza Westminster Bridge has now opened just across the road.

Premier Inn London County Hall

County Hall, Belvedere Road, SE1 7PB (0870 238 3300, www.premierinn. com). Waterloo tube/rail. **££**.
A position right by the London Eye (p67) and friendly, efficient staff make this refurbished chain hotel the acceptable face of budget convenience. Check-in is quick; rooms are spacious, clean and warm, with comfortable beds and decent bathrooms with good showers, although some are quite dark. Buffet-style breakfast is extra and wireless internet access costs £10 a day.

Ecclestone Square Hotel

NEW *37 Ecclestone Square, SW1V 1PB (3489 1000, www.ecclestonesquare hotel.com). Pimlico tube or Victoria tube/rail.* **£££**.
Due to open as this guide goes to press, this Grade II-listed Georgian house has been transformed to the tune of £6.5m into an ultra-modern boutique hotel. The focus is on high-spec technology – with 46-inch 3D flatscreens, an iPad2 to control the room environment and electronically adjustable Hastens beds in each of the 39 rooms.

Haymarket Hotel

1 Suffolk Place, St James's, SW1Y 4BP (7470 4000, www.firmdale.com). Piccadilly Circus tube. **££££**.
A terrific addition to Kit Kemp's Firmdale portfolio, this block-size building was designed by John Nash, the architect of Regency London. The public spaces are a delight, with Kemp's trademark combination of contemporary arty surprises (a giant lightbulb over the library's chessboard, a gothic little paper-cut of layered skulls above the free afternoon canapés) and impossible-to-leave, acid green, plump, floral sofas. Wow-factors include the bling basement swimming pool and bar (shiny sofas, twinkly roof) and the couldn't-be-more central location.

Mint Westminster

30 John Islip Street, Westminster, SW1P 4DD (7630 1000, www.mint hotel.com). Pimlico tube. **£££**.
There's nothing particularly flashy about this rebranded chain, but it is neatly designed, well run and obliging: the rooms have all the added extras you'd want (iMacs, CD/DVD library for your in-room player, wireless internet, flatscreen TVs) and the floor-to-ceiling windows mean that river-facing suites on the 12th and 13th floors have superb

ESSENTIALS

Haymarket Hotel

night views – when the business people go home for the weekend you might grab one at a bargain rate.

Trafalgar

2 Spring Gardens, Westminster, SW1A 2TS (7870 2900, www.thetrafalgar. com). Charing Cross tube/rail. **£££**.
In an imposing building, the Trafalgar is a Hilton – but you'd hardly notice. The mood is young and dynamic at what was the chain's first 'concept' hotel. To the right of the open reception is the cocktail bar, with DJs most nights, while breakfast downstairs is accompanied by gentle live music. The good-sized rooms (a few corner suites look into Trafalgar Square) have a masculine feel, with white walls and walnut furniture.

South Kensington & Chelsea

B+B Belgravia

64-66 Ebury Street, Belgravia, SW1W 9QD (7259 8570, www.bb-belgravia. com). Victoria tube/rail. **££**.
B+B Belgravia have taken the B&B experience to a new level, although you pay a bit more for the privilege of staying somewhere with a cosy lounge that's full of white and black contemporary furnishings. It's sophisticated and fresh without being hard-edged, and there are all kinds of goodies to make you feel at home: an espresso machine for 24/7 caffeine, an open fireplace, newspapers and DVDs.

Gore

190 Queen's Gate, South Kensington, SW7 5EX (7584 6601, www.gorehotel. com). South Kensington tube. **££££**.
This fin-de-siècle period piece was founded by descendants of Captain Cook in two grand Victorian town houses. The lobby and staircase are close hung with old paintings, and the bedrooms all have carved oak beds, sumptuous drapes and old books. The suites are spectacular: the Tudor Room has a huge stone-faced fireplace and a minstrels' gallery; tragedy queens love the Venus room, with Judy Garland's old bed and replica ruby slippers.

Halkin

Halkin Street, Belgravia, SW1X 7DJ (7333 1000, www.halkin.como.bz). Hyde Park Corner tube. **££££**.
Gracious and discreet behind a Georgian-style façade, Christina Ong's first hotel (a sister to the more famous Metropolitan) was well ahead of the

ESSENTIALS

East-meets-West design trend when it opened in 1991 and its subtle marriage of European luxury and oriental serenity looks more current than hotels half its age. Off curving black corridors, each room has a touchscreen bedside console to control everything from the 'Do not disturb' sign to the air-con.

Lanesborough

1 Lanesborough Place, Knightsbridge, SW1X 7TA (7259 5599, www. lanesborough.com). Hyde Park Corner tube. **£££££**.

Considered one of London's historic luxury hotels, the Lanesborough was in fact impressively redeveloped only in the 1990s. Occupying an 1820s Greek Revival hospital building, its luxurious guest rooms are traditionally decorated (antique furniture, Carrera-marble bathrooms) but with electronic keypads to change the air-con or call on the superb 24hr room service. Rates include high-speed internet, movies and calls within the EU and to the US; complimentary personalised business cards state you are resident here.

Lux Pod

38 Gloucester Road, South Kensington, SW7 4QT (7460 3171, www.theluxpod. com). Gloucester Road tube. **££**.

This little hideaway is the pride and joy of its owner, Judith Abraham, with many of the features purpose-designed. Little is the operative word: it's a tiny space that ingeniously packs in a bathroom, slide-top kitchenette and lounge, with the comfy bed high up above the bathroom and accessible only by a heavy ladder. All is shiny and modern, and the room is packed with gadgets and high-style details. The tight space is ideal for one, a little bit fiddly to get round for two, but terrific fun for any design fan, tech-geek or traveller bored of samey hotels.

Morgan House

120 Ebury Street, Belgravia, SW1W 9QQ (7730 2384, www.morganhouse. co.uk). Pimlico tube or Victoria tube/ rail. **£**.

The Morgan has the understated charm of the old family home of a posh but unpretentious English friend: a pleasing mix of nice old wooden or traditional iron beds, pretty floral curtains and coverlets in subtle hues, the odd chandelier or big gilt mirror over original mantelpieces, padded wicker chairs and sinks in every bedroom. Though there's no guest lounge, guests can sit in the little patio garden.

Number Sixteen

16 Sumner Place, South Kensington, SW7 3EG (7589 5232, www.firmdale. com). South Kensington tube. **£££**.

This may be Firmdale's most affordable hotel, but there's no slacking in style – witness the fresh flowers and origami-ed birdbook decorations in the comfy drawing room, with its inviting fireplace. Bedrooms are generously sized, bright and light, and carry the Kit Kemp trademark mix of bold and traditional. By the time you finish breakfast in the sweet and calming conservatory, which looks out on the delicious back garden with its central water feature, you'll have forgotten you're in the city.

West End

Charlotte Street Hotel

15-17 Charlotte Street, Fitzrovia, W1T 1RJ (7806 2000, www.firmdale.com). Goodge Street or Tottenham Court Road tube. **£££££**.

This gorgeous Firmdale hotel is a fine exponent of Kit Kemp's fusion of traditional and avant-garde – you won't believe it was once a dental hospital. Public rooms contain Bloomsbury Set paintings (Duncan Grant, Vanessa Bell), while the bedrooms mix English understatement with bold decorative flourishes. The huge beds and trademark polished granite bathrooms are suitably indulgent, and some rooms have unbelievably high ceilings. The bar-restaurant buzzes with media types, for whom the screening room must feel like a home comfort.

Claridge's

55 Brook Street, Mayfair, W1K 4HR (7629 8860, www.claridges.co.uk). Bond Street tube. **££££**.
Claridge's is sheer class and pure atmosphere, its signature art deco redesign still dazzling. Photographs of Churchill and sundry royals grace the grand foyer, as does an absurdly over-the-top Dale Chihuly chandelier. Without departing too far from the traditional, Claridge's bars and restaurant are actively fashionable – Gordon Ramsay is the in-house restaurateur, and the A-listers can gather for champers and sashimi in the bar. The rooms divide evenly between deco and Victorian style, with period touches balanced by high-tech bedside panels.

Clink78

78 King's Cross Road, King's Cross, WC1X 9QG (7183 9400, www.clink hostels.com). King's Cross tube/rail. **£**.
In a former courthouse, the Clink sets the bar high for hosteldom. There's the setting: the original wood-panelled lobby and courtroom where the Clash stood before the beak (now filled with backpackers surfing the web). Then there's the urban chic ethos, with new graffiti-styled decor and a refurbished bar. The smaller, quieter Clink261 (261-265 Gray's Inn Road, 7833 9400), refurbished last year, is nearby.

Connaught

Carlos Place, Mayfair, W1K 2AL (7499 7070, www.the-connaught.co.uk). Bond Street tube. **££££**.
It isn't the only London hotel to provide butlers, but there can't be many that offer 'a secured gun cabinet room' for hunting season. This is traditional British hospitality for those who love 23-carat gold leaf and stern portraits in the halls, but all mod cons in their room, down to free wireless and

flatscreens in the en suite. Both of the bars – gentleman's club cosy Coburg and cruiseship deco Connaught (p108) – and the Hélène Darroze restaurant are impressive. There's also a less atmospheric new wing, which not only doubled the guestrooms, but added a swish spa and 60sq m swimming pool.

Covent Garden Hotel

10 Monmouth Street, Covent Garden, WC2H 9LF (7806 1000, www. firmdale.com). Covent Garden or Leicester Square tube. **££££**.
On the ground floor, the 1920s Paris-style Brasserie Max and its retro zinc bar continues to buzz – testament to the deserved popularity of Firmdale's snug and stylish 1996 establishment. Its Covent Garden location and tucked-away screening room ensure it still attracts starry customers, and guests needing a bit of privacy can retreat upstairs to the lovely panelled private library, with honesty bar. In the individually styled guest rooms, pinstriped wall-paper and floral upholstery are mixed with bold, contemporary elements. All round, a stunner.

Dean Street Townhouse & Dining Room

69-71 Dean Street, Soho, W1D 3SE (7434 1775, www.sohohouse.com). Leicester Square or Piccadilly Circus tube. **£££**.
This is the latest winning enterprise from the people behind Soho House members' club. To one side of a buzzy ground-floor restaurant are four floors of bedrooms that run from full-size rooms with early Georgian panelling and reclaimed oak floors to half-panelled 'Tiny' rooms barely bigger than their double beds – but available for from £95. The atmosphere is gentleman's club cosy (there are cookies in a cute silver Treats container in each room), but modern types are reassured by rainforest showers, 24hr service, Roberts DAB radios, free wireless internet and big flatscreen TVs.

Renaissance in St Pancras

The amazing old hotel that's been born anew.

At last, the Midland Grand hotel at St Pancras station (now run by Marriott as the **St Pancras Renaissance**, p200) has opened. The gorgeously romantic Gothic Revival railway hotel – built by George Gilbert Scott between 1869 and 1876 – had been mothballed since it closed almost eight decades back.

To celebrate the auspicious unveiling, the hotel invited *Time Out*'s travel editor Chris Moss to be among the first journalists to sleep in one of the suites that overlooks the Eurostar platforms. The view is, of course, unique, breathtaking, inspiring, but even more impressive is the £200m refurb, which has turned a former taxi lane into a bright, beautiful lobby, the old Booking Office into a smart bar-restaurant serving comfort food and the former Ladies Smoking Room into a chic event venue. Chef Marcus Wareing is in charge of the hotel's haute cuisine British brasserie, the Gilbert Scott, which is reviving such unusual dishes as 'tweed

kettle' – a fish dish dating back to 19th-century Edinburgh. There's a dedicated pastry bar at the front of the restaurant, welcoming diners with stacks of desserts such as Cambridge burnt cream and bakewell pudding.

All of the 38 suites are in the original 'Chambers' building, but some of the additional 207 'ordinary' rooms are located in a cleverly cantilevered extension behind the station. Throughout, the attention to detail is superlative: there is original art from the Royal Academy in the suites, gold-leaf stencilling on ceilings, old-school tipples and fizzes in the bar, and stylish lighting that apes the original Victorian gasoliers.

Rates for rooms start at £300 a night (plus VAT), but rise to around £14,000 for the rock star-size Royal Suite. Mere mortals might just want to nose in to the bar or restaurant, but consider arranging a 90-minute tour with the hotel's historian, Royden Stock (07778 932359 mobile; £20 per person, maximum group size of six).

Dorchester

*53 Park Lane, Mayfair, W1K 1QA
(7629 8888, www.thedorchester.com).
Hyde Park Corner tube.* **££££.**
A Park Lane fixture since 1931, the
Dorchester's interior is opulently classical, but its attitude is cutting-edge,
with a terrific level of personal service.
The hotel employs no fewer than 90
chefs at the Grill Room, Alain Ducasse
and China Tang. With one of the best
lobbies in town, amazing park views,
state-of-the-art mod cons and a magnificently refurbished spa, it's small wonder the hotel has always welcomed film
stars (from the departed Liz Taylor to
Tom Cruise) and political leaders
(Eisenhower planned D-Day here).

45 Park Lane

NEW *45 Park Lane, Mayfair, W1K
1PN (7629 4848, www.45parklane.com).
Green Park or Hyde Park Corner tube.*
££££.
A new hotel from the Dorchester
Collection is due to open in late 2011.
Situated directly across from the
stately entrance of the Dorchester, 45
will feel very different from its predecessor: on a site that used to be the
Playboy Club, its decor is more retro-
modern and masculine than its elder
sister. Of the (45, naturally) rooms,
Premium and above will have fine
views of Hyde Park. Star American
chef Wolfgang Puck is in charge of the
hotel's Cut restaurant and bar.

Harlingford Hotel

*61-63 Cartwright Gdns, Bloomsbury,
WC1H 9EL (7387 1551, www.
harlingfordhotel.com). Russell Square
tube or Euston tube/rail.* **££.**
An affordable hotel with bundles of
charm in the heart of Bloomsbury, the
Harlingford has light airy rooms with
boutique aspirations. Decor is lifted
from understated sleek to quirky with
the help of vibrant colour splashes
from the glass bathroom fittings and
the mosaic tiles. The crescent it's set in
has a lovely, leafy private garden.

Hazlitt's

*6 Frith Street, Soho, W1D 3JA
(7434 1771, www.hazlittshotel.com).
Tottenham Court Road tube.* **£££.**
Four Georgian townhouses comprise
this charming place, named after
William Hazlitt, a spirited 18th-century
essayist who died here in abject
poverty. With flamboyance and stag-
gering attention to detail the rooms
evoke the Georgian era, all fireplaces,
heavy fabrics, free-standing tubs and
exquisitely carved half-testers, yet
modern luxuries – air-con, TVs in
antique cupboards, free Wi-Fi and
triple-glazed windows – have also been
attended to. It gets creakier and more
crooked the higher you go, culminating
in enchanting garret single rooms.

Montagu Place

*2 Montagu Place, Marylebone, W1H
2ER (7467 2777, www.montagu-
place.co.uk). Baker Street tube.* **£££.**
A stylish small hotel in a pair of Grade
II-listed Georgian townhouses, catering
primarily for the midweek business
traveller. All rooms have pocket-
sprung beds, as well as cafetières and
flatscreen TVs (DVD players are available from reception). The look here is
boutique-hotel sharp, except for an
uneasy overlap of bar and reception –
though you can simply get a drink and
retire to the graciously modern lounge.

Morgan

*24 Bloomsbury Street, Bloomsbury,
WC1B 3QJ (7636 3735, www.morgan
hotel.co.uk). Tottenham Court Road
tube.* **££.**
This brilliantly located, comfortable
budget hotel looks better than it has for
a while after recent renovations. The
rooms have ditched floral for neutral,
and are equipped with free wireless,
voicemail, air-conditioning and flatscreen televisions with Freeview. A
slap-up English breakfast is served in
a good-looking room with wood panelling, decorated with London prints
and blue-and-white china plates.

ESSENTIALS

No.5 Maddox Street

*5 Maddox Street, Mayfair, W1S 2QD
(7647 0200, www.living-rooms.co.uk).
Oxford Circus tube.* **£££**.

A bit different, this: for your money,
you get a chic, self-contained apartment. Shut the discreet brown front
door, climb the stairs and flop into a
well-furnished home from home with
all mod cons, including new flatscreen
TVs. Each apartment has a fully
equipped kitchen, but room service will
shop for you in addition to the usual
hotel services. The East-meets-West
decor is classic 1990s minimalist, but
bright and clean after refurbishment.

One Aldwych

*1 Aldwych, on the Strand, WC2B 4RH
(7300 1000, www.onealdwych.com).
Covent Garden or Temple tube, or
Charing Cross tube/rail.* **££££**.

You only have to push through the
front door and enter the breathtaking
Lobby Bar to know you're in for a treat.
Despite its weighty history – the 1907
building was designed by the men
behind the Ritz – One Aldwych is thoroughly modern, from Frette linen
through bathroom mini-TVs to envi-
ronmentally friendly loo flushes. The
location is perfect for Theatreland, but
the cosy screening room and swimming pool may keep you indoors.

Rough Luxe

*1 Birkenhead Street, King's Cross,
WC1H 8BA (7837 5338, www.rough
luxe.co.uk). King's Cross tube/rail.* **££**.

In a bit of King's Cross that's choked
with ratty B&Bs, this Grade II-listed
property has walls artfully distressed,
torn wallpaper, signature works of art,
old-fashioned TVs that barely work
and even retains the sign for the hotel
that preceded Rough Luxe: 'Number
One Hotel'. Each room has free wireless
internet, but otherwise have totally different characters. It's all rather hip and
fun, but also has quite a hand-made
feel – the sleeping arrangements are a
classy take on on a sofa bed, pulled out

by your host each night. The owners
are more than happy to chat over a
bottle of wine in the back courtyard
where a great breakfast is served.

St John Hotel

NEW *1 Leicester Street, off Leicester
Square, WC2H 7BL (7251 0848,
www.stjohnhotellondon.com). Leicester
Square or Piccadilly Circus tube.* **£££**.

When one of London's finest restaurants, St John (p156), decides to move
into the hotel trade, it's worth taking
notice. Co-owner Trevor Gulliver
described the 16-room hotel as 'that
rare thing – a hotel where people would
actually want to eat'. To which end, the
first floor, ground floor and basement
are given over to a bar and restaurant
(p134); above them are 15 rooms and a
three-bedroom rooftop suite – the bathroom's round window looks west to
Big Ben. The decor is in keeping with
the white, masculine, minimalist style
of the original Smithfield venue.

St Pancras Renaissance

NEW *Euston Road, King's Cross, NW1
2AR (7841 3540, www.marriott.com).
King's Cross tube/rail.* **££££**.

Even at a busy time for grand new
hotel openings in London, the St
Pancras Renaissance is managing to
stand out. See box p198.

Sanderson

*50 Berners Street, Fitzrovia, W1T 3NG
(7300 1400, www.morganshotelgroup.
com). Oxford Circus tube.* **££££**.

This Schrager/Starck statement creation takes clinical chic to new heights.
The only touch of colour in our room
was a naïve landscape painting nailed
to the ceiling over the silver sleigh bed.
Otherwise, it's all flowing white net
drapes, glass cabinets and retractable
screens. The residents-only Purple Bar
sports a button-backed purple leather
ceiling and fabulous cocktails; the 'bil-
liard room' has a purple-topped pool
table and weird tribal adaptations of
classic dining-room furniture.

Savoy

NEW *Strand, WC2R 0EU (7836 4343, www.fairmont.com). Covent Garden or Embankment tube, or Charing Cross tube/rail.* **££££**.

The superluxe, Grade II-listed Savoy finally reopened in late 2010 after more than £100m of renovations – the numerous delays testimony to the difficulty of recreating a listed building, loved by generations of visitors for its discreet mix of Edwardian neo-classical and art deco, as a modern luxury hotel. Built in 1889 to put up theatregoers from Richard D'Oyly Carte's Gilbert & Sullivan shows in the attached theatre (p147), the Savoy is the hotel from which Monet painted the Thames, where Vivien Leigh met Laurence Olivier, where Londoners met the martini. There's topiary at the famous cul-de-sac entrance, a new tearoom with glass-roofed conservatory and the leather counter of the new Beaufort champagne bar is set on a former stage for big bands, but the Savoy Grill (p143) and American Bar have barely changed. Seamless service whisks you to your room almost before you notice you've arrived.

Sumner

54 Upper Berkeley Street, W1H 7QR (7723 2244, www.thesumner.com). Marble Arch tube. **££**.

The Sumner's cool, deluxe looks have earned it many fans – and several awards. You won't be at all surprised: from the soft dove and slatey greys of the lounge and halls you move up to glossily spacious accommodation with brilliant walk-in showers. The breakfast room feels soft and sunny, with a lovely, delicate buttercup motif and vibrant Arne Jacobsen chairs, whereas the stylishly moody front sitting room is a cosy gem.

22 York Street

22 York Street, Marylebone, W1U 6PX (7224 2990, www.22yorkstreet.co.uk). Baker Street tube. **££**.

Imagine one of those bohemian French country houses you see in *Elle Decor* – all pale pink lime-washed walls, wooden floors and quirky antiques. That's the feel of this graceful, unpretentious bed and breakfast. There's no sign on the door and the sense of staying in a hospitable home continues when you're offered coffee in the spacious breakfast room-cum-kitchen with its curved communal table. Many of the rooms have en suite baths.

W London Leicester Square

NEW *10 Wardour Street, Leicester Square, W1D 6QF (7758 1000, www.wlondon.co.uk). Leicester Square tube.* **££££**.

The old Swiss Centre building on the edge of Leicester Square has been demolished and in its place is the UK's first W Hotel. The W brand has made it's name with a series of hip hotels around the world that offer glamorous bars, classy food and functional but spacious rooms. The London W is no exception: Spice Market (p134) gets its first UK site within the hotel; Wyld is a large nightclub/bar space aiming to become the Met Bar for a new decade, and the W lounge aims to bring New York's cocktail lounge ethos to London. The rooms – 192 of them, across ten storeys – are well-equipped and decent-sized, and SWEAT (the hotel's state-of-the-art fitness facility) offers fine views over Soho. Also of note is the W's gob-smacking exterior: the entire hotel is veiled in translucent glass, which is lit in different colours through the day.

YHA London Central

104 Bolsover Street, Fitzrovia, W1W 5NU (0845 371 9154, www.yha.org. uk). Great Portland Street tube. **££**.

The Youth Hostel Association's newest hostel is one of its best – as well as being one of the best hostels in London. The friendly and well-informed receptionists are stationed at a counter to the left of the entrance, in a substantial

ESSENTIALS

café-bar area. The basement contains a well-equipped kitchen and washing areas; above it, five floors of clean, neatly designed rooms, many en suite. Residents have 24hr access (by individual key cards), there's free wireless internet and the quiet location is an easy walk from most of the West End.

The City

Apex London Wall
7-9 Copthall Avenue, EC2R 7NJ (7562 3030, www.apexhotels.co.uk). Bank tube or Moorgate tube/rail. **££**.
The mini-chain's newest London hotel shares the virtues of its predecessor (Apex City of London, 1 Seething Lane, 7702 2020). The service is obliging, the rooms are crisply designed with all mod cons, and there are comforting details – rubber duck in the impressive bathrooms, free jelly beans, free local calls. From the suites, a terrace peers into offices, but the view from the restaurant and breakfast room – of the flamboyant sculptures on the business institute next door – is as good.

Boundary
2-4 Boundary Street, E2 7DD (7729 1051, www.theboundary.co.uk). Liverpool Street tube/rail or Shoreditch High Street rail. **£££**.
In a converted warehouse, Conran's latest combines restaurant, rooftop bar, ground-floor café (p174) and excellent hotel rooms, the whole establishment clearly a labour of love. Each room has a wet room and hand-made bed, but are otherwise coolly individual, with classic furniture and original art. The five split-level suites range in style from the bright and sea-salt fresh Beach to a new take on Victoriana, while the remaining rooms are themed by design style: Mies van der Rohe, Shaker and so on. Good rates too on a Sunday.

Fox & Anchor
115 Charterhouse Street, EC1M 6AA (0845 347 0100, www.foxandanchor.
com). Barbican tube or Farringdon tube/rail. **££**.
No more than a few atmospheric, well-appointed and luxurious rooms above a bustling, darkly panelled pub, this has been one of our most enjoyable stays in London. Each en suite room differs, but the high-spec facilities (big flatscreens, clawfoot bath, drench shower) and quirky attention to detail (bottles of ale in the minibar, 'Nursing hangover' signs to hang out if you want some privacy) are common throughout. Expect some clanking market noise in the early mornings.

Hoxton Hotel
81 Great Eastern Street, EC2A 3HU (7550 1000, www.hoxtonhotels.com). Old Street tube/rail. **££**.
Everything you've heard is true. First, there's the hip location. Then there are the great design values: the foyer is a sort of postmodern country lodge (with stag's head) and rooms that are small but well thought-out and full of nice touches (Frette linens, free fresh milk in the mini-fridge, free mini-breakfast hung on your door handle in the morning). Above all, it's the budget-airline pricing system, by which you might catch a £1-a-night ultra-bargain – but, assuming you can book far enough ahead to beat demand, ensures you get a great-value room. See box p204.

Malmaison
Charterhouse Square, EC1M 6AH (7012 3700, www.malmaison.com). Barbican tube. **£££**.
It's part of a chain, but the Malmaison is a charming hotel, beautifully set in a cobblestone square near the lively restaurants and bars of Smithfield Market. The reception is stylish with its lilac-and-cream checked floor, exotic plants and petite champagne bar; purples, dove-grey and black wood dominate the rooms, where you'll find free broadband and creative lighting. The gym and a subterranean brasserie complete the picture.

Shoredich Rooms

Mint Tower of London

NEW *7 Pepys Street, EC3N 4AF (7709 1000, www.minthotel.com). Tower Hill tube.* **£££**.

As you turn from the Tower of London and Tower Bridge (for both, see p161) among anonymous modern buildings to reach the new Mint, you might feel your heart sink. Keep your spirits up: the hotel has unexpectedly brilliant views. Even if you aren't lucky enough to stay in the spacious Thames Suite, the 12th-floor SkyLounge bar, with its outside terrace, looks over the rooftops to provide a fine Thames vista. As at Mint Westminster (p194), service is smooth and smiley, and the room technology and fittings top-class.

Rookery

12 Peter's Lane, Cowcross Street, EC1M 6DS (7336 0931, www.rookery hotel.com). Farringdon tube/rail. **£££**.

The front door of the Rookery is satisfyingly hard to find, especially when the streets are teeming with Fabric (p157) devotees (the front rooms can be noisy on these nights). Once inside, guests enjoy a warren of creaky rooms, individually decorated in the style of a Georgian townhouse: clawfoot baths, elegant four-posters. The split-level Rook's Nest suite has views of St Paul's

(p159). At the rear, a cosy honesty bar opens on to a sweet little patio.

Shoreditch Rooms

NEW *Ebor Street, E1 6AW (7739 5040, www.shoreditchhouse.com). Shoreditch High Street rail.* **££**.

The most recent hotel from Soho House members' club (see also Dean Street Townhouse, p197) might be the best, perfectly catching the local atmosphere with its unfussy, slightly retro design. The rooms feel a bit like urban beach huts, with pastel-coloured tongue-and-groove and swing doors to the en suite showers. They feel fresh and comfortable, even though they're furnished with little more than a bed, DAB radio and old-fashioned phone, and a solid dresser (minibar, hairdryer and treats within, flatscreen TV on top). Guests get access to the eating, drinking and fitness facilities (there's an excellent rooftop pool) in the members' club next door. Tiny rooms start from just £75.

Zetter

86-88 Clerkenwell Road, EC1M 5RJ (7324 4444, www.thezetter.com). Farringdon tube/rail. **£££**.

Zetter is a fun, laid-back, modern hotel with interesting design notes, a refreshing lack of attitude, friendly staff and

ESSENTIALS

Budget Style

London's hippest, most affordable new rooms.

The **Hoxton** (p202) has led the London hotel pack for years when it comes to budget style. The original ethos was so simple it seemed odd no one else was doing it. The rather small, well-equipped, utilitarian-chic rooms are identical, and provide the essentials for free; inessentials are available in the foyer at supermarket prices. Most important, though, was the pricing: room rates adjusted to meet demand, which meant early birds could snap up some impressive bargains.

At these prices, what could be improved? It turns out, some of those rooms. Reflecting the hotel's arty surroundings – Shoreditch is still a centre for young London trendiness – the owners decided to make over some former office space into individually designed new bedrooms. Unsurprisingly, they've done a superb job.

The new rooms are actually slightly smaller than the originals, but the designs are eye-poppingly fun. We particularly enjoyed one that's styled like a Swinging London film set, all passionate reds and naughty posters, with a spotlight on a camera tripod, big, up-ended steamer trunks to serve as wardrobes, and cushions scattered all over the bed. All the functional details are taken care of, naturally, but opt for one of these new rooms and you'll know you're on holiday.

firm eco-credentials (such as occupancy detection systems in the bedrooms). The rooms, stacked up on five galleried storeys overlooking the intimate bar area, are smoothly functional, but cosied up with choice home comforts like hot-water bottles and old Penguin paperbacks, as well as having walk-in showers with Elemis smellies. Bistrot Bruno Loubet (p152) is thriving, and the new 13-room Townhouse – a Georgian house on the rear square – has an ace cocktail bar (p157).

Neighbourhood London

Base2Stay

25 Courtfield Gardens, Earl's Court, SW5 0PG (7244 2255, www.base 2stay.com). Earl's Court tube. **££**.
Base2Stay looks good, with its modernist limestone and taupe tones, and keeps prices low by removing inessentials: no bar, no restaurant. Instead, there's a 'kitchenette' (microwave, sink, silent mini-fridge, kettle), with all details carefully attended to (plenty of kitchenware, including corkscrew and can opener). The rooms, en suite (with power showers) and air-conditioned, are as carefully thought-out, with desks, free wireless and flatscreens, but the single/bunkbed rooms are barely wider than the beds themselves.

40 Winks

109 Mile End Road, Stepney, E1 4UJ (7790 0259, 07973 653944 mobile, www.40winks.org). Stepney Green tube. **££**. No credit cards.
Opposite a housing estate and cheap Somali diners, the flamboyantly camp and fashionable family home of an interior designer has become the B&B of choice for movie stars and fashion movers. The 'micro-boutique hotel' 40 Winks looks extraordinary (kitchen frescoes, a music room with Beatles drumkit, a lion's head tap in the bath), but each stay is made individual by

owner David Carter's commitment to his guests. You'll feel like you're staying with an ingenious friend, rather than just renting a room.

Mayflower Hotel

26-28 Trebovir Road, Earl's Court, SW5 9NJ (7370 0991, www.mayflower-group.co.uk). Earl's Court tube. **££**.
The Mayflower Group – the other properties are New Linden (59 Leinster Square, Bayswater, 7221 4321, www. newlinden.co.uk) and Twenty Nevern (20 Nevern Square, Earl's Court, 7565 9555, www.twentynevernsquare.co.uk) – has been leading the budget style revolution for years, but here's where the contemporary house style evolved, proving affordability can be opulently chic and perfectly equipped. Cream walls and sleek dark woods are an understated background for richly coloured fabrics and intricate wooden architectural fragments, like the lobby's imposing Jaipuri arch.

Pavilion

34-36 Sussex Gardens, Paddington, W2 1UL (7262 0905, www.pavilion hoteluk.com). Edgware Road tube or Marylebone or Paddington tube/rail. **£**.
Behind a deceptively modest façade is what could be the city's funkiest, most original hotel. A voluptuously exotic paean to excess and paint effects, the Pavilion's madly colourful themed rooms ('Highland Fling', 'Afro Honky Tonk', 'Casablanca Nights') have become a celeb-magnet and are often used for fashion shoots. Not for lovers of minimalism and 'facilities' – though it's got most of the usual necessities.

Portobello Hotel

22 Stanley Gardens, W11 2NG (7727 2777, www.portobellohotel.com). Holland Park or Notting Hill Gate tube. **£££**.
With half a century of celebrity status, the Portobello has hosted Johnny Depp, Kate Moss and Alice Cooper, who used his tub to house a boa constrictor. It

remains a pleasingly unpretentious place, with a more civilised demeanour than its legend might suggest. There is now a lift to help rockers who are feeling their age up the five floors, but there's still a 24hr guest-only bar downstairs for those who don't yet feel past it. The rooms are themed – the superb basement Japanese Water Garden, for example, has an elaborate spa bath, its own private grotto and a small private garden – but all are stylishly equipped.

Stylotel

160-162 Sussex Gardens, Paddington, W2 1UD (7723 1026, www.stylotel. com). Edgware Rd tube, or Marylebone or Paddington tube/rail. **£**.
Stylotel is a retro-futurist dream: metal floors and panelling, lots of royal blue (the hall walls, the padded headboards) and pod bathrooms. But the real deal is its new bargain-priced studio and apartment (respectively, £120-£150 and £150-£200, including breakfast), designed – like the hotel – by the owner's son. These achieve real minimalist chic with sleek brushed steel or white glass wall panels and simply styled contemporary furniture upholstered in black or white.

Town Hall Hotel

NEW *Patriot Square, Bethnal Green, E2 9NF (7871 0460, www.townhall hotel.com). Bethnal Green tube.* **£££**.
A Grade II-listed, early 20th-century town hall has been transformed into a classy aparthotel – despite its location beside a council estate. The decor is minimal, retaining many features (walnut panelling, marble, stained glass, fire hoses on old brass reels) that would be familiar to the departed bureaucrats, but jazzed up with art and a patterned aluminium 'veil' that covers the new top floor. The spacious apartments are well equipped for self-catering, but luxuries such as free wireless internet, TV/DVD players, a narrow basement swimming pool and the fine Viajante (p175) restaurant are also in place.

ESSENTIALS

The 2012 Games

Tickets

The initial application phase for tickets for the London 2012 **Olympic Games** was in spring 2011. There will be a similar phase from 9 to 30 September 2011 for the 2m tickets for the **Paralympic Games**. To get the latest ticketing news and information, simply register at **www.tickets.london2012.com**.

UK residents and residents of designated European countries can apply for tickets online. If you're not resident in these countries, apply through your National Olympic Committee or National Paralympic Committee.

More than 20m applications were made for 6.6m Olympic tickets before the deadline, with headline sports and events such as the Opening and Closing Ceremonies, Track Cycling, Swimming and Athletics finals heavily oversubscribed; when any remaining tickets go on sale in winter 2011, look for team sports in large venues with lots of sessions, such as earlier rounds of the Football. The only **official resale site** for London 2012 Olympic and Paralympic tickets opens in early 2012.

There are also several **unticketed events**: in Athletics, the Marathon and Race Walk; in Cycling, the Road Race and Road Time Trial; and also the Cycling section of the Triathlon.

Beware of **bogus websites**. Only the official website (above) and designated partner organisations (Thomas Cook, Prestige Ticketing and Jet Set Sports) can sell London 2012 tickets.

Orientation & venues

Getting Around

The venues for the 2012 Games can be thought of as three concentric rings: east London's **Olympic Park venues** (map p208); **London venues**, spread across the city (map p213) and venues

outside London. They are all listed below, with closest transport links – normal transport arrangments might change in the run up to the Games, so check precise details nearer the time. On the website **www.london2012. com**, click on 'Visiting in 2012', then 'Getting to the Games' for detailed information. Our succinct advice on travel is on p207; general information on city transport is on p214. The back flap has a London underground map.

Olympic Park venues

Stratford tube/DLR/rail or West Ham tube/rail. **Map** pp179-181.

Olympic Stadium *Stadium Island, south section of the Park, beside the Aquatics Centre.* Refreshments and information desks will be located around the perimeter of the Stadium.

Aquatics Centre & Water Polo Arena *South-east of the Park, between the Olympic Stadium & Westfield Stratford City.*

Velodrome & BMX Track *North end of the North-East Concourse, between the Basketball Arena & Eton Manor.*

Basketball Arena *North-east of the Park, between the Velodrome & the Athletes' Village.*

Eton Manor *North of the Park.*

Handball Arena *West of the Park, off the North-West Concourse, between the Olympic Stadium & the Hockey Centre.*

Hockey Centre *North end of North-West Concourse, west of the Velodrome.*

London venues

The **Central Zone** takes the 2012 Games into the heart of tourist London, mixing sights (Horse Guards Parade, the Mall, Hyde Park) and sporting history (Lord's, Earls Court).

River Zone venues are scattered north and south of the Thames in the east of town, with Greenwich Park, the North Greenwich Arena and the Royal

Artillery Barracks on the south side, and ExCeL north of the river.

Finally, there are four venues in **west London**: Hampton Court Palace, Wembley Stadium, Wimbledon, and the Wembley Arena concert hall.

Earls Court *Warwick Road, SW5 9TA. Earl's Court tube or West Brompton tube/rail.* Just west of the South Kensington museums (pp89-93).

ExCeL *1 Western Gateway, Royal Victoria Dock, E16 1XL. Arrivals: Custom House or West Silvertown DLR; departures: Prince Regent or Pontoon Dock DLR.* Between Canary Wharf and London City Airport.

Greenwich Park *Greenwich, SE10 8XJ. Greenwich DLR/rail or Blackheath rail.* See pp181-184.

Hampton Court Palace *Hampton Court rail, or riverboat to Hampton Court Pier (Apr-Oct).* See p188.

Horse Guards Parade *Green Park or Piccadilly Circus tube, or Charing Cross, Victoria or Waterloo tube/rail.* See p85.

Hyde Park *Green Park, Hyde Park Corner, Knightsbridge or Marble Arch tube, or Paddington or Victoria tube/rail.* See p95.

Lord's Cricket Ground *St John's Wood tube, or Marylebone or Paddington tube/rail.* See p169.

The Mall *Between Buckingham Palace (p85) & Trafalgar Square (p83). Green Park or Piccadilly Circus tube, or Charing Cross, Victoria or Waterloo tube/rail.*

North Greenwich Arena *Millennium Way, North Greenwich, SE10 0PH. North Greenwich tube or Charlton rail.* Hosts concerts as the O2 Arena (p184).

The Royal Artillery Barracks *Greenwich, SE18 4BH. Woolwich Arsenal DLR/rail.* South of the Thames, east of the Greenwich sights (pp181-184).

Wembley Arena *Arena Square, Engineers Way, Wembley, Middx HA9 0DH. Wembley Park tube, Wembley Central tube/rail, or Wembley Stadium rail.* Close to Wembley Stadium (p188).

Wembley Stadium *Wembley Park tube, Wembley Central tube/rail, or Wembley Stadium rail.* See p188.

Wimbledon *Southfields tube or Wimbledon tube/rail.* See p189.

Outside London

These venues range from those on the fringes of London (Hadleigh Farm, Eton Dorney, Lee Valley White Water Centre) to the south coast, a hundred miles away (Weymouth & Portland). The Olympic Football competition might take you further yet: in addition to Wembley Stadium there are games in Scotland (Hampden Park, Glasgow), Wales (the Millennium Stadium, Cardiff), the north of England (Old Trafford, Manchester; St James' Park, Newcastle) and the Midlands (City of Coventry Stadium).

Brands Hatch *Fawkham, Longfield, Kent DA3 8NG (01474 872331, www. motorsportvision.co.uk). Swanley rail (approx 1hr from London Victoria).*

Eton Dorney *Dorney Lake, off Court Lane, Dorney, Windsor, Berks SL4 6QP. Maidenhead, Slough or Windsor & Eton Riverside rail (approx 15-45mins from London Paddington).*

Hadleigh Farm *Castle Lane, Benfleet, Essex SS7 2AP. Leigh-on-Sea rail (approx 45-50mins from London Fenchurch Street station).*

Lee Valley White Water Centre *Cheshunt rail.* See box p190.

Weymouth & Portland *Osprey Road, Portland, Dorset DT5 1SA. Weymouth rail (approx 2hrs 40mins to 3hrs from London Waterloo station).*

Transport

In summer 2012, events starting with the Queen's Diamond Jubilee (2-5 June 2012) and continuing through both the Olympic Games and the Paralympic Games will add up to what Transport for London has described as 'around 100 continuous days of extraordinary operation'. In fact, the Olympic Delivery

ESSENTIALS

Indicative map of the Olympic Park at Games time

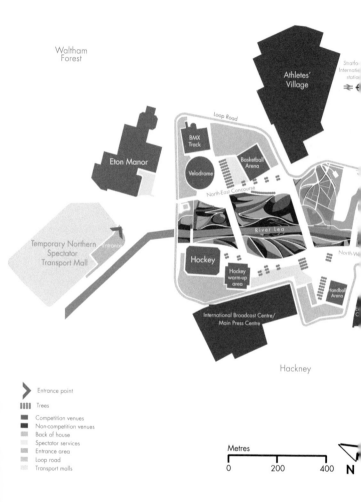

Waltham
Forest

Athletes'
Village

Stratford
International
station

Loop Road

BMX
Track

Basketball
Arena

Velodrome

North-East Concourse

Eton Manor

River Lea

North-We

Temporary Northern
Spectator
Transport Mall

Entrance

Hockey

Hockey
warm-up
area

Handball
Arena

International Broadcast Centre/
Main Press Centre

Hackney

> Entrance point

|||| Trees

▇ Competition venues

▇ Non-competition venues

▇ Back of house

▇ Spectator services

▇ Entrance area

▇ Loop road

▇ Transport malls

Metres

0   200   400

N

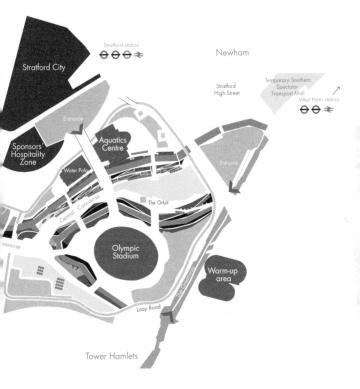

Stratford station

Newham

Stratford City

Stratford
High Street

Temporary Southern
Spectator
Transport Mall

West Ham station

Entrance

Sponsors'
Hospitality
Zone

Aquatics
Centre

Water Polo

Entrance

Central Concourse

The Orbit

Concourse

Olympic
Stadium

Warm-up
area

The Greenway

Loop Road

Tower Hamlets

Take home a memory of London

From a great selection of gifts available at the London 2012 Shops, conveniently located at Paddington Station, Heathrow Terminal 5, St Pancras International, Liverpool Street Station and John Lewis Oxford Street.

london2012.com/shop

Authority expects an additional 1m journeys to be taken across just the nine busiest days of the Games, with the usage of public transport likely to peak on 4 Aug 2012 with some 750,000 spectators moving between different venues around town. We recommend you think carefully about your travel arrangements and plan your journey as early as possible.

■ Allow plenty of time to travel to and between venues, because London's transport system will be much busier than usual. Remember to allow extra time to get through the transport system – which will be very busy – and substantial time for queuing and walking within large venues.

■ Do not drive. There is no public parking available at, or in the vicinity of, any Olympic or Paralympic venue. To travel to and from venues use public transport, walk or cycle.

■ Spectators with a ticket for a Games event in London or at certain venues outside London will receive a one-day 'Games Travelcard' for the day of that event with their event ticket. The Games Travelcard will entitle you to travel in zones 1 to 9 in London and by National Rail between London and the recommended stations for certain venues outside London (Eton Dorney, Hadleigh Farm and Lee Valley White Water Centre), but not journeys by taxi or on the Heathrow, Stansted or Gatwick Express trains. Ticket holders will also be entitled to a one-third discount on boat services in London.

■ London 2012 ticket holders have been able to book travel from around Great Britain to venues since summer 2011 on several additional, Games-specific travel services. These include National Rail (for journeys from any National Rail station in the country to London and the co-Host Cities), dedicated park-and-ride for venues, specially organised coach services (to the Olympic Park, Greenwich Park, ExCeL and Weymouth & Portland) and even Blue Badge parking.

Visit www.london2012.com/getting-to-the-games for information and travel tools and tips that will make planning your travel easier. Details of transport in London are on p214. Underground, Overground, DLR and some mainline rail services from the Olympic Park will run until around 1am. Many buses will operate 24 hours a day.

Health & safety

For health information and advice visit NHS Choices at **www.nhs.uk/2012** or call NHS Direct on **0845 4647**. For health emergencies, see p219.

■ If you're on any medication, bring your supply and take it as prescribed.
■ You will be spending lots of time outside, so regularly apply generous amounts of sunscreen (at least SPF15, with a four- or five-star rating).
■ Drink plenty of water, especially when the sun is out or when drinking alcohol. Drink alcohol responsibly.
■ Don't bring or take illegal drugs. There will be police within and outside of the Olympic Park.
■ Walk as much as you can – it's the best way to enjoy London's sights.

Accommodation

People have worried about being able to find accommodation for the 2012 Games. There's no need to be concerned. More than 200 new hotels have opened in London over the last five years; many more are due before the Games, including several hotels near the Olympic Park – you're unlikely to find anywhere closer to it than the three hotels being built in Westfield Stratford City (p181). By 2012, there will be over 123,000 rooms in London. Our favourite places, across town and to suit all pockets, are on pp192-205.

If you are staying in central London, we advise that you plan your journey carefully and allow plenty of time for travelling around the city (p207).

ESSENTIALS

Discover
the world's
greatest cities

London 2012 venues: Greater London area

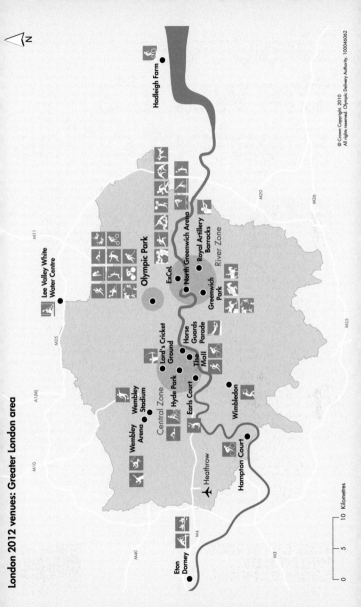

N

Hadleigh Farm

Lee Valley White
Water Centre

Olympic Park

ExCeL

North Greenwich Arena

Royal Artillery
Barracks

River Zone

Greenwich
Park

Lord's Cricket
Ground

Horse
Guards
Parade

The
Mall

Central Zone

Hyde Park

Earls Court

Wembley
Stadium

Wembley
Arena

Wimbledon

Heathrow

Hampton Court

Eton
Dorney

M11

M25

A1(M)

M10

M40

M4

M3

M20

M26

M25

Kilometres

0   5   10

Getting Around

We've provided succinct travel advice and tips for the **London 2012 Olympic & Paralympic Games** on p207.

Airports

Gatwick Airport
0844 335 1802, www.gatwickairport. com. About 30 miles south of central London, off the M23.

The quickest rail link to London is the **Gatwick Express** (0845 850 1530, www.gatwickexpress.com) to Victoria; it runs 3.30am-12.30am daily and takes 30mins. Tickets cost £16.90 single or £28.70 open return (valid for 30 days).

Southern (0845 748 4950, www. southernrailway.com) also runs trains to Victoria, every 5-10mins (every 30mins 1am-4am). It takes about 35mins, and costs £11.30 single.

Thameslink trains (0845 748 4950, www.firstcapitalconnect.co.uk) run to St Pancras. Tickets cost £8.90 single or £17 for a 30-day open return.

A **taxi** to central London takes a bit over an hour and costs around £100.

Heathrow Airport
0844 335 1801, www.heathrowairport. com. About 15 miles west of central London, off the M4.

The **Heathrow Express** (0845 600 1515, www.heathrowexpress.co.uk) runs to Paddington every 15mins (5.10am-11.25pm daily) and takes 15-20mins. The train can be boarded from Terminals 1 and 3 (Heathrow Central tube station) or Terminal 5 (which has its own tube station); from Terminal 4, get a shuttle to Heathrow Central. Tickets are £16.50 single, £32 return (£1 less online, £2 more on board).

The journey by **tube** into central London is longer but cheaper. The 50-60min Piccadilly Line ride into central London costs £5 one way (less with

Oyster, p216). Trains run every few minutes from about 5am to 11.57pm daily (6am-11pm Sun).

The **Heathrow Connect** (0845 678 6975, www.heathrowconnect.com) rail service offers direct access to stations including Ealing Broadway and Paddington. The trains run every half-hour, terminating at Heathrow Central; from there to Terminal 4 get the free shuttle; between Central and Terminal 5, there's free use of the Heathrow Express. A single to Paddington is £7.90, an open return £15.80.

By road, **National Express** (0871 781 8181, www.nationalexpress.com) runs coaches daily to London Victoria (90mins, 5am-9.35pm daily) from Heathrow Central bus terminal every 20-30mins. It's £5 for a single or £9 for a return. A **taxi** to central London costs £45-£65 and takes 30-60mins.

London City Airport
7646 0000, www.londoncityairport.com. About 9 miles east of central London.

The **Docklands Light Railway** now has a stop for London City Airport, which is often less chaotic than the city's other airports. The journey to Bank station in the City takes around 20mins, and trains run 5.30am-12.30am Mon-Sat or 7.30am-11.30pm Sun. A **taxi** costs roughly £30 to central London, but less to the City or Canary Wharf.

Luton Airport
01582 405100, www.london-luton.com. About 30 miles north of central London, J10 off the M1.

A short bus ride links the airport to Luton Airport Parkway station, from which **Thameslink** trains (0845 748 4950, www.firstcapitalconnect.co.uk) depart for stations including St Pancras and City, taking 35-45mins. Trains leave every 15mins (hourly through the night) and cost £13.50 single and £23 return.

ESSENTIALS

By coach, Luton to Victoria takes 60-90mins. **Green Line** (0870 608 7261, www.greenline.co.uk) runs a 24hr service (£14 single, £19 return). A **taxi** to central London costs £70-£80.

Stansted Airport

0870 000 0303, www.stanstedairport. com. About 35 miles north-east of central London, J8 off the M11.

The **Stansted Express** (0845 748 4950, www.stanstedexpress.com) runs to Liverpool Street station, taking 40-45mins and leaving every 15mins. Tickets are £19.80 single, £28.70 return.

The **Airbus** (0871 781 8181, www. nationalexpress.com) is one of several coach services; it takes at least 80mins to reach Victoria, with coaches running roughly every 30mins (24hrs daily), more frequently at peak times. A single is £10, a return is £17. A **taxi** to central London costs around £100.

Arriving by coach

Coaches run by National Express (0871 781 8181, www.nationalexpress.com), the biggest coach company in the UK, arrive at **Victoria Coach Station** (164 Buckingham Palace Road, SW1W 9TP, 0843 222 1234, www.tfl.gov.uk).

Arriving by rail

Trains from mainland Europe run by Eurostar (0843 218 6186, www. eurostar.com) arrive at **St Pancras International** station (7843 7688, www.stpancras.com).

Mainline stations

For times and prices, call 0845 748 4950 or visit www.nationalrail.co.uk. All the major stations are served by the tube.

Public transport

Travel Information Centres give help with the tube, buses and Docklands Light (DLR; p216). Call 0843

222 1234 or visit www.tfl.gov.uk/journeyplanner for more information.
Camden Direct *Camden Town Hall, Argyle Street (opposite King's Cross St Pancras).* **Open** 9am-5pm Mon-Fri.
Euston rail station Open 7.15am-9.15pm Mon-Fri; 7.15am-6.15pm Sat; 8.15am-6.15pm Sun.
Heathrow Terminals 1, 2 & 3 tube station Open 7.15am-9pm daily.
Liverpool Street tube station Open 7.15am-9.15pm Mon-Sat; 8.15am-8pm Sun.
Piccadilly Circus tube station Open 9.15am-7pm daily.
Victoria rail station Open 7.15am-9.15pm Mon-Sat; 8.15am-8.15pm Sun.

London Underground

Delays are fairly common, with lines closing most weekends for engineering works. Trains are hot and crowded in rush hour (8-9.30am, 4.30-7pm Mon-Fri). Even so, the colour-coded lines of the Underground ('the tube') are the quickest way to get about. Underground, Overground and DLR lines are shown on the **tube map** on the back flap.

Using the Underground

Tube and DLR fares are based on a system of six zones, stretching 12 miles from the centre of London. A flat **cash fare** of £4 per journey applies across zones 1-4 on the tube, £5 for zones 1-6; customers save up to £2.30 per journey with a pre-pay Oyster card (p216). Anyone caught with neither ticket nor Oyster will be fined £25 (£50 if you fail to pay within three weeks).

To enter and exit the tube using an **Oyster card**, touch it to the yellow reader, which opens the gate. You must also touch the card to the reader when you exit, or you'll be charged a higher fare when you next use your card. On certain lines, you'll see a pink reader (the 'validator') – touch it in addition to the yellow entry/exit readers and on some routes it will reduce your fare.

ESSENTIALS

To enter using a **paper ticket**, place it in the slot with the black magnetic strip facing down, then pull it out of the top to open the gates. Exit in the same way; tickets for single journeys will be retained by the gate on final exit.

Oyster cards

A pre-paid smartcard, Oyster is the cheapest way of getting round on buses, tubes and the DLR. You can get Oyster cards from www.tfl.gov.uk/oyster, Travel Information Centres (p215), tube stations, and some newsagents and rail stations. A £3 refundable deposit is payable on new cards. A tube journey in zone 1 using Oyster pay-as-you-go costs £1.90; single journeys from zones 1-6 using Oyster are £4.50 (6.30am-9.30pm Mon-Fri) or £2.70 (all other times, including public holidays).

Travelcards

If you're only taking the tube, DLR, buses and trams, using Oyster to pay as you go will always be capped at the same price as an equivalent Day Travelcard. However, if you're also using National Rail services, Oyster may not be accepted: opt instead for a Day Travelcard, a ticket that allows travel across all the London networks. **Anytime Day Travelcards** can be used all day. They cost £8 for zones 1-2. Tickets are valid for journeys started by 4.30am the next day. The **Off-Peak Day Travelcard** is only for travel after 9.30am Mon-Fri (all day for weekends and public holidays). It costs £6.60 for zones 1-2.

Travelling with children

Under-5s travel free on buses and trams. **Under-11s** can also travel free, but need to obtain a 5-10 Oyster photocard. An 11-15 Oyster photocard is needed by **under-16s** to pay as they go on the tube/DLR and to buy 7-Day, monthly or longer period Travelcards.

For details, see www.tfl.gov.uk/fares or call 0845 330 9876.

Visitors can apply for a **photocard** (www.tfl.gov.uk/photocard) in advance. Photocards are not required for adult rate 7-Day Travelcards, Bus Passes or for any adult rate Travelcard or Bus Pass charged on an Oyster card.

Underground timetable

Tube trains run daily from around 5am (except Sunday, when they start an hour or so later depending on the line, and Christmas Day, when there's no service). You shouldn't have to wait more than ten minutes for a train; during peak times, services should run every two or three minutes. Times of last trains vary; they're usually around 12.30am (11.30pm on Sun). The tube runs all night only on New Year's Eve; otherwise, get the night bus (right).

Docklands Light Railway

DLR trains (7363 9700, www.tfl.gov.uk/dlr) run from Bank station (on the Central tube line) or Tower Gateway, close to Tower Hill tube (Circle and District lines). At Westferry station, the line splits east and south via Island Gardens to Greenwich and Lewisham; a change at Poplar can take you north to Stratford (perfect for the Olympic Park; for details, see p179). The easterly branch forks after Canning Town either to Beckton or, via London City Airport (p214), to Woolwich Arsenal. Trains run 5.30am-12.30am daily. With very few exceptions, adult single **fares** on the DLR are exactly the same as for the Underground (p215).

Rail & Overground

Independently run commuter services coordinated by National Rail (0845 748 4950, www.nationalrail.co.uk) leave from the city's main rail stations. Visitors heading to south London, or to more remote destinations such as

Hampton Court (p188), will need to use these overground services. Travelcards are valid within the right zones, but not all routes accept Oyster pay-as-you-go.

The orbital **London Overground** line continues to open piecemeal. It already runs through north London from Stratford in the east to Richmond in the south-west, and new spurs connect Willesden Junction in the north-west to Clapham Junction in the south-west, Gospel Oak in the north to Barking in the east, and north from New Cross through Shoreditch High Street, Dalston Junction and Highbury & Islington. Trains run about every 20mins. We've listed Overground stations as 'rail', but the trains all accept Oyster and prices are, almost always, the same as the Underground (p215).

Buses

All London buses are now low-floor vehicles accessible to wheelchair-users and passengers with buggies. The only exceptions are Heritage Route 9 and 15 Routemasters (p80). Articulated, long single-decker 'bendy buses' are being phased out on most routes, following one of Mayor Boris Johnson's election pledges, and the first few new Routemasters (officially, the 'New Bus for London') come into service in 2012.

You must have a ticket or valid pass before boarding any bus in zone 1 and 'bendy buses' anywhere in the city. You can buy a **ticket** (or 1-Day Bus Pass) from machines at bus stops, but they're often not working; it's better to travel with an Oyster or Travelcard (p216). Using Oyster pay-as-you-go costs £1.30 a trip; your total daily payment, regardless of how many journeys you make, will be capped at £4. Paying cash costs £2.20 single. Under-16s travel for free (but must use an Oyster photocard; p216). A 7-Day Bus Pass gives unlimited bus and tram travel for £17.80. Inspectors patrol buses at random; if you don't have a ticket, you may be fined £50.

Many buses operate 24 hours a day, seven days a week. There are also some special **night buses** with an 'N' prefix, which run from about 11pm to 6am. Most night services run every 15-30mins, but busier routes run a service around every 10mins. They all feel a lot less frequent after a heavy night.

Water transport

Most river services operate every 20-60mins from 7am to 9pm, more often and later in the summer months; see the website www.tfl.gov.uk. A River Roamer day ticket with **Thames Clippers** (0870 781 5049, www.thamesclippers.com), which runs a service between Embankment Pier and Royal Arsenal Woolwich Pier, boarded at Blackfriars, Bankside, London Bridge, Canary Wharf and Greenwich, costs £12.60; there are reductions if you hold an Oyster or travelcard.

Taxis & minicabs

If a **black cab**'s orange 'For Hire' sign is lit, it can be hailed. If it stops, the cabbie must take you to your destination if it's within seven miles. It can be hard to find an empty cab, especially just after the pubs close. Fares rise after 8pm on weekdays and at weekends. You can book black cabs from the 24hr **Taxi One-Number** (0871 871 8710; a £2 booking fee applies, plus 12.5% on credit cards), **Radio Taxis** (7272 0272) and **Dial-a-Cab** (7253 5000; credit cards only, booking fee £2).

Minicabs (saloon cars) are often cheaper than black cabs, but only use licensed firms (look for a disc in the front and rear windows), and avoid anyone who illegally touts for business in the street: such drivers may be unlicensed, uninsured and dangerous. Trustworthy, fully licensed firms include **Addison Lee** (7387 8888), which will text you when the car arrives, and **Lady Cabs** (7272 3300), **Ladybirds** (8295 0101) and **Ladycars** (8558 9511), which all employ

ESSENTIALS

only women drivers. Otherwise, text HOME to 60835 ('60tfl'; 35p plus standard call rate) for the numbers of the two nearest licensed minicab operators and the number for Taxi One-Number, which provides licensed black cabs. No matter who you choose, always ask the price when you book and confirm it with the driver.

Driving

Congestion charge

Driving into central London 7am-6pm Mon-Fri costs £10 (£9 by Auto Pay); the restricted area is shown at www.cclondon.com, but watch for signs and roads painted with a white 'C' on a red circle. Expect a fine of £60 if you fail to pay (£120 if you fail to pay within 14 days). Passes can be bought from garages, newsagents and NCP car parks; you can also pay at www.cclondon.com, on 0845 900 1234 or (after pre-registering on the website) by SMS. You can pay any time during the day or, for £2 more, until midnight on the next charging day.

Parking

Parking on a single or double yellow line, a red line or in residents' parking areas during the day is illegal, and you may be fined, clamped or towed. In the evening (from 7pm in much of central London) and at various weekend times parking on single yellow lines is legal and free. If you find a clear spot on a single yellow during the evening, look for a sign giving local regulations. During the day meters cost around £1.10/15mins, limited to two hours, but they are free at certain evening and weekend times. Parking on double yellows and red routes is always illegal.

NCP **24hr car parks** (0845 050 7080, www.ncp.co.uk) are numerous but cost £2-£7.20/120mins: try Arlington House, Arlington Street, in St James's, W1; Snowsfields in Southwark, SE1; and 4-5 Denman Street in Soho, W1.

Vehicle removal

If your car has disappeared, it's either been stolen or, if it was illegally parked, towed to a car pound. A release fee of £200 is levied for removal, plus £40 per day from the first midnight after removal. You'll also probably get a parking ticket of £60-£100 when you collect the car (£30-£50 if paid within 14 days). To find out how to retrieve your car, call 7747 4747.

Vehicle hire

Alamo (0870 400 4562, www.alamo. co.uk), **Budget** (0844 544 3439, www. budget.co.uk) and **Hertz** (0870 844 8844, www.hertz.co.uk) all have airport branches. Shop around for the best rate and always check the level of insurance.

Cycling

London isn't the friendliest town for cyclists, but the **London Cycle Network** (www.londoncyclenetwork. org.uk) and **London Cycling Campaign** (7234 9310, www.lcc.org. uk) help to keep things improving, and **Transport for London** (0843 222 1234, www.tfl.gov.uk) has been giving riders some great support, including online and printable route-finders.

Cycle hire

A City Hall-sponsored bike rental scheme launched in 2010, see box p81. South Bank's **London Bicycle Tour Company** (7928 6838, www.london bicycle.com) and **Velorution** (7637 4004, www.velorution.biz) in Fitzrovia are handy for longer rentals.

Walking

The best way to see London is on foot, but the street layout is complicated. There are street maps in the By Area chapters (pp61-190). For route advice, see www.tfl.gov.uk/gettingaround.

Resources A-Z

For information on **London 2012**, see pp206-213. See http://europa.eu/travel for information on travelling to the UK from within the EU, including visa regulations and details of healthcare provision.

Accident & emergency

If you require treatment for an illness or injury that is not critical or life-threatening, go to your nearest urgent care or walk-in centre. No appointment is necessary. For a non-urgent police enquiry call **0300 123 1212**.

Guy's Minor Injury Unit *Great Maze Pond, SE1 9RT (7188 7188). London Bridge tube/rail.*
St Barts Minor Injury Unit *West Smithfield, EC1A 7BE (7377 7000). St Paul's or Barbican tube.*
Soho Walk-In Centre *1 Frith Street, W1D 3HZ (7534 6500). Tottenham Court Road tube.*
Victoria Walk-In Centre *63 Buckingham Gate, SW1E 6AS (7340 1190). St James's Park tube.*

If you are so seriously ill or injured you need emergency care fast, call **999** or **112** free from any phone, including payphones – and ask for an ambulance, the fire service or police. For other emergencies, use the 24hr A&E departments at:

Chelsea & Westminster *369 Fulham Road, Chelsea, SW10 9NH (8746 8000, www.chelwest.nhs.uk). South Kensington tube.*
Royal London *Whitechapel Road, E1 1BB (7377 7000, www.bartsandthelondon.nhs.uk). Whitechapel tube.*
St Thomas's *Lambeth Palace Road, SE1 7EH (7188 7188, www.guysandstthomas.nhs.uk). Westminster tube or Waterloo tube/rail.*

University College *235 Grafton Road, Bloomsbury, NW1 2BU (0845 155 5000, www.uclh.nhs.uk). Euston Square or Warren Street tube.*

Credit card loss

American Express *01273 696933, www.americanexpress.com.*
Diners Club *0870 190 0011, www.dinersclub.co.uk.*
MasterCard/Eurocard *0800 964 767, www.mastercard.com.*
Visa *7795 5777, www.visa.co.uk.*

Customs

For allowances, see www.hmrc.gov.uk.

Dental emergency

Dental care is free for the under-18s, students resident in this country and people on benefits, but all other patients must pay (NHS-eligible patients at a subsidised rate).

Disabled

London is a difficult place for disabled visitors, although legislation is slowly improving access and general facilities. The bus fleet is now low-floor for easier wheelchair access, but the tube remains escalator-dependent. The *Tube Access Guide* booklet is free; call 0843 222 1234 for more details.

Most major attractions and hotels have good accessibility, though provisions for the hearing- or sight-disabled are patchier. The inclusive London website (www.inclusivelondon.com) gives details about the accessibility across town. *Access in London* is an invaluable reference book for disabled travellers, available for a £10 donation from **Access Project** (www.accessproject-phsp.org).

Electricity

The UK uses 220-240V, 50-cycle AC voltage and three-pin plugs.

Embassies & consulates

American Embassy *24 Grosvenor Square, Mayfair, W1A 2LQ (7499 9000, http://london.usembassy.gov). Bond Street or Marble Arch tube.* **Open** *8.30am-5.30pm Mon-Fri.*
Australian High Commission *Australia House, Strand, Holborn, WC2B 4LA (7379 4334, www.uk. embassy.gov.au). Holborn or Temple tube.* **Open** *9am-5pm Mon-Fri.*
Canadian High Commission *38 Grosvenor Street, Mayfair, W1K 4AA (7258 6600, www.canada.org.uk). Bond Street or Oxford Circus tube.* **Open** *8am-4pm Mon-Fri.*
Embassy of Ireland *17 Grosvenor Place, Belgravia, SW1X 7HR (7235 2171, 7225 7700 passports & visas, www.embassyofireland.co.uk). Hyde Park Corner tube.* **Open** *9.30am-5.30pm Mon-Fri.*
New Zealand High Commission *New Zealand House, 80 Haymarket, St James's, SW1Y 4TQ (7930 8422, www.nzembassy.com). Piccadilly Circus tube.* **Open** *9am-5pm Mon-Fri.*

Internet

Most hotels have broadband and/or wireless access, and many cafés now offer wireless surfing.

Insurance

There's access to free or reduced-cost healthcare for residents in the European Economic Area and Switzerland (bring a valid European Health Insurance Card, www.ehic.org. uk), as well as some countries with bilateral agreements with the UK. We still recommend you take out appropriate travel insurance – it's essential for all visitors from any other country.

Left luggage

Bus and rail stations have left-luggage desks rather than lockers; call 0845 748 4950 for details.

Gatwick Airport *01293 502014 South Terminal, 01293 569900 North Terminal.*
Heathrow Airport *8745 5301 Terminal 1, 8759 3344 Terminal 3, 8897 6874 Terminal 4, 8759 3344 Terminal 5.*
London City Airport *7646 0162.*
Stansted Airport *01279 663213.*

Opening hours

Banks 9am-4.30pm (some close at 3.30pm, some 5.30pm) Mon-Fri; sometimes also Saturday mornings.
Businesses 9am-5pm Mon-Fri.
Post offices 9am-5.30pm Mon-Fri; 9am-noon Sat.
Pubs & bars 11am-11pm Mon-Sat; noon-10.30pm Sun.
Shops 10am-6pm Mon-Sat; many also open noon-6pm Sun.

Pharmacies

For advice on over-the-counter medication, sometimes including emergency contraception and sexual health advice, visit a pharmacist. Text 'pharmacy' to 64746 to find your nearest). Most pharmacies open 9am-6pm Mon-Sat.

Police

Look up 'Police' in the phone book or call 118 118, 118 500 or 118 888 if none of these police stations are convenient.

Charing Cross *Agar Street, Covent Garden, WC2N 4JP (0300 123 1212). Charing Cross tube/rail.*
Chelsea *2 Lucan Place, SW3 3PB (0300 123 1212). South Kensington tube.*
West End Central *27 Savile Row, Mayfair, W1S 2EX (0300 123 1212). Piccadilly Circus tube.*

Post

For general enquiries, call 0845 722 3344 or consult www.royalmail.com. Post offices are usually open 9am-6pm Mon-Fri and 9am-noon Sat, although the **Trafalgar Square Post Office** (24-28 William IV Street, WC2N 4DL, 0845 722 3344) opens 8.30am-6.30pm Mon-Fri and 9am-5.30pm Sat.

Smoking

Smoking is banned in enclosed public spaces, such as clubs, hotel foyers, shops, restaurants and public transport.

Telephones

London's dialling code is 020; standard landlines have eight digits after that. If you're calling from outside the UK, dial your international access code, then the UK code, 44, then the full London number, omitting the first 0 (Australia 61, Canada 1, New Zealand 64, Republic of Ireland 353, South Africa 27, USA 1). **US cellphone users** need a tri- or quad-band handset.

Public payphones take coins and/or credit cards. International calling cards are widely available.

Tickets

Advice concerning tickets for the **London 2012 Games** is on p206.

For most London events, book ahead – even obscure acts sell out, major gigs and sport events do so in seconds. Agencies include **Ticketmaster** (0844 844 0444, www.ticketmaster.co.uk) and **See Tickets** (0871 220 0260, www.seetickets.com); they both charge booking fees, so it is usually cheaper to go direct to the venue's box office. For West End tickets use **tkts** (p139).

Time

Greenwich Mean Time (GMT) is five hours ahead of US Eastern Standard time. In autumn (30 Oct 2011, 28 Oct 2012) the clocks go back an hour to GMT; they go forward to British Summer Time on 25 Mar 2012.

Tipping

Tip in taxis, minicabs, restaurants, hotels, hairdressers and some bars (but not pubs). Ten per cent is normal, with some restaurants adding as much as 15%. Always check whether service has already been included in your bill.

Tourist information

Britain & London Visitor Centre *1 Lower Regent Street, SW1 4XT (7808 3800, www.visitbritain.com). Piccadilly Circus tube.* **Open** 9.30am-6pm Mon; 9am-6pm Tue-Fri; 9am-5pm Sat; 10am-4pm Sun.
City of London Information Centre *St Paul's Churchyard, EC4M 8BX (7332 1456, www.cityoflondon.gov.uk). St Paul's tube.* **Open** 9.30am-5.30pm Mon-Sat; 10am-4pm Sun. Also offers tours with specialist City-trained guides.
Greenwich Tourist Information Centre *Discover Greenwich, Pepys House, 2 Cutty Sark Gardens, SE10 9LW (0870 608 2000, www.greenwichwhs.org.uk). Cutty Sark DLR.* **Open** 10am-5pm daily.

Visas

Citizens of the EU don't require a visa to visit the UK; for limited tourist visits, citizens of the USA, Canada, Australia, New Zealand and South Africa can also enter the UK with only a passport. But *always* check the current situation at www.ukvisas.gov.uk well before you travel.

What's on

Time Out remains London's only quality listings magazine. It gives listings for the week from Thursday.

ESSENTIALS

Index

ESSENTIALS